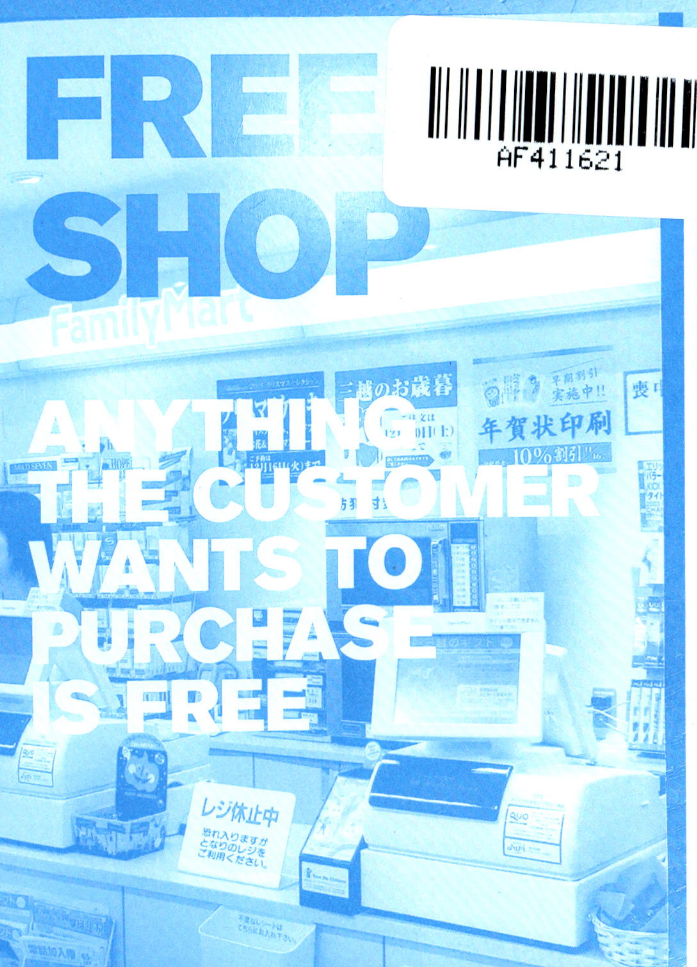
FREE
SHOP
FamilyMart
ANYTHING
THE CUSTOMER
WANTS TO
PURCHASE
IS FREE
AF411621

Rohmilchkäse
aus biologischer Landwirtschaft

Abt. 1   Waage 1   # 002369
30.09.2003 9:52:43   74/2   Verk.   1

kg	€/kg	€
MerLot Pays d'Oc 0.5		2,95
Urberger 12 Monate		
0,278	17,50	4,87
Montsurais 1/1		4,90
HEIDE CAMEMBERT		
0,178	18,50	3,29
Parmiggiano Reggiano		
0,416	26,80	11,15
Minuseingabe		-27,16

6 Pos. Summe   €   0,00

In der Summe enthalten sind: Brutto
7,00% Mehrwertsteuer   -0,19   -2,95
16,00% Mehrwertsteuer   0,41   2,95

30.09.2003 9:57:00

****

-ökologisch handeln-

-bewußt genießen-

Es bediente Sie:
MICHAEL NUSSBAUM

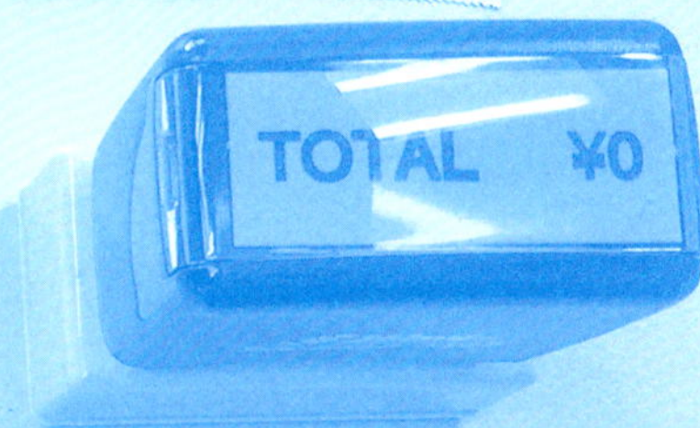

DOLCEVITA
73
Pappelstraße 73
28199 Bremen
Telefon + Fax:
0421/59 77 11 3
FEINKOST
MIR
W02   0009
4:50   B01
0,00   €/kg
0,50
* €   0,50
421-705413
M DOBBEN 110
TOTAL   ¥0
ZONE   六本木ビル
豆狸
TEL 03 3475 1619
2003年10月28日(火)No0
2個 X 単80
豆狸   ¥160
2個 X 単70
たこちび   ¥140
きのこいた
きのこいなり   ¥120
小 計   ¥540
外税売   ¥540
外 税   ¥27
合   計   ¥567
お預り   ¥567
お釣り   ¥0
10責   4248 12時45分

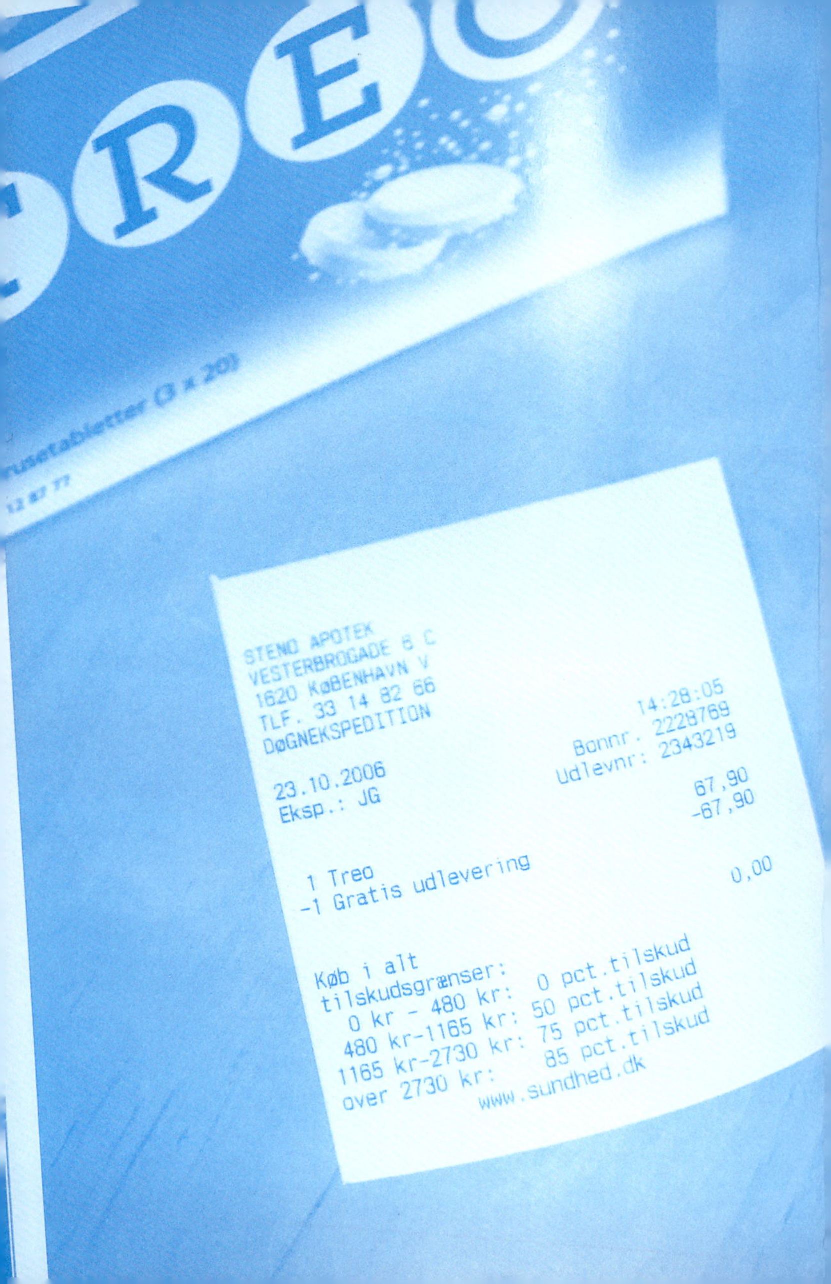

STENO APOTEK
VESTERBROGADE 8 C
1620 KØBENHAVN V
TLF. 33 14 82 66
DØGNEKSPEDITION

                              14:28:05
                    Bonnr. 2228769
                    Udlevnr: 2343219

23.10.2006
Eksp.: JG   67,90
                               -67,90

 1 Treo
-1 Gratis udlevering   0,00

Køb i alt
tilskudsgrænser: 0 pct.tilskud
  0 kr - 480 kr: 50 pct.tilskud
480 kr-1165 kr: 75 pct.tilskud
1165 kr-2730 kr: 85 pct.tilskud
over 2730 kr: www.sundhed.dk

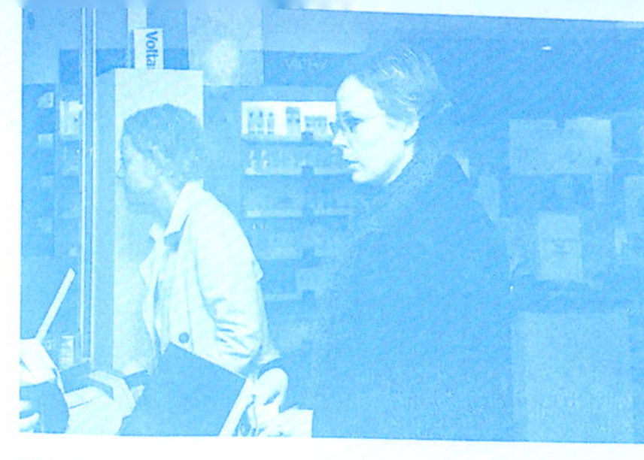

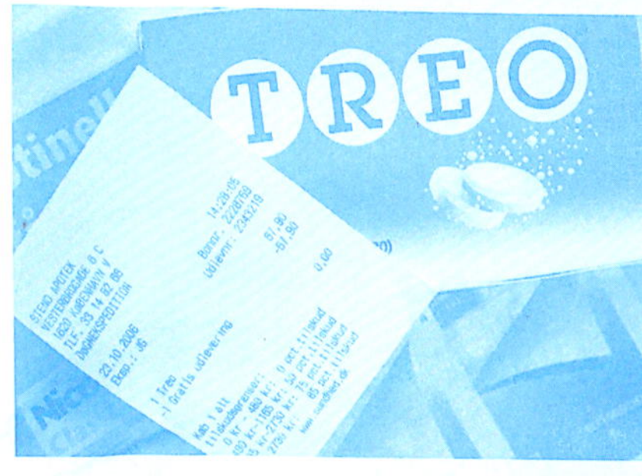

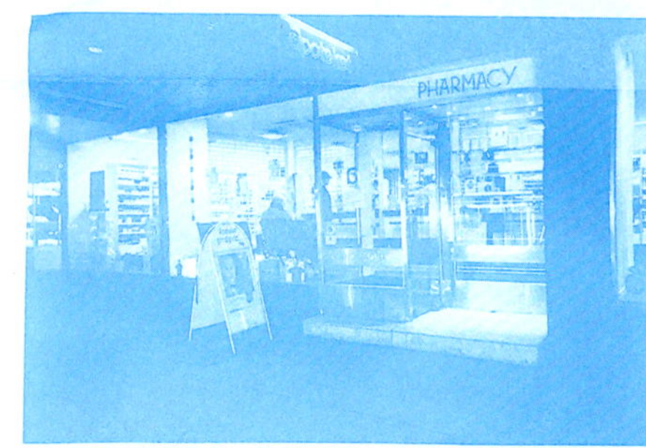

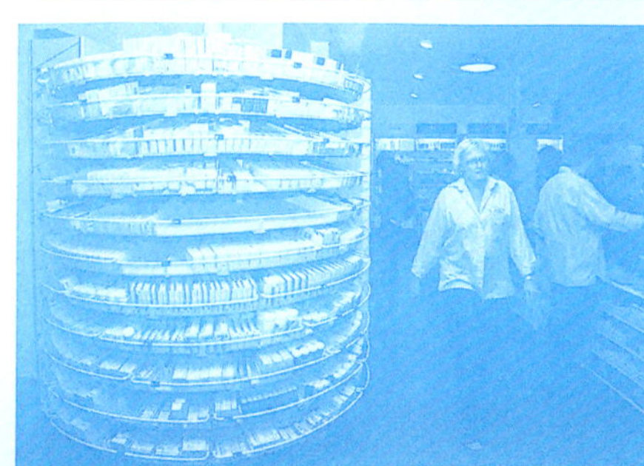

c, 2007
m/Berlin

006

out your permission.
.

Fabricius

pay you 1 LØN

A Day at a Pharma

By Toke Lykkeberg Nielsen, Co

On Monday the items in the St
Station were available for free
their first Danish Free Shop.

"I'm gobsmacked!" exclaims a
outside the pharmacy opposit
girlfriend, "I'd have bought a lo

Great was the general bewilde
Monday morning, the first cus
Shop in Denmark. The idea, wh
in Germany and Japan, is simp
tomers come in for cost them

"And today it's free of charge,"
sales assistant after the other
ing, collect a ticket from the di
comes up on the electronic dis

Monday is a busy day and an e
to the pharmacy in central Co
ing through the city swing thr

A middle-aged Norwegian cou
smiles. They're in high spirits,
didn't have to pay. They've bee
principles but are surprised t

"They must be doing it to at
– a bit like sponsors," the we
husband.

"But a sponsor normally con
But here it was more than a p
concludes, sounding puzzled
so he'd better talk to her abo

Superflex's interventions in t
of the logic of the market.

"Normally, when you give son
in return. In the Free Shop tha
group's members, explains ov
vals of the day during which t
arily suspended.

Superflex's previous Free Sh
that sell convenience goods.
Free Shop, there's a differen
pharmacy do so of necessity

An assistant observes that re
keen on the project herself. I
and why. "People don't becor
about," she says. They are gr

An American from L.A., hidde
and with long dark hair, is ea
he learns that the idea spran

"So many artists are self-ab
Mendoza, a bassist in the ne

Superflex, Superf
17. April – 29. Mai 2005
Vernissage 16. April 2005, 19 Uhr
Gratis
Eintritt
+
2 Fr.
kriegen
KUNSTHALLE BASEL
Gratis
Eintrit
+
2 Fr.
kriege
KUNSTHALLE BASE

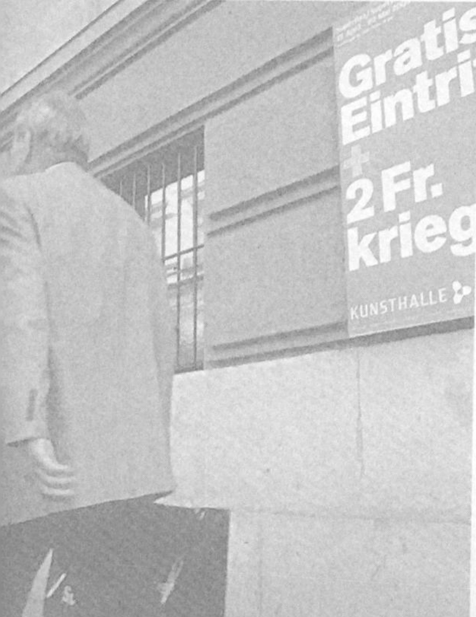
Gratis
Eintrit
+
2 Fr.
krieg
KUNSTHALLE

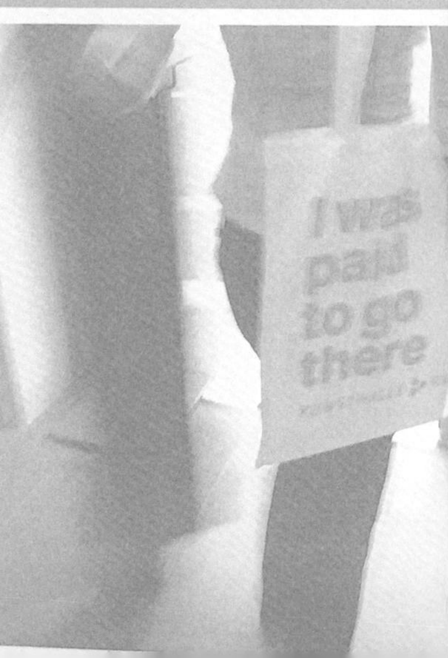
i was
paid
to go
there

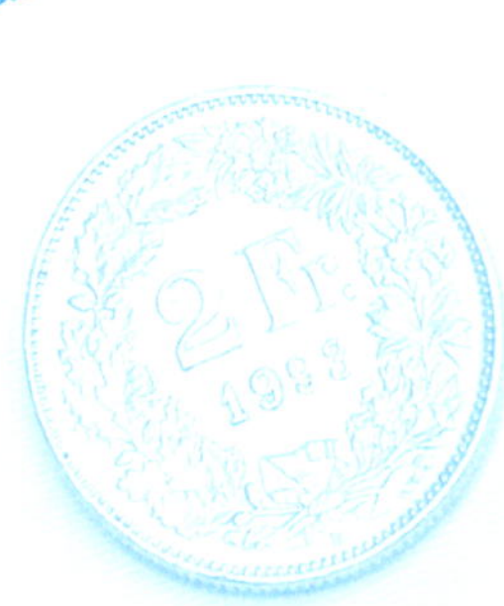
Gratiseintritt
11.05.2005
Superflex / Supershow
17.04 – 29.05.2005
+ 2 Fr.
2 Fr.
1999

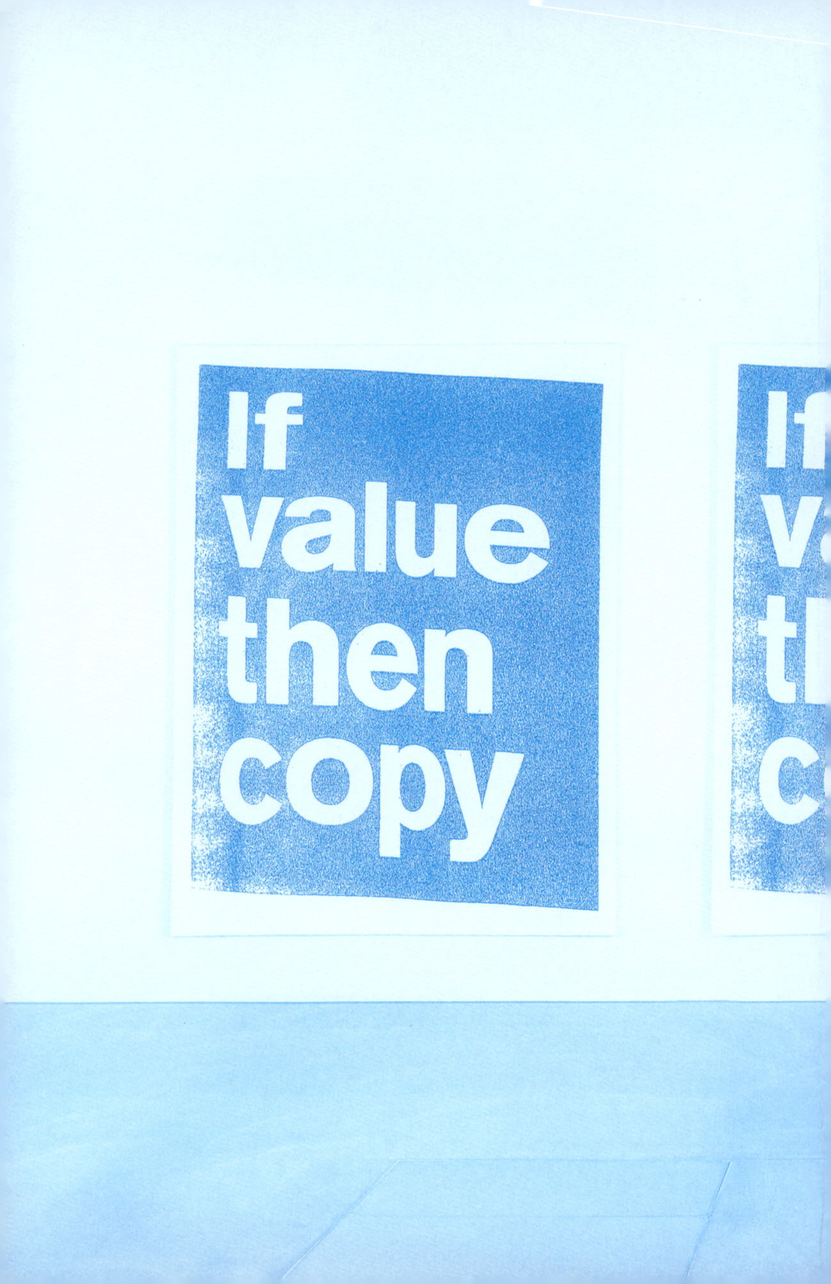

If
value
then
copy

lue
en
py

If
value
then
copy

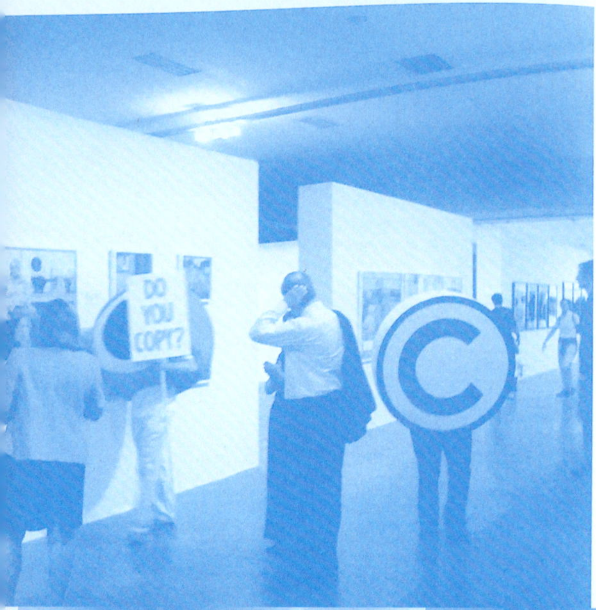

CULTURE
IS BEEN
HARMED BY
TRADEMARKS

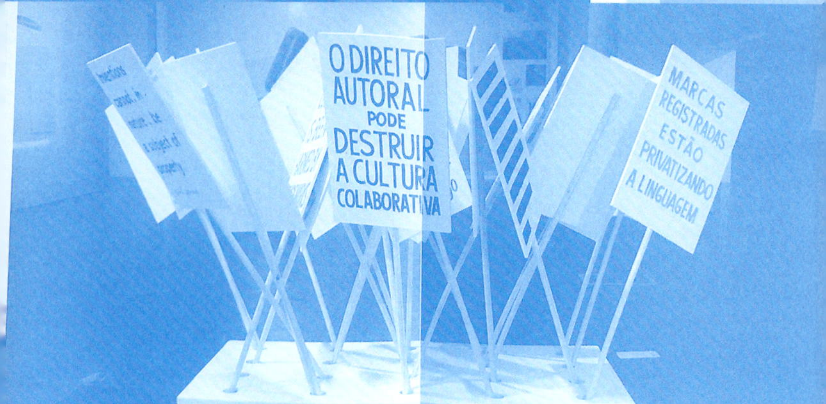

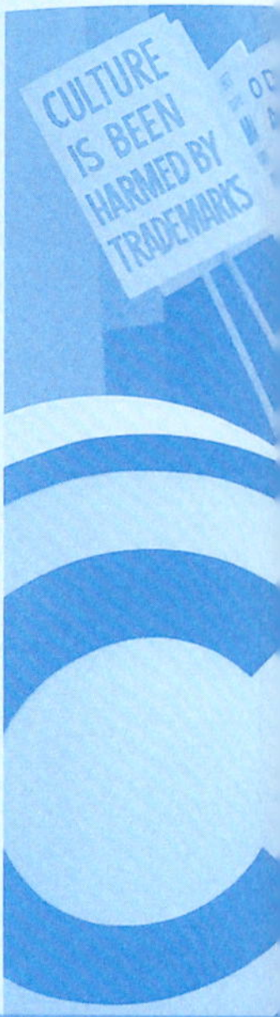

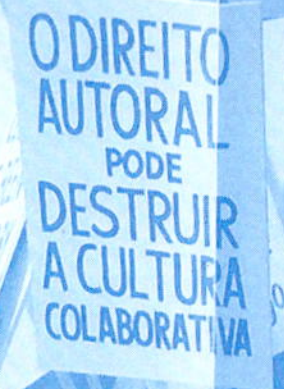
O DIREITO
AUTORAL
PODE
DESTRUIR
A CULTURA
COLABORATIVA

IF VALUE, THEN COPY

COPY IS A RIGHT!

DO YOU COPY?

FREE SPEECH

COPYRIGHT IS PREVENTING ACCESS TO KNOWLEDGE

CULTURE IS BEEN HARMED BY TRADEMARKS

COPYRIGHT SHOULD NOT DESTROY COLLABORATIVE CULTURE

TRADEMARKS ARE PRIVATIZING LANGUAGE

FREE SPEECH IS MORE IMPORTANT THAN TRADEMARKS

The intellectual products held in the developing world rest in a global public domain, while the intellectual products of the developed world are held closely by corporations.
— Anupam Chander & Madhavi Sunder

© GO TO HELL!

Good Copy, Bad Copy

FIGHT FOR YOUR RIGHT TO COPY

There has never been a time in history when more of our "culture" was as "owned" as it is now.
And yet there has never been a time when the concentration of power to control the uses of culture has been as unquestioningly accepted as it is now.
— Lawrence Lessig

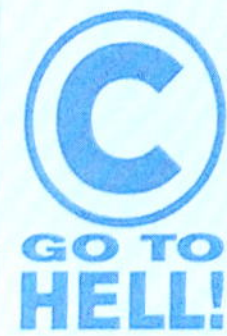

Intellectual property is the oil of the 21st century.
— Mark Getty, grandson of oil magnate J. Paul Getty

Inventions cannot, in nature, be a subject of property.
— Thomas Jefferson

Intellectual Property is a victory of lawyers over economists
— The Money Economist Associatie schitteren van macht, juni 2003

STOP PATENTING TRADITIONAL KNOWLEDGE

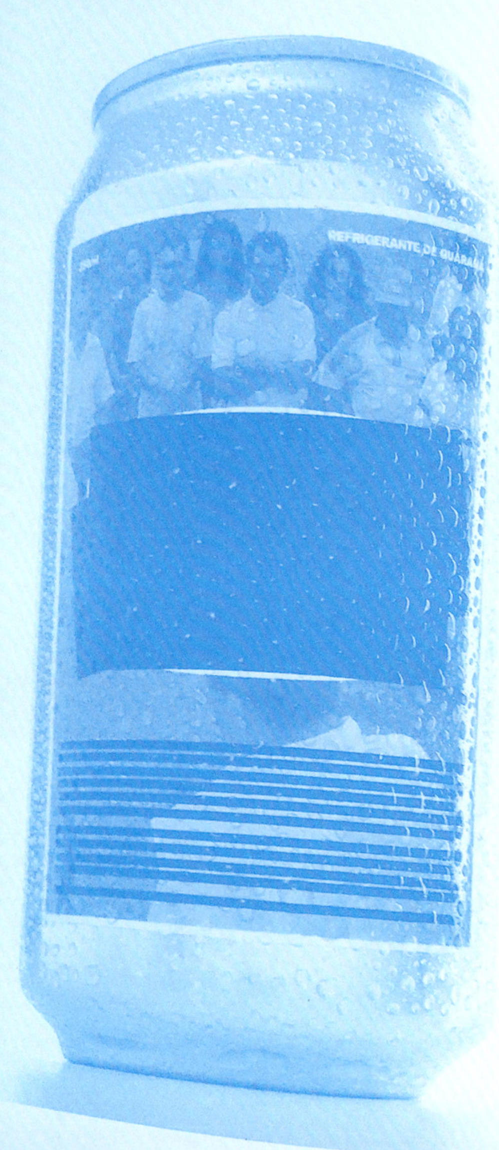
REFRIGERANTE DE GUARAN

The Art work that Brazilians are not allowed to see at the biennial.

The President of the Bienal Foundation, Manoel Francisco Pires da Costa censors an international well-known art Work for the Brazilian audience.

Superflex was invited by the group of curators of the 27th Bienal of São Paulo to show their work and, in particular, was asked to present their internationally known work ███████ ███████ - a social and political work that deals with the curatorial concept of this biennial, "how to live together".

However, the president of the Bienal Foundation, Manoel Francisco Píres da Costa, annulled the invitation made by the group of curators to show this particular work. Mr Pires da Costa stated that ███████ ███████ is not a piece of art but "a product whose foremost aim is commercialism" and therefore cannot be shown at the biennial. According to the definition of Píres da Costa, the work ███████ ███████ is not considered "artistic activity" and goes against the "purposes foreseen" in the laws of the foundation.

The use of the word "guaraná" was even prohibited, arguing that it could upset possible "third party interests".

"We have, however, not been able to get a clear answer as to which third party interests mr. Costa refers to and how those are linked to the biennial", says Superflex

"It's a contradiction that the president of the biennial censors a political work that was originally created in Brazil and deals directly with a local, political and social conflict", says Superflex.

███████ ███████ has been shown at numerous important art institutions and international biennials. The work was first shown at the Venice Biennial in Italy in 2003 and has later been shown at, among other art institutions, the Stedeljlik Museum in Amsterdam, Netherlands, and Kiasma, Museum of Modern Art in Helsinki, Finland. The work has been discussed and critiqued in several art magazines and books around the world.

The work ███████ ███████ uses global brands and their strategies as raw material for a counter-economic positioning. ███████ ███████ reclaims the Maués guaraná plant as a powerful natural tonic, not just as a symbol of a brand name.

The ███████ ███████ softdrink is produced by a guaraná farmers cooperative in Maués in the Brazilian Amazon, in collaboration with Superflex. The farmers have organized themselves in response to the activities of the Brazilian and multinational corporations ███████ and ███████, whose ███████ ███ position on the purchase of the raw material has driven the price of guaraná berries down 80%, while the income from the end products to the consumer has risen.

███████ ███████ contains original Maués guaraná for energy and empowerment.

Although being censored from the São Paulo Bienal by Mr. Píres da Costa, a new version of ███████ ███████ is being produced in collaboration with Galeria Vermelho. It will be available for free for tasting at numerous events in Brazil during the coming months.

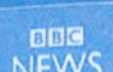 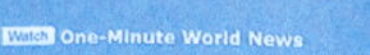 One-Minute World News

'Free' Danish beer makes a splash

Last Updated: Thursday, 28 July, 2005, 08:38 GMT 09:38 UK

E-mail this to a friend   Printable version

By Clark Boyd
Technology correspondent

The Danes love their beer, but increasingly they are looking beyond the old Danish standby, Carlsberg, to quench their thirst.

Students from the Information Technology University in Copenhagen are trying to help by releasing what they are calling the world's first open source beer recipe.

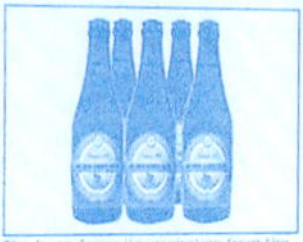

It is called Vores Oel, or Our Beer, and the recipe is proving to be a worldwide hit.

The beer draws its inspiration from the open source movement

The idea behind the beer comes from open source software. This is software whose code is made publicly available for anyone to change and improve, provided that those changes and improvements are then shared in turn.

Perhaps the most well-known example of open source software is the Linux operating system.

Microsoft, on the other hand, creates proprietary software, meaning the company does not tend to let others see how its software works.

The Danish brewer Carlsberg takes a similar approach to beer.

BBC.co.uk, 2005
(news)

July 20, 2005   Print | Send this article | Feedback

SPIEGEL'S DAILY TAKE

Tony Blair Wants to Root Out the Heart of Terrorism

British Prime Minister Tony Blair has on called Muslim leaders to help stop Islamic extremism. The best way, say Muslim leaders, is to reach out to the marginalized and often inaccessible "nutters" who preach hate to youths. Plus, free beer recipes online as open source beer hits the Internet and Britain's Naked Chef, Jamie Oliver, meets his twin.

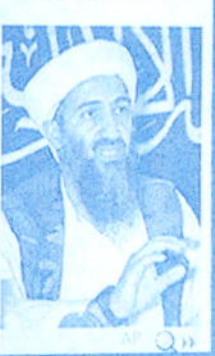

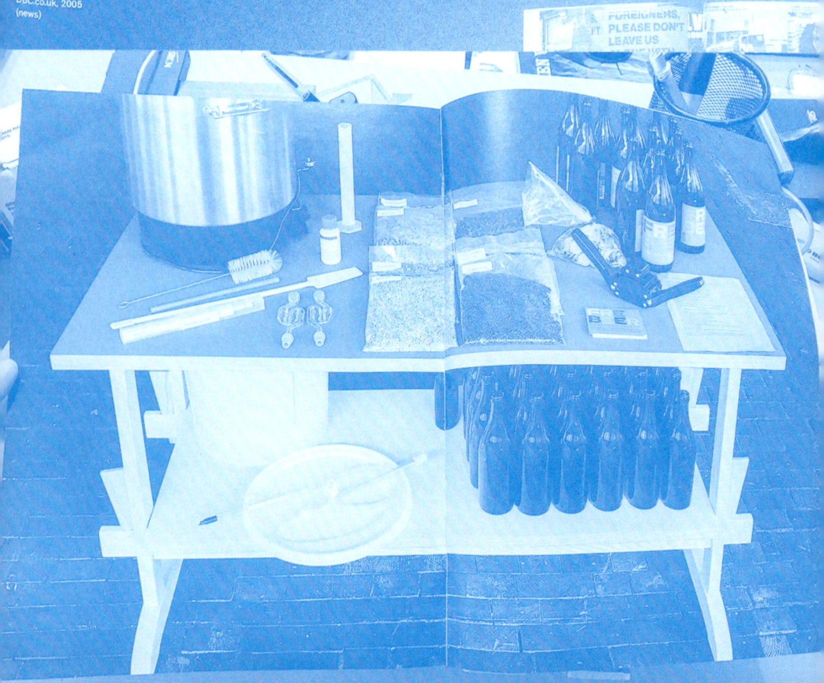

FREE BEER
– øllets svar på LINUX

FREE BEER er verdens første Open source-øl. Med inspiration i computernørdernes stille oprør mod Microsoft, monopoler og ensretning, er det en øl, som bliver bedre ved at deles. Forvirret? Så læs videre her...

FREE BEER
Taiwan Brewing Process

Ingredients:
6 liter water, 5g Ale Yeast, fructose 2cc/bottle

FREE BEER is an open source beer, based on classic ale brewing traditions.

The recipe and branding elements of FREE BEER is published under a Creative Commons license (Attribution-ShareAlike 2.5). This license gives anyone the permission to use the recipe or create a derivative of the recipe to brew their own FREE BEER and to use and modify the design and branding elements. Anyone is free to earn money from FREE BEER, but they must publish the changes and results under the same license and credit our work.

Recipe, branding elements and more information at:
www.freebeer.org

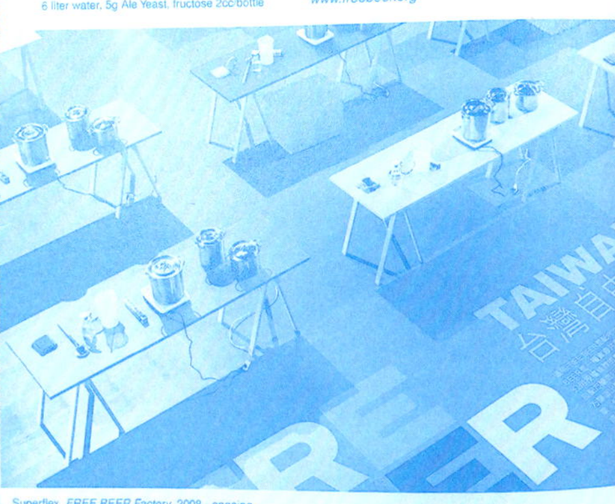

Superflex, *FREE BEER Factory*, 2008 - ongoing
Mixed media installation with platform, tables, cooking equipment, brewing kits incl. beer ingredients, microphone/headset, empty bottles, bottled bottles, refrigerator, vinyl text.
Courtesy of the Artists and Gallery Nils Staerk/Copenhagen

FREE BEER (version 1.0) is an open source beer. FREE BEER is based on classic ale brewing traditions but with added guaraná for a natural energy-boost.
The recipe and the whole brand of FREE BEER is published under a Creative Commons license (Attribution-ShareAlike 2.0) meaning that anyone can use the recipe to brew the beer or to create a derivative of our recipe. You are free to earn money from FREE BEER, but you have to publish the recipe under the same license (e.g. on your website) and credit our work. You can use all our design and branding elements, and are free to change them at will provided you publish your changes under the same license. Free Beer is based on Vores Øl (version 1.0)

Recipe, logos and info of FREE BEER are available at:
http://www.superflex.net/projects/freebeer

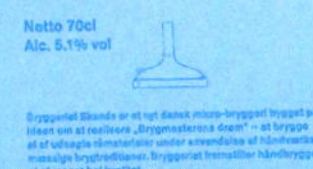

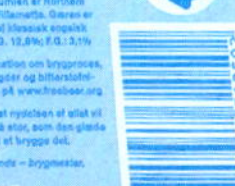

FREE
Creative Commons Birthday Free Beer
This batch of Free Beer is produced in limited
quantities to celebrate Creative Commons
Birthday (December 16, 2006).
www.creativecommons.org
Edition no. 83/886
FREE BEE

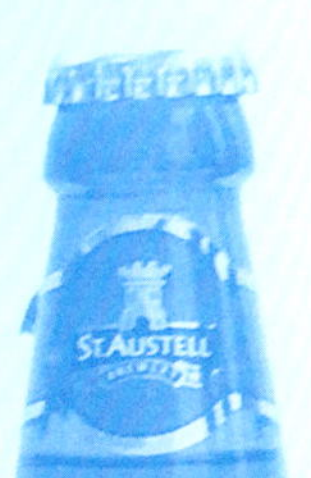

ST.AUSTELL
BREWERY
FREE
BEER
FREE
BEE

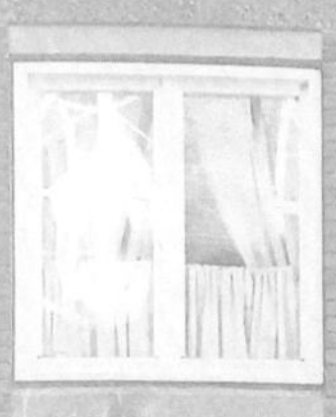
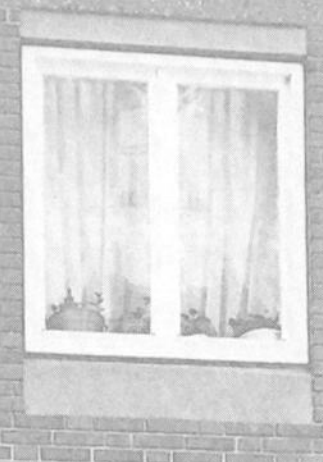
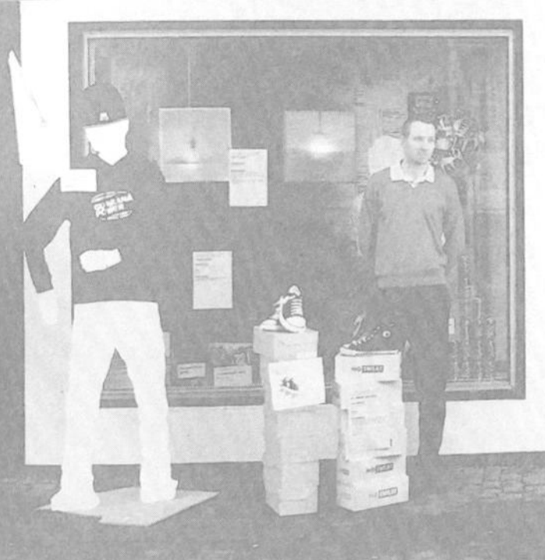

COPYSHOP
COPYSHOP
If value, then copy

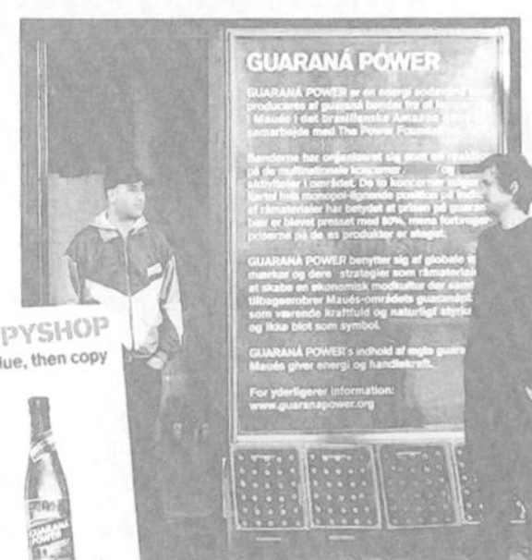

GUARANÁ POWER

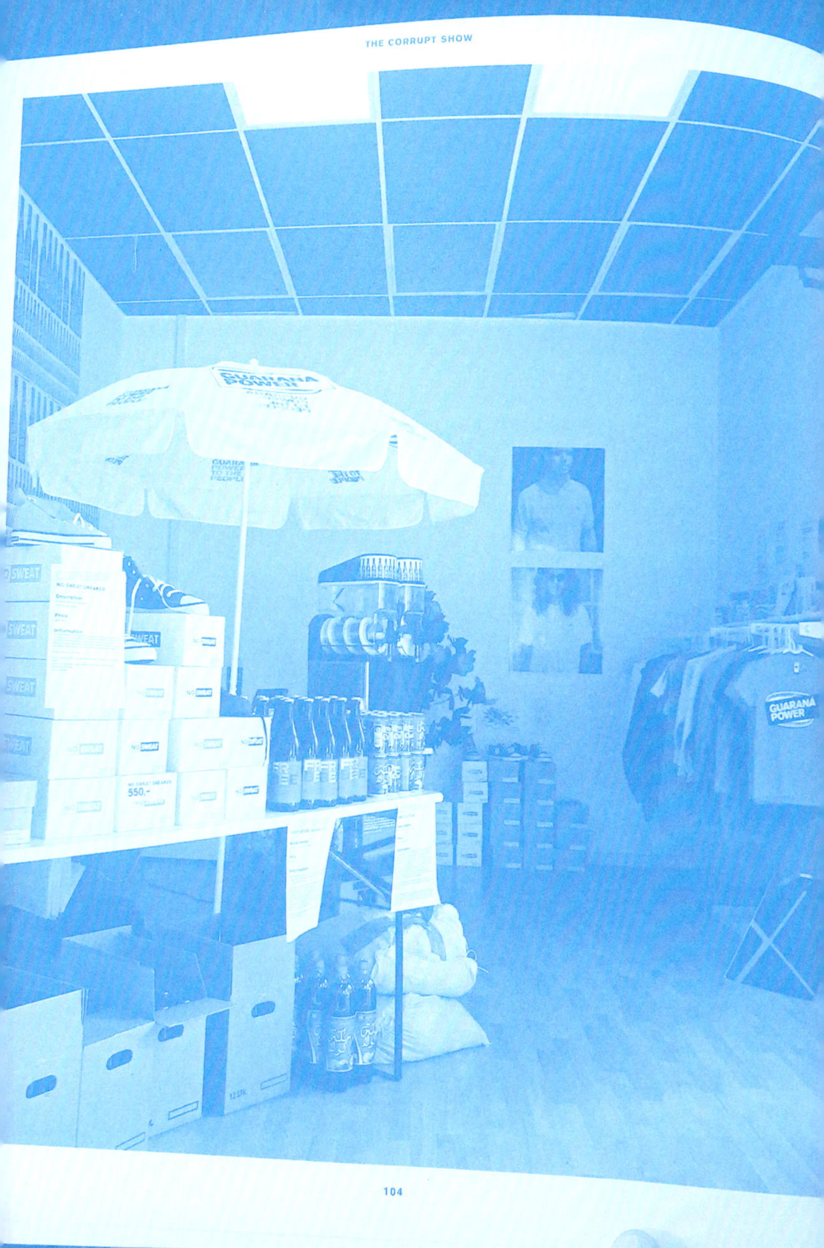

GUARANÁ POWER
NO SWEAT SNEAKER
SWEAT
550,-
GUARANÁ POWER

If value, then co

COPYSHOP is a place where you can photocopy everything
to images. We use this name for a shop and information foru
will investigate the phenomena of copying.

COPYSHOP presents products that challenges intellectual p
can be modified originals, improved copies, political anti-bra
a SUPERCOPY as the new original.

COPYSHOP will discuss the control of value in the same pla
it is produced and distributed: the market. As an active p
function of COPYSHOP will be as an ordinary shop. Fur
COPYSHOP will function as a gathering point and networl
verse group who share a critical view on intellectual propert

COPYSHOP produces, promotes and sells products that
the concept 'If value then right'.

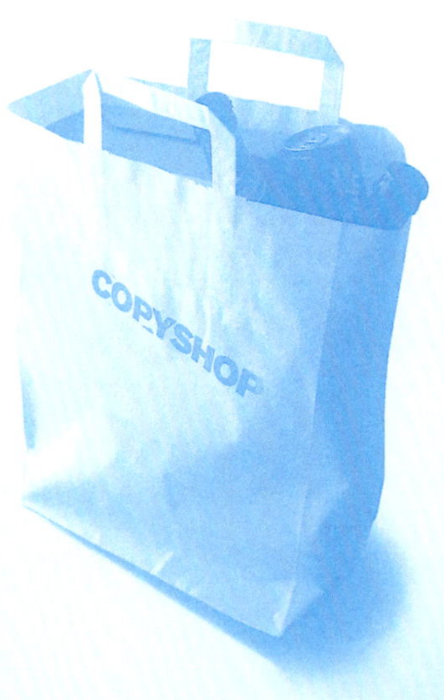

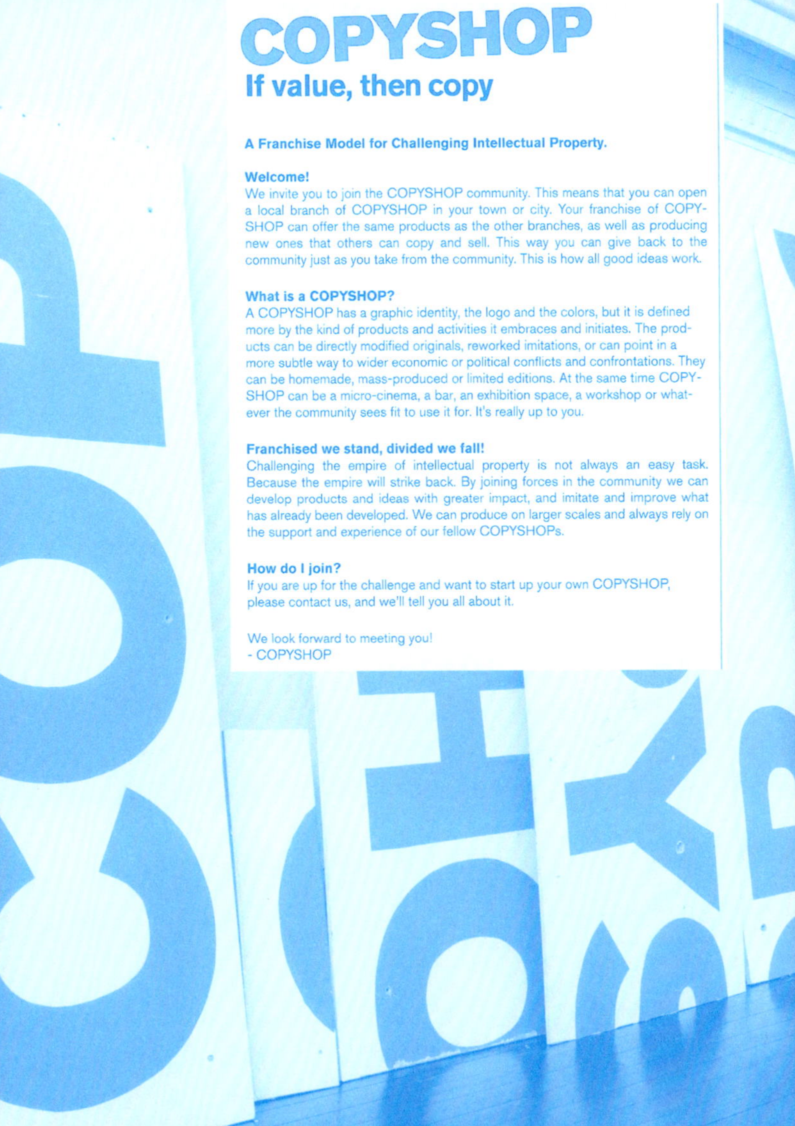

COPYSHOP
If value, then copy

A Franchise Model for Challenging Intellectual Property.

Welcome!
We invite you to join the COPYSHOP community. This means that you can open a local branch of COPYSHOP in your town or city. Your franchise of COPYSHOP can offer the same products as the other branches, as well as producing new ones that others can copy and sell. This way you can give back to the community just as you take from the community. This is how all good ideas work.

What is a COPYSHOP?
A COPYSHOP has a graphic identity, the logo and the colors, but it is defined more by the kind of products and activities it embraces and initiates. The products can be directly modified originals, reworked imitations, or can point in a more subtle way to wider economic or political conflicts and confrontations. They can be homemade, mass-produced or limited editions. At the same time COPYSHOP can be a micro-cinema, a bar, an exhibition space, a workshop or whatever the community sees fit to use it for. It's really up to you.

Franchised we stand, divided we fall!
Challenging the empire of intellectual property is not always an easy task. Because the empire will strike back. By joining forces in the community we can develop products and ideas with greater impact, and imitate and improve what has already been developed. We can produce on larger scales and always rely on the support and experience of our fellow COPYSHOPs.

How do I join?
If you are up for the challenge and want to start up your own COPYSHOP, please contact us, and we'll tell you all about it.

We look forward to meeting you!
- COPYSHOP

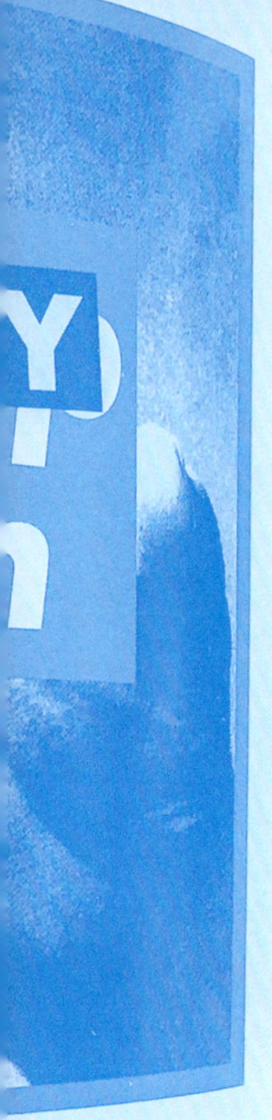

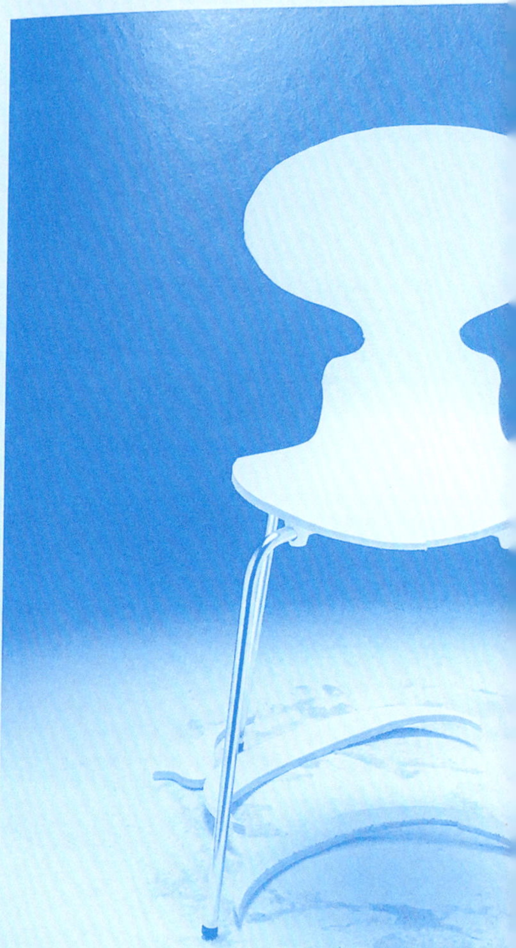

Copy Right (Photo Copy) 2006
C-print, dibond and framed, 120 × 90 cm

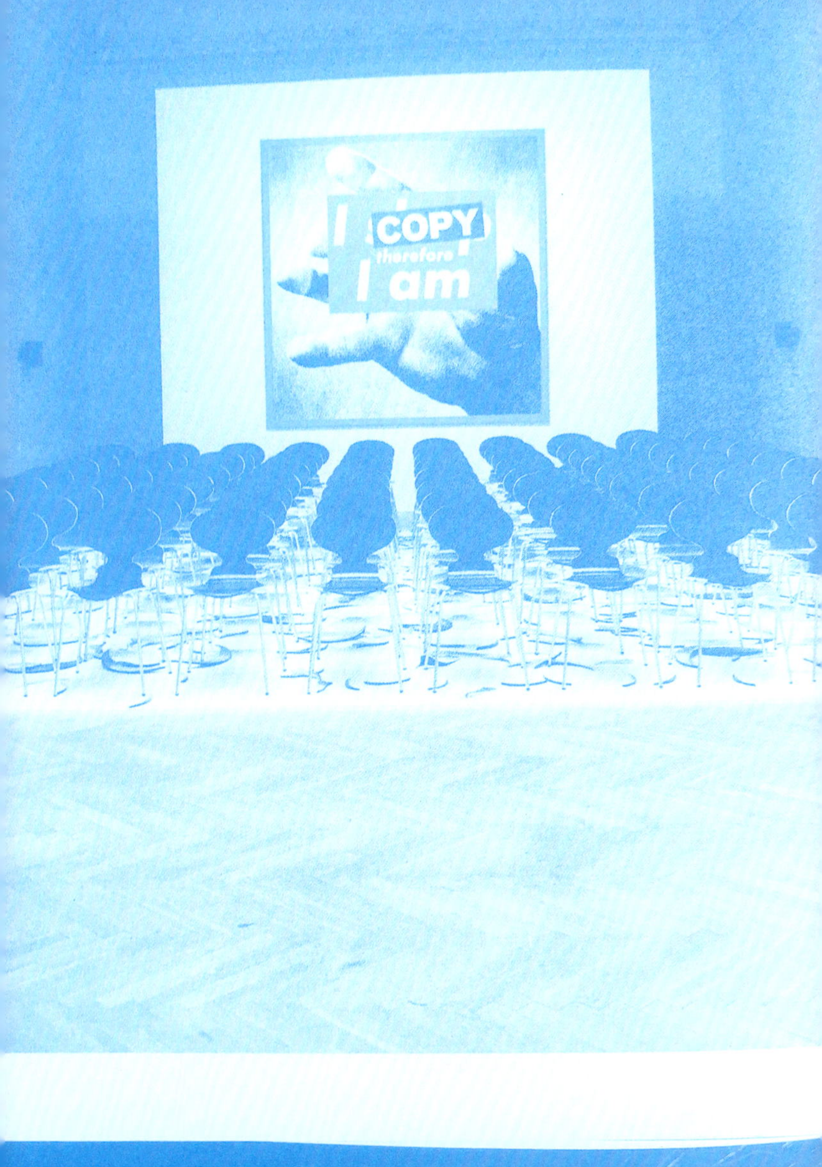
COPY
therefore
I am

Yves Klein, *Untitled Orange Monochrome (M6)* 1956,
dry pigment and synthetic resin on canvas mounted on panel, 37 × 57 cm.

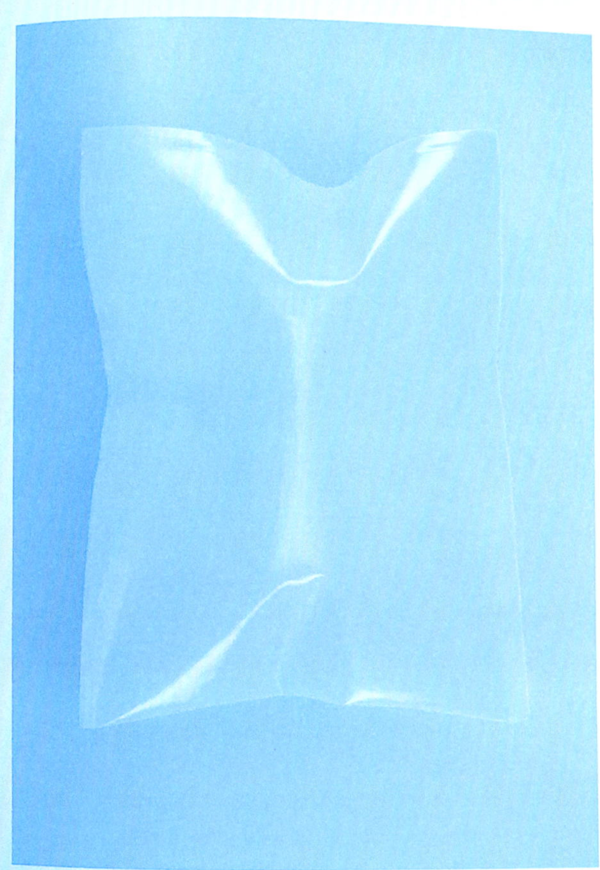

SUPERFLEX, *The Campaign* 1994. An object, presented as an invention and concealed in orange PVC, is used as the point of departure for potential SUPERFLEX collaborations.

INTELLECTUAL PROPERTY LAW

BENTLY, SHERMAN, GANGJEE, & JOHNSON

5TH EDITION

FROM GOODS TO A GOOD LIFE

Intellectual Property and Global Justice

MADHAVI SUNDER

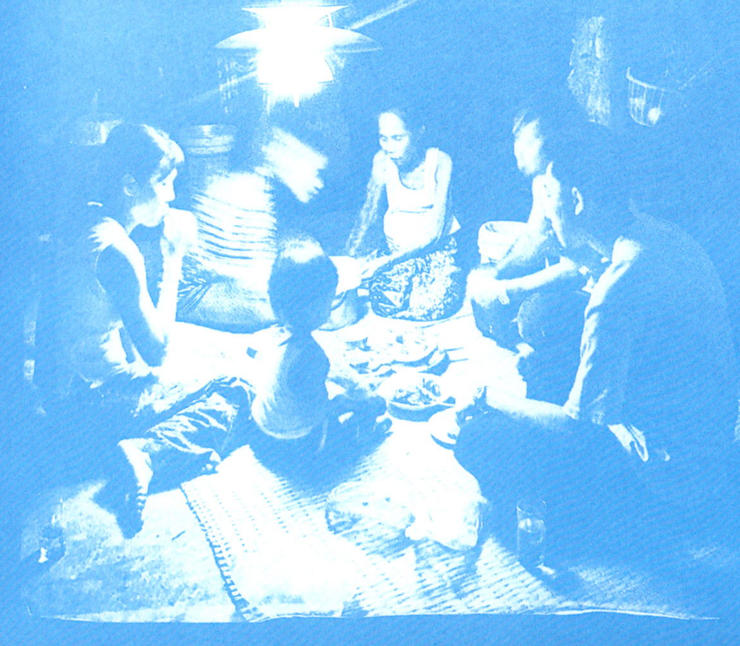

From Goods to a Good Life, 2012
(book)

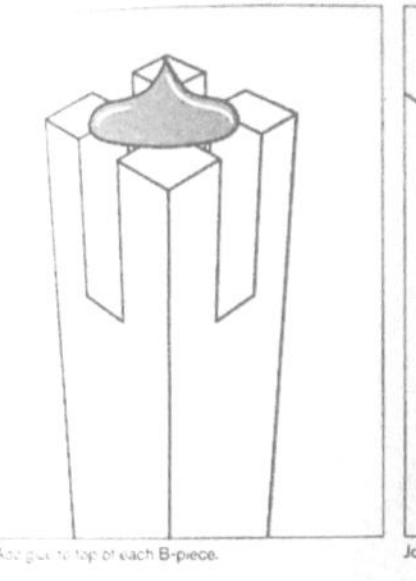

4 Add glue to top of each B-piece.

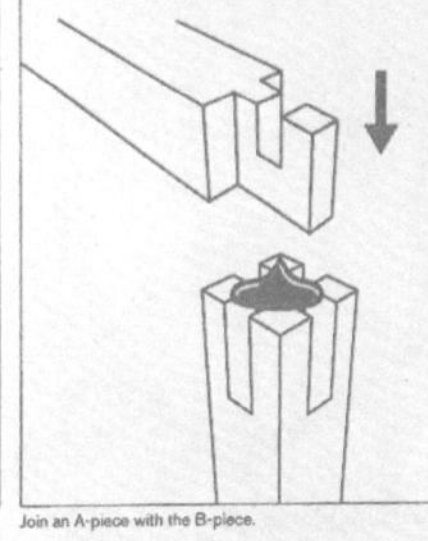

Join an A-piece with the B-piece.

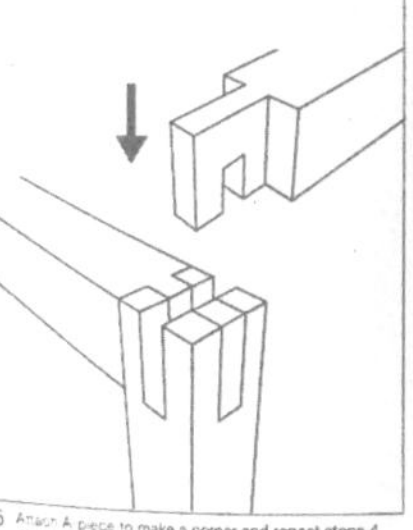

5 Attach A-piece to make a corner and repeat steps 4
   and 5 for remaining corners.

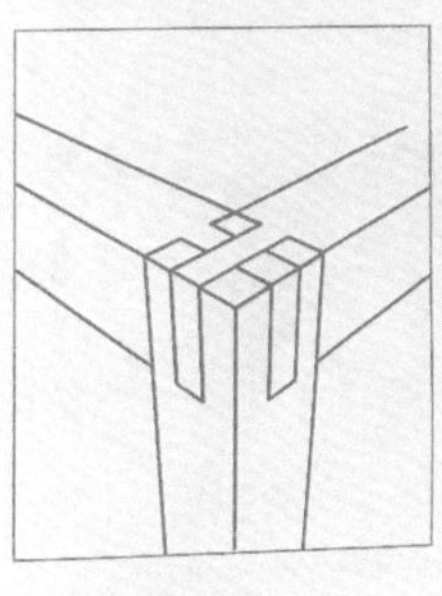

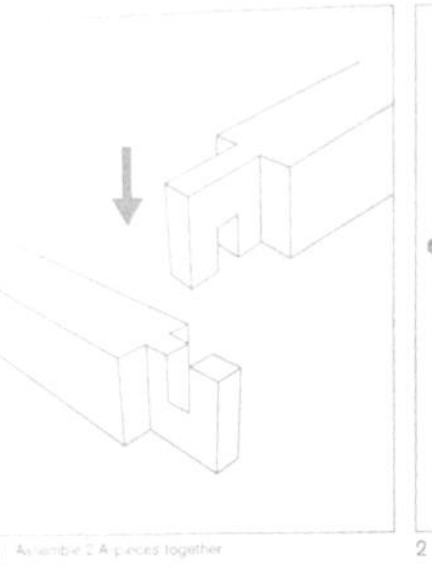

1 Assemble 2 A-pieces together

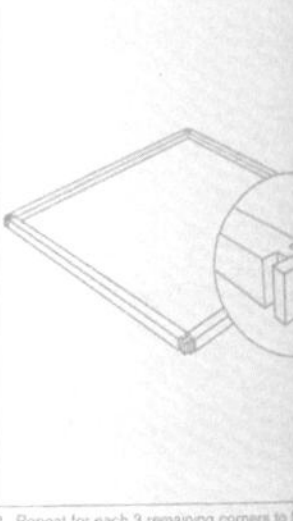

2 Repeat for each 3 remaining corners to for

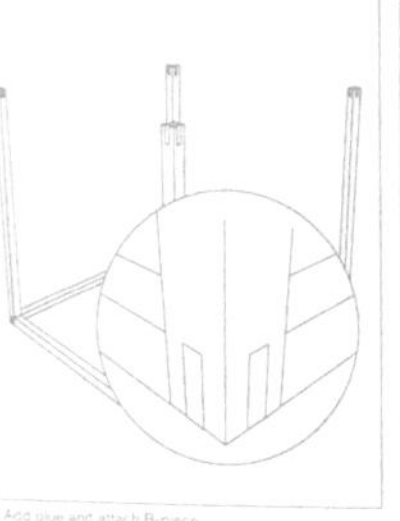

3 Add glue and attach B-piece.

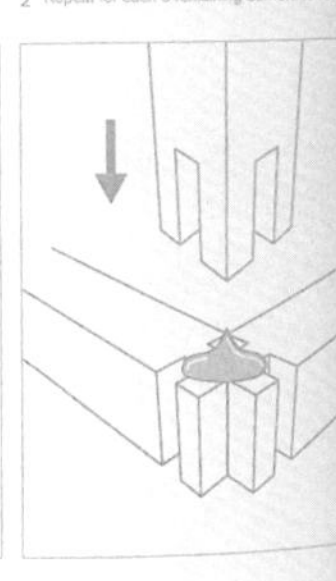

rap print around the structure and glue the two
ds together onto the wood.

Installation

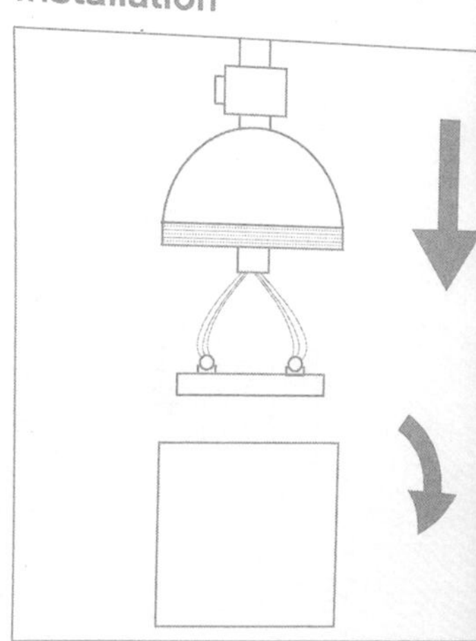

14 Place piece S2 into piece S3, and screw together
    pieces S1 and S3. Screw in the fastner to position
    the light bulb at the desired length.

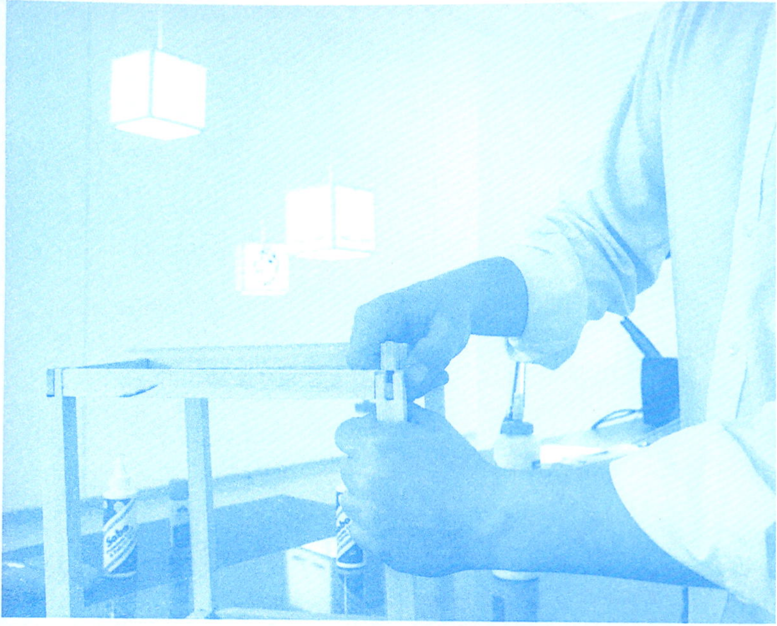

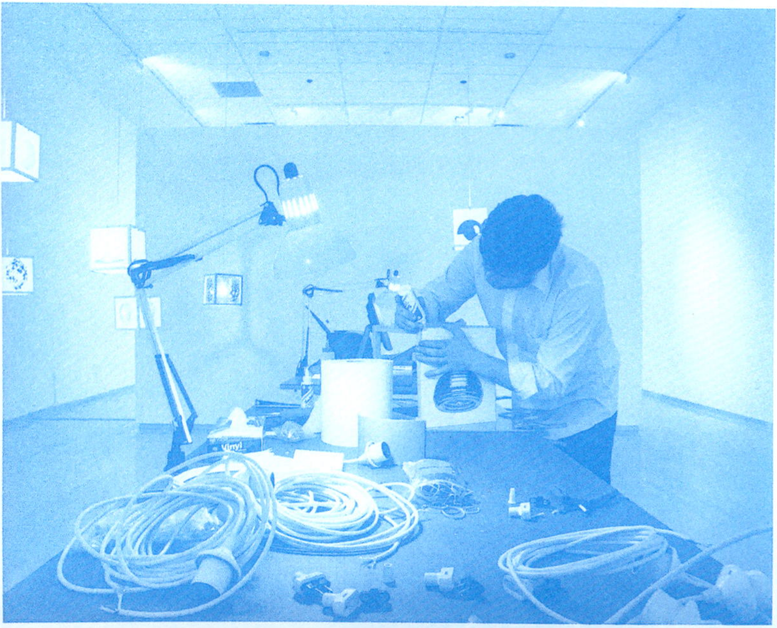

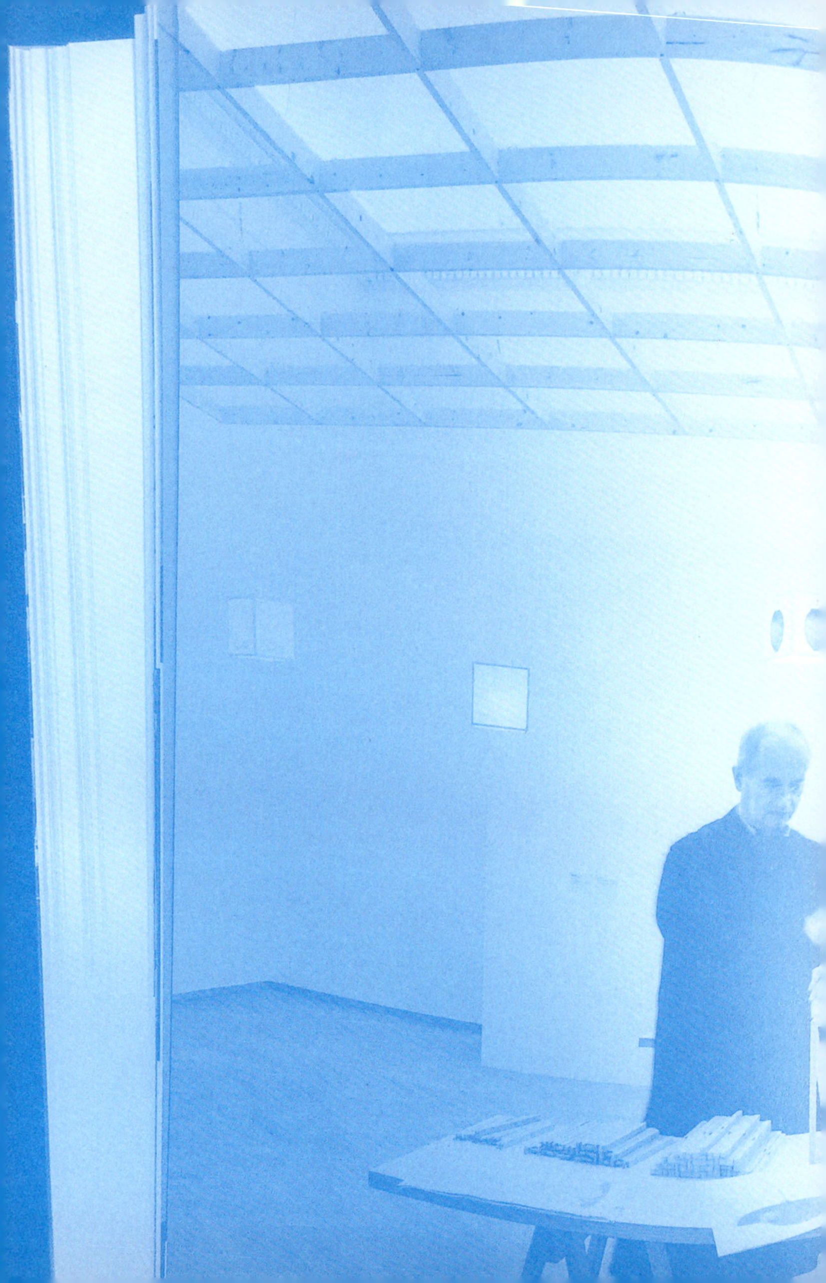

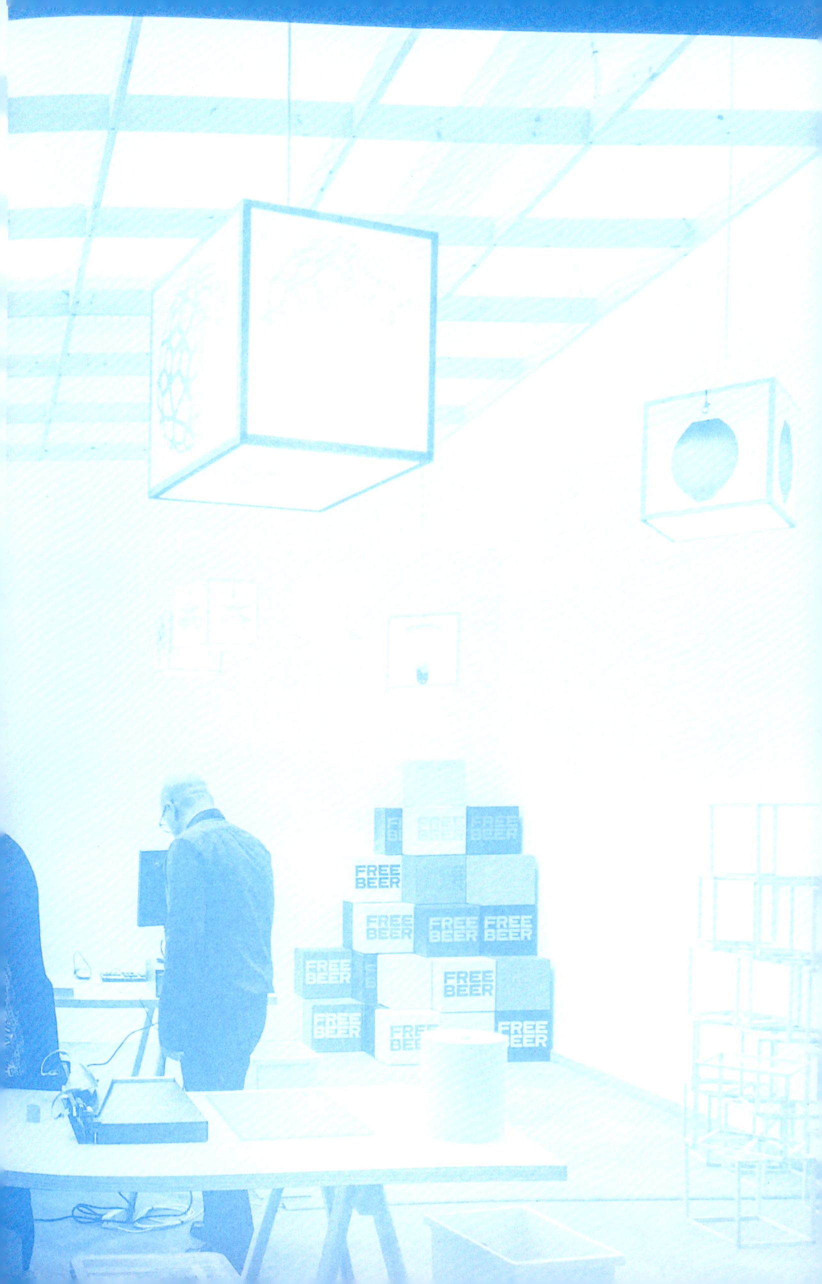

FREE BEER
FREE BEER
FREE BEER
FREE BEER
FREE BEER
FREE BEER
FREE BEER
FREE BEER
FREE BEER

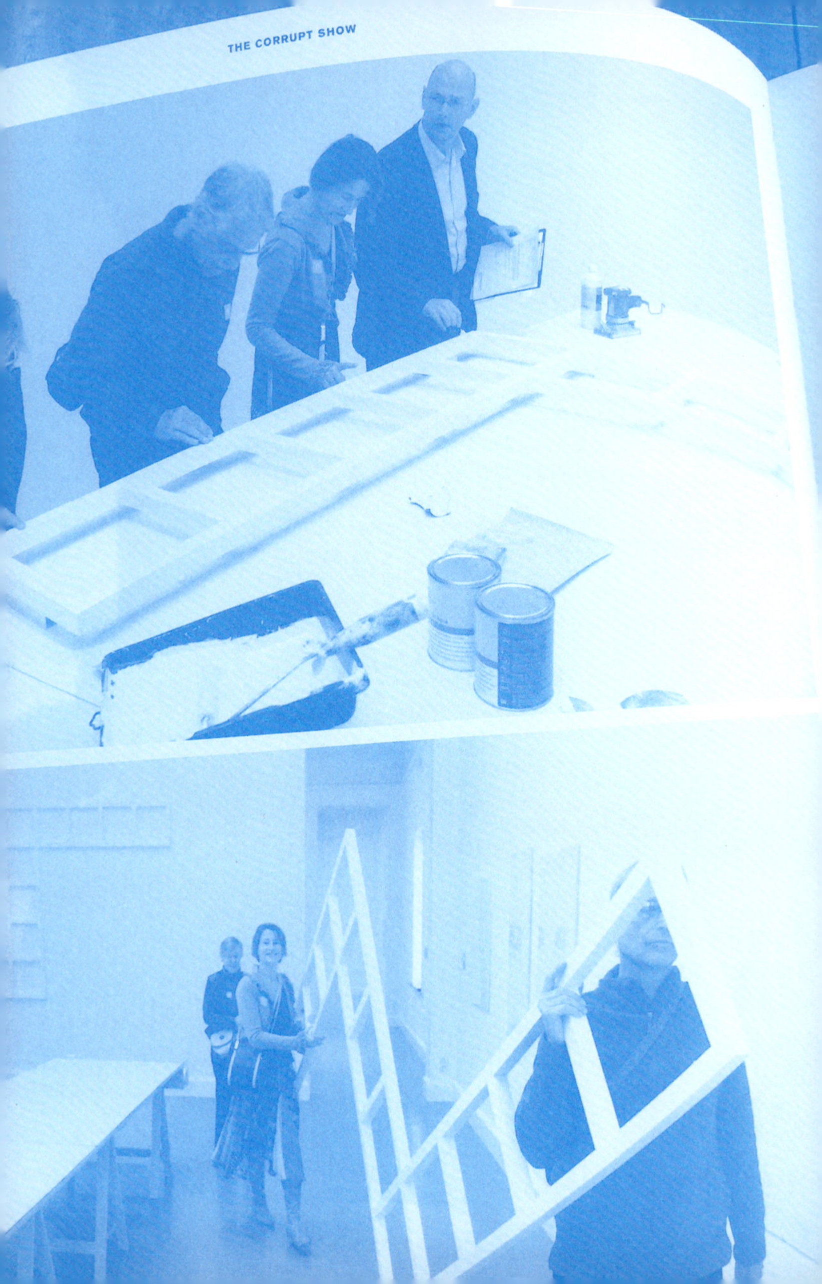

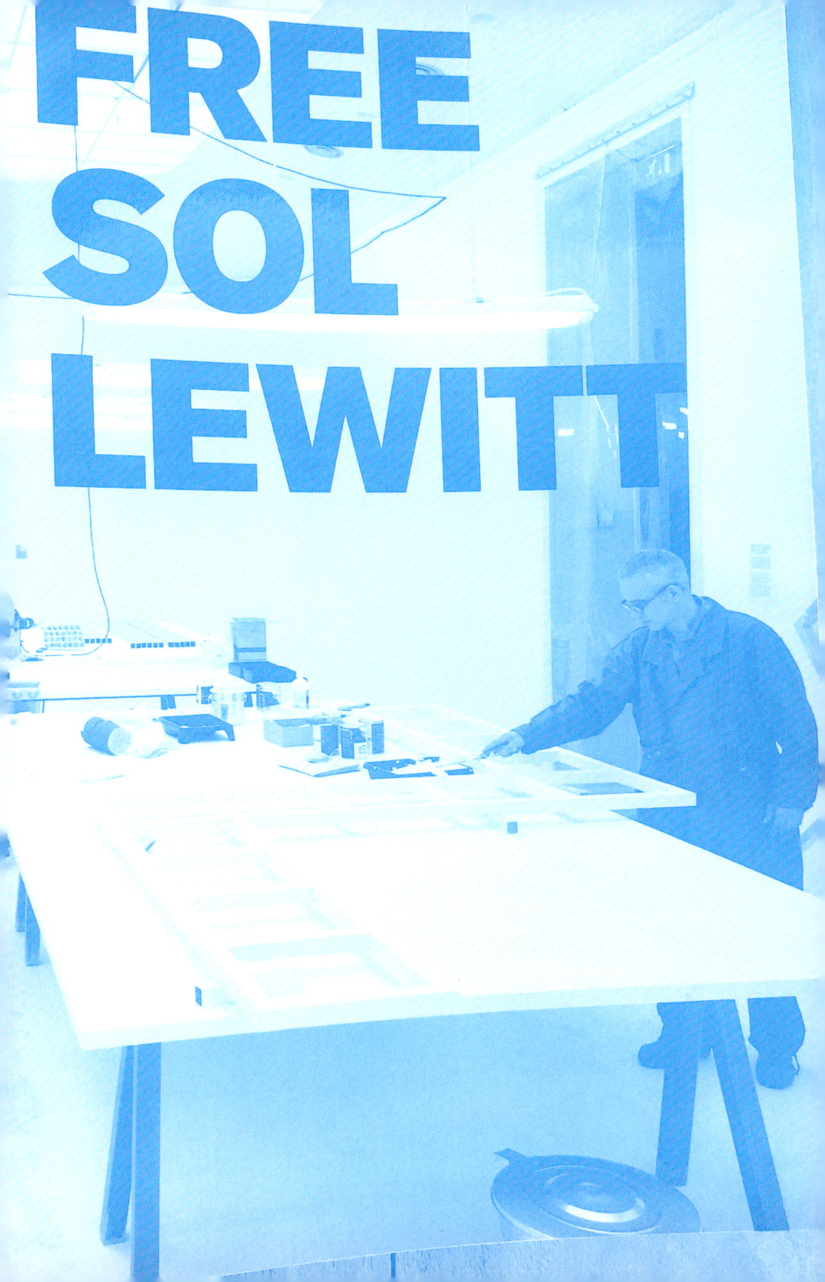
FREE
SOL
LEWITT

Power Toilets/ UNESCO

Superflex

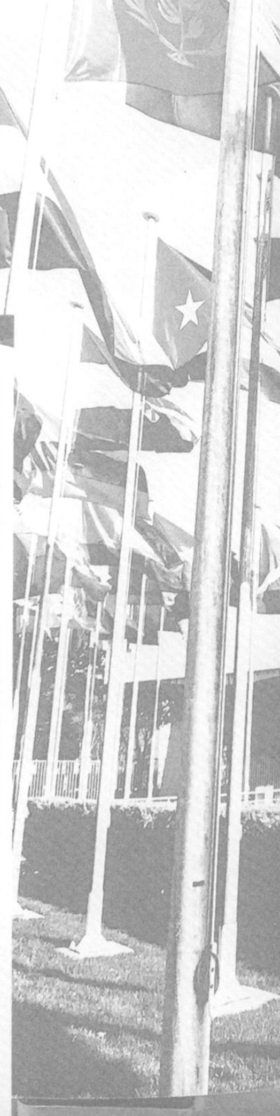

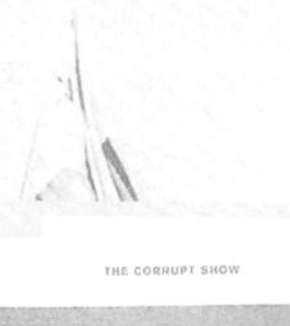

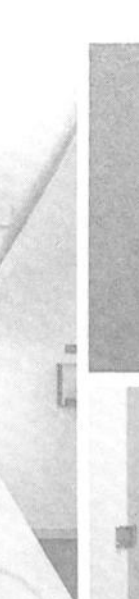

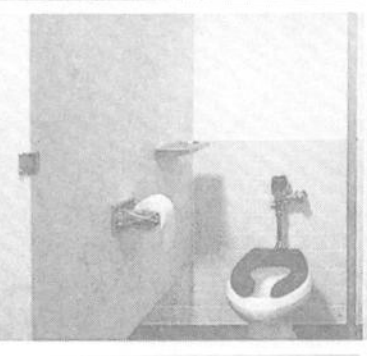

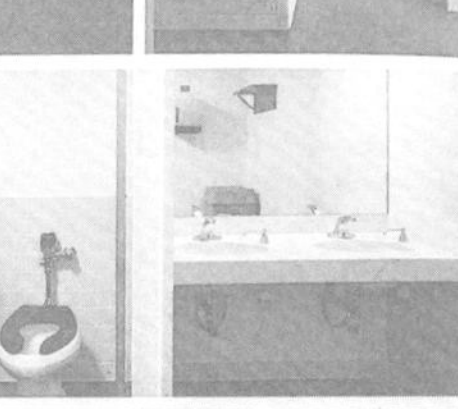

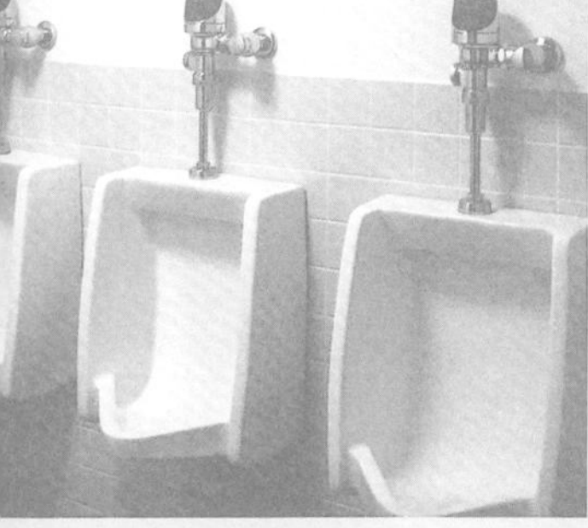

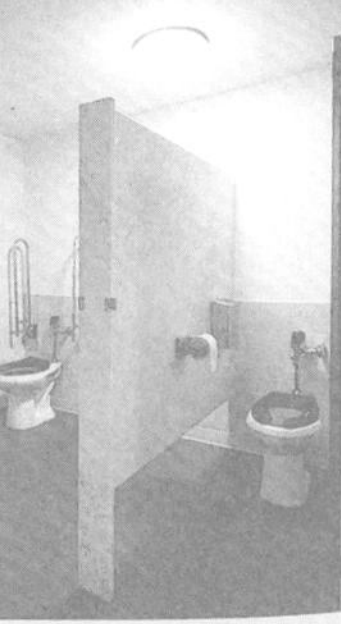

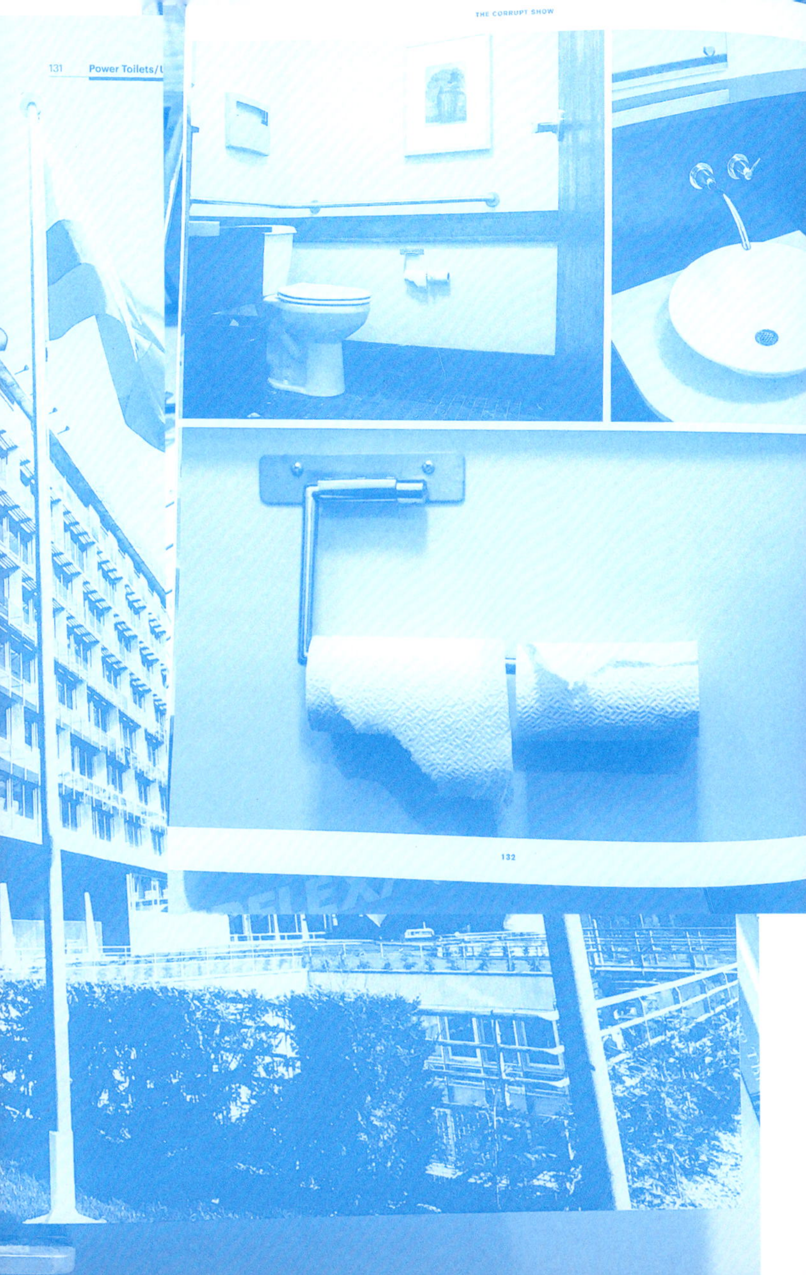

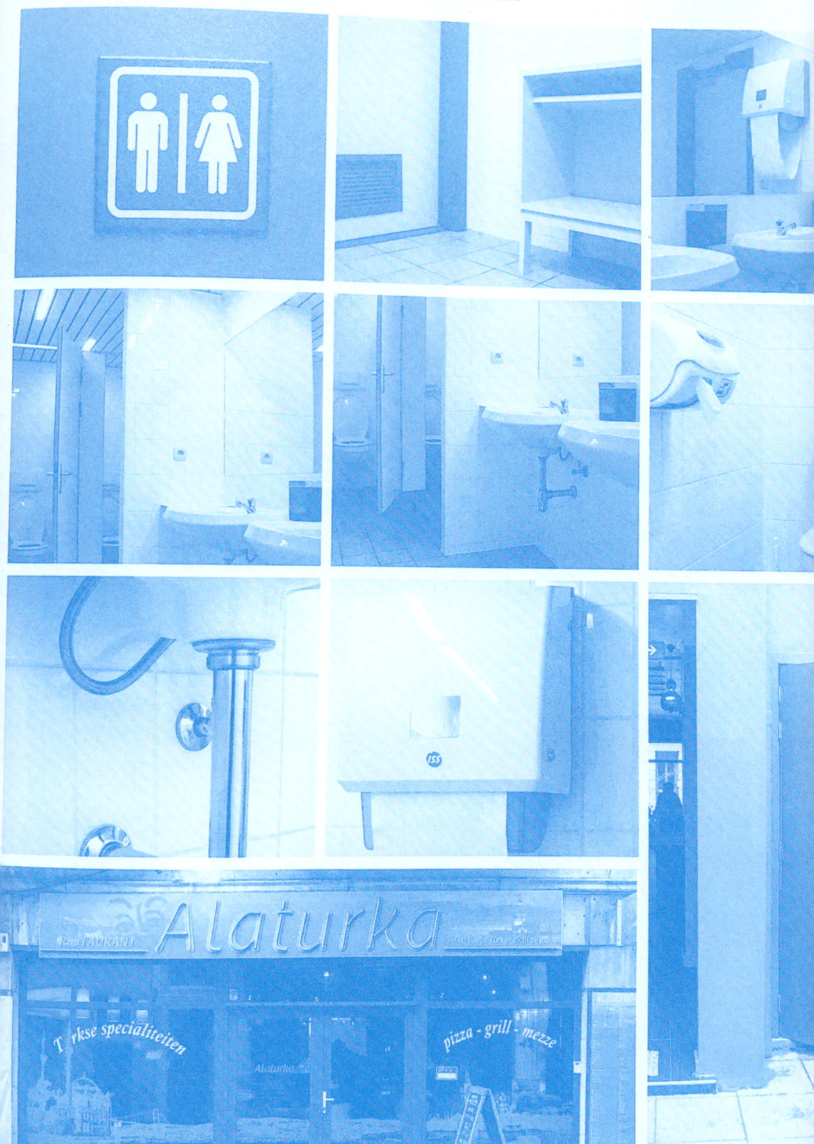
Alaturka
RESTAURANT
T rkse specialiteiten
pizza - grill - mezze
Alaturka

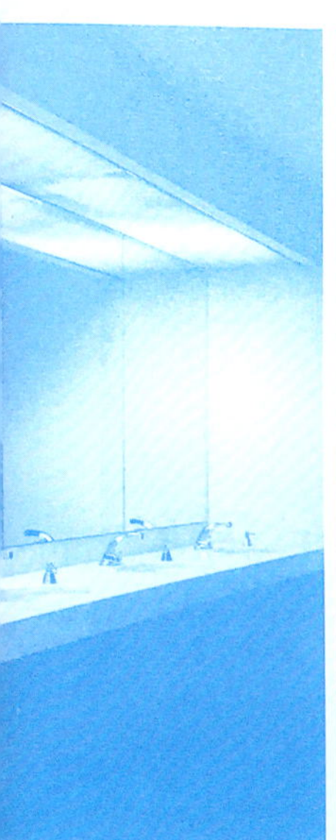

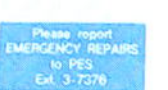
Please report
EMERGENCY REPAIRS
to PES
Ext. 3-7376

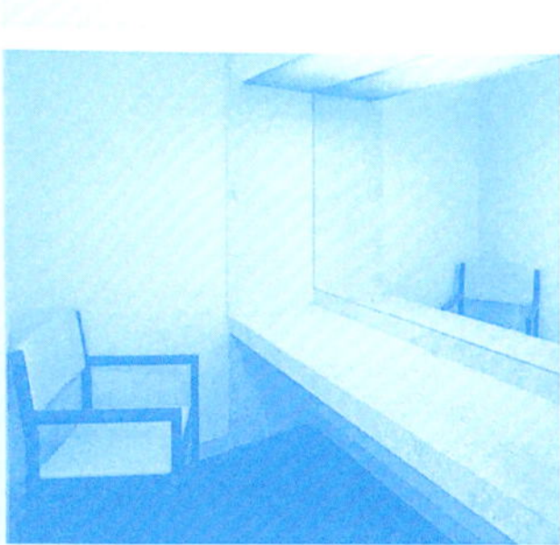

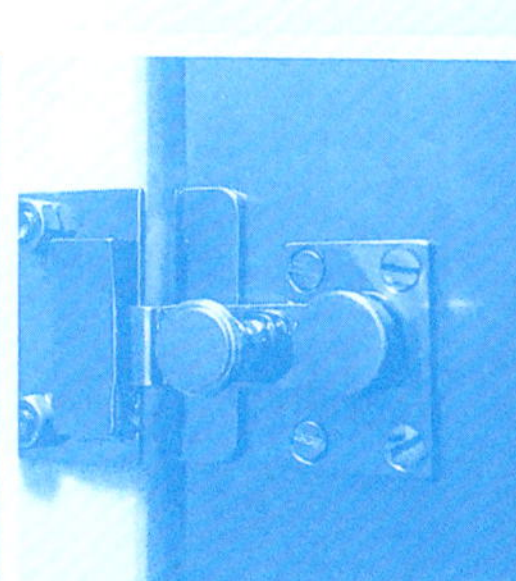

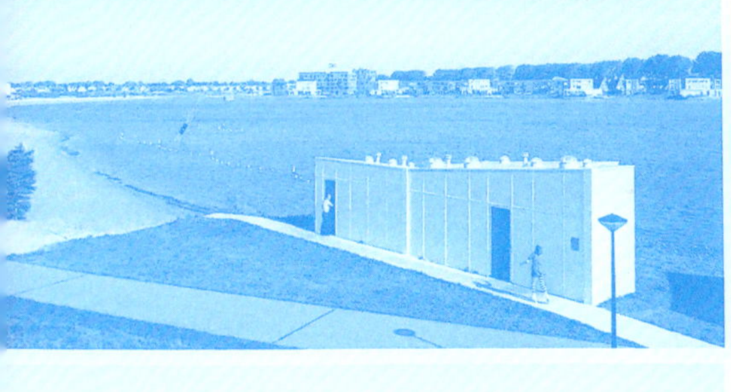

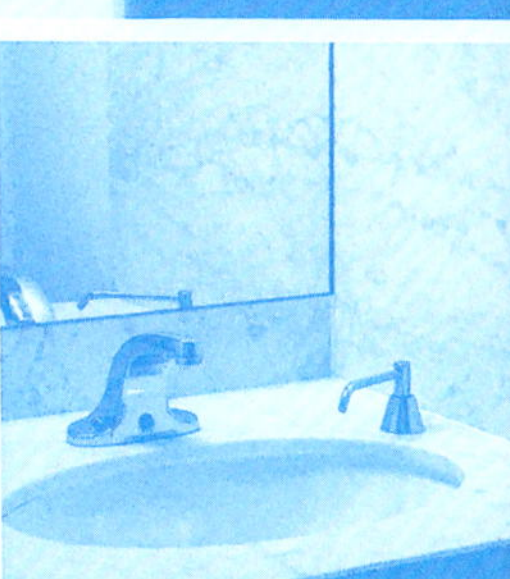

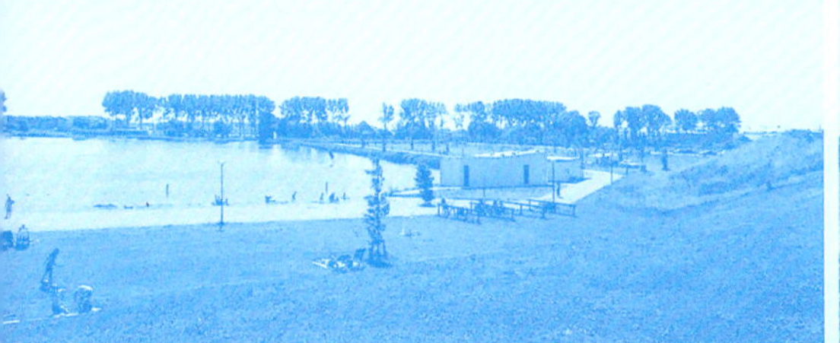

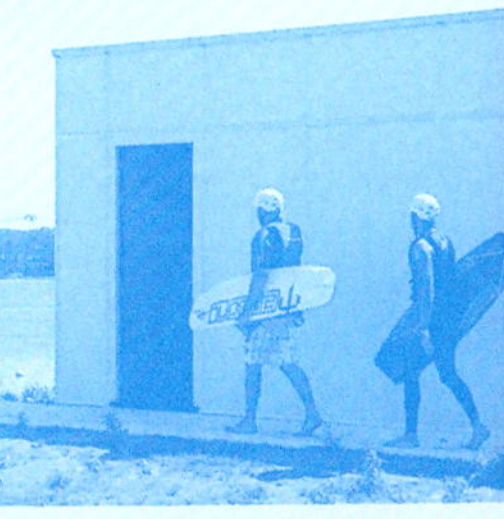

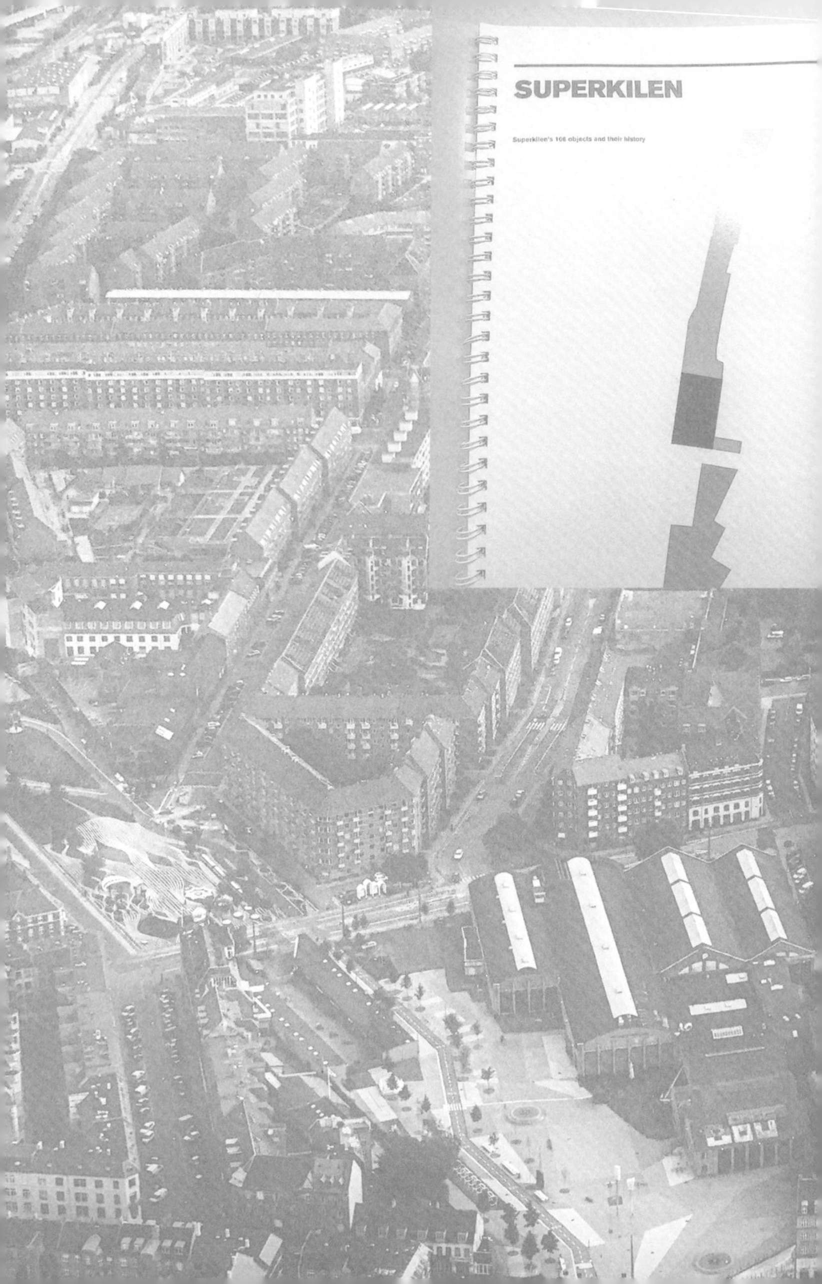

SUPERKILEN
Superkilen's 106 objects and their history

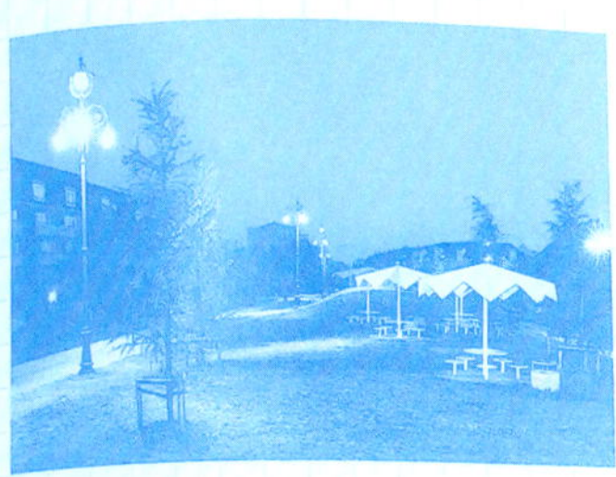

〈緑の公園〉
Green Park
Photo: Mike Magnussen

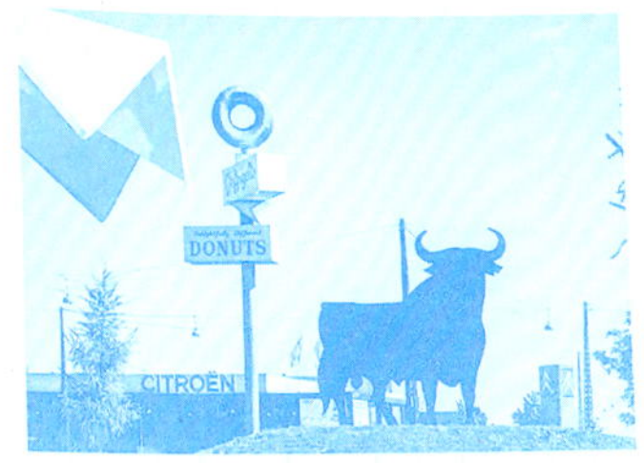

〈コスタ・デル・ソルのオズボーン社の牛〉
Osborne bull, Costa del Sol
Photo: Jens Lindhe

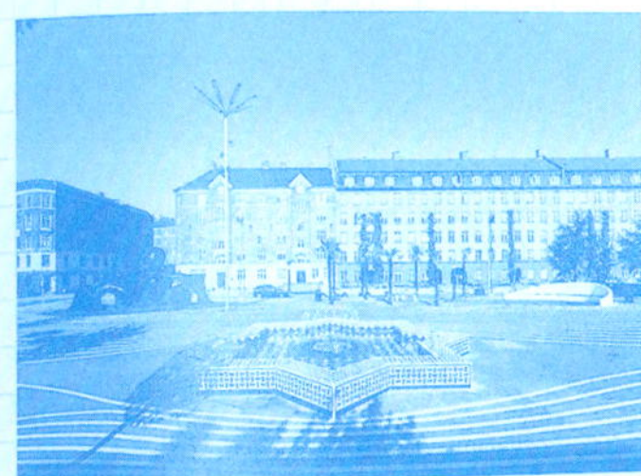

〈黒の広場〉
The Black Square
Photo: Torben Eskerod

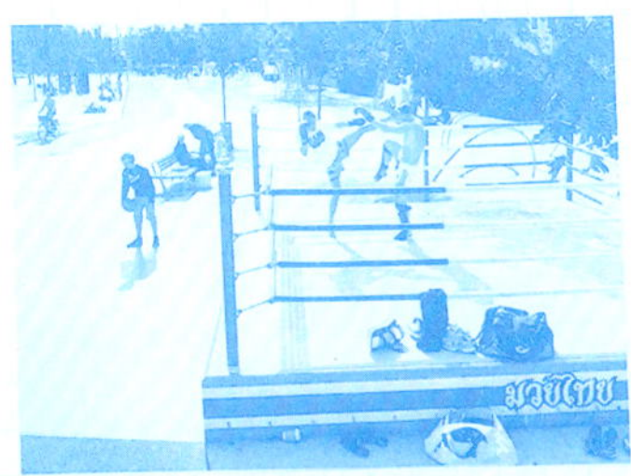

〈バンコクのタイ・ボクシング〉
Thai-boxing, Bangkok
Photo: SUPERFLEX

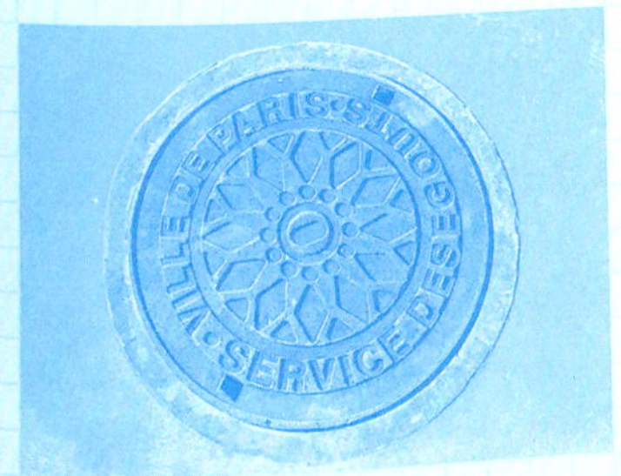

〈パリのマンホール〉
Manhole, Paris
Photo: Torben Eskerod

〈ブラック・マーケット〉
Black Market
Photo: Torben Eskerod

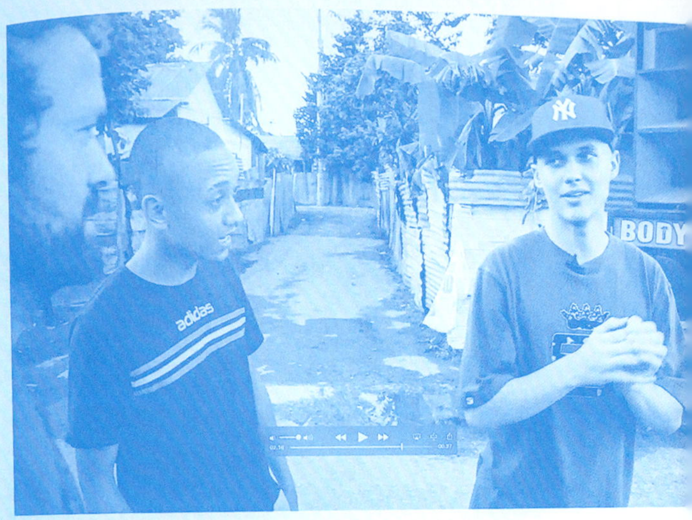

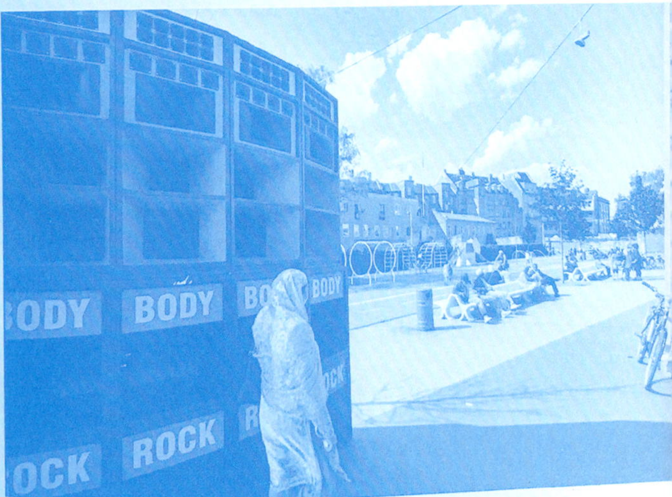

top:
SUPERFLEX in Kingston, Jamaica with Nørrebro residents and rappers Niklas and Benjamin in search of a sound system for Superkilen during Extreme Participation

above:
The nominated sound system 'Body Rock' recreated at a 1:1 scale for installation in Superkilen

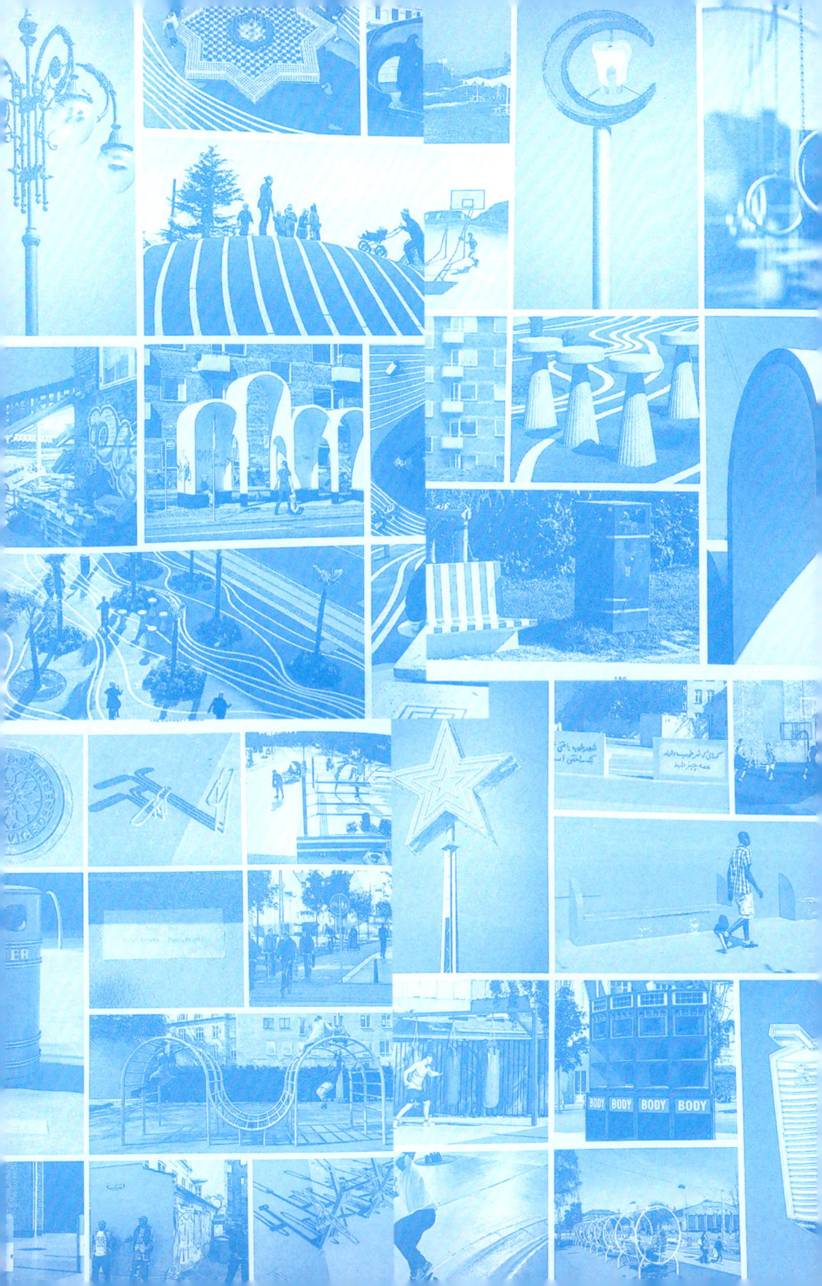

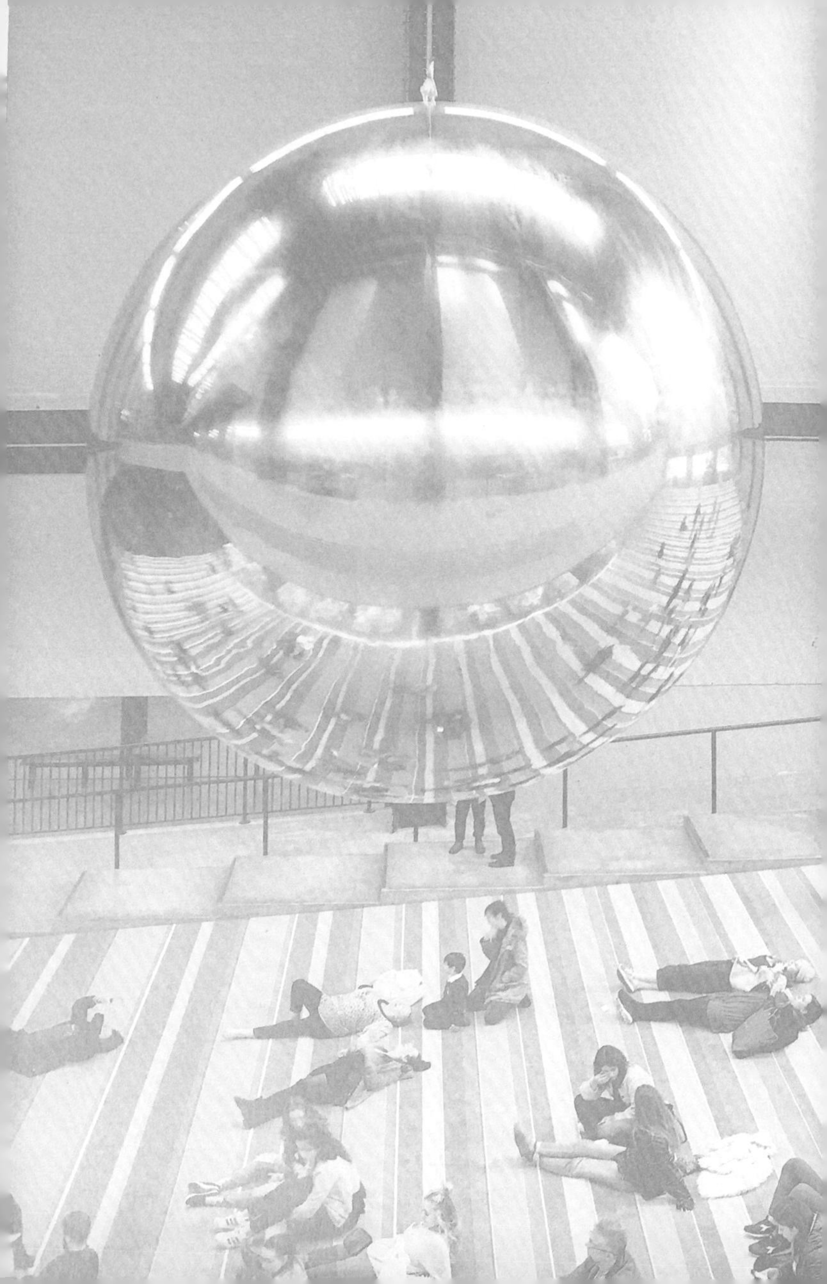

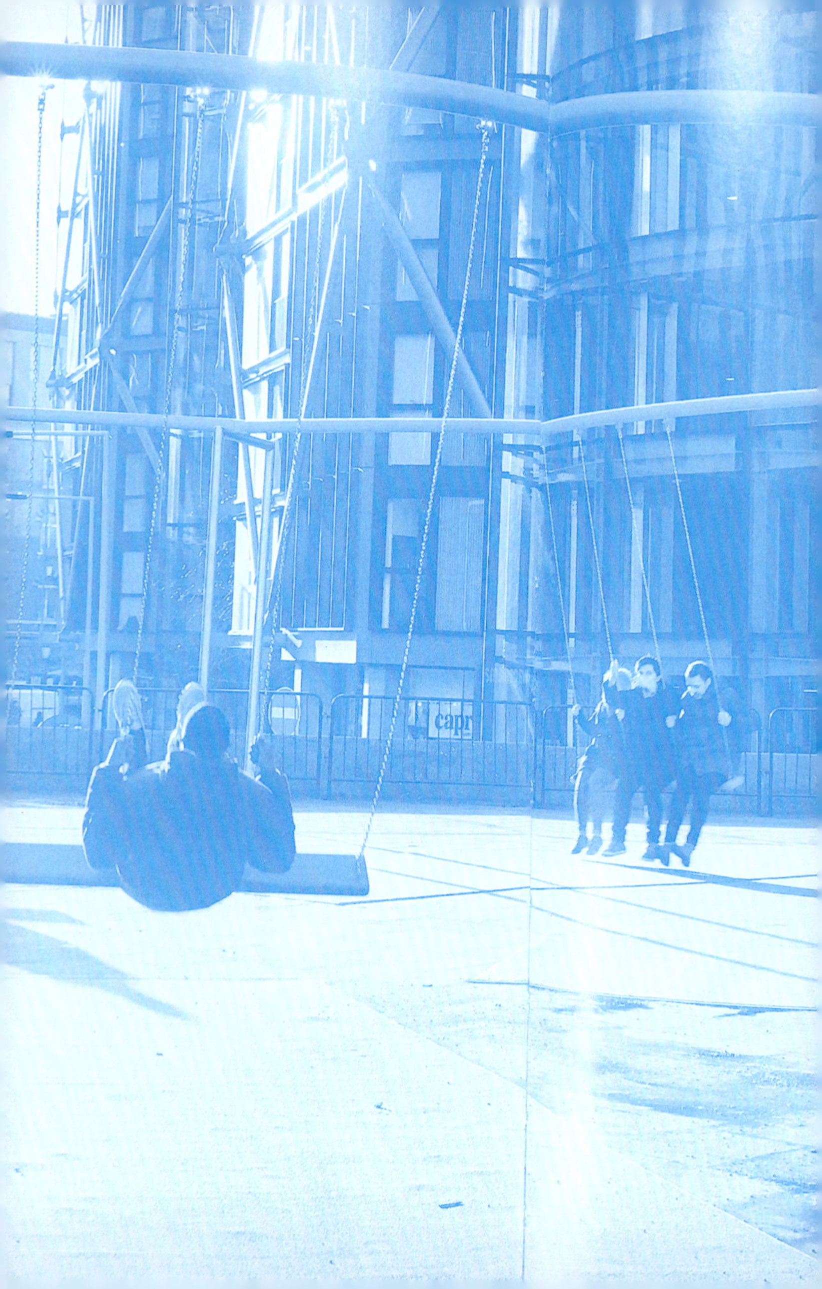

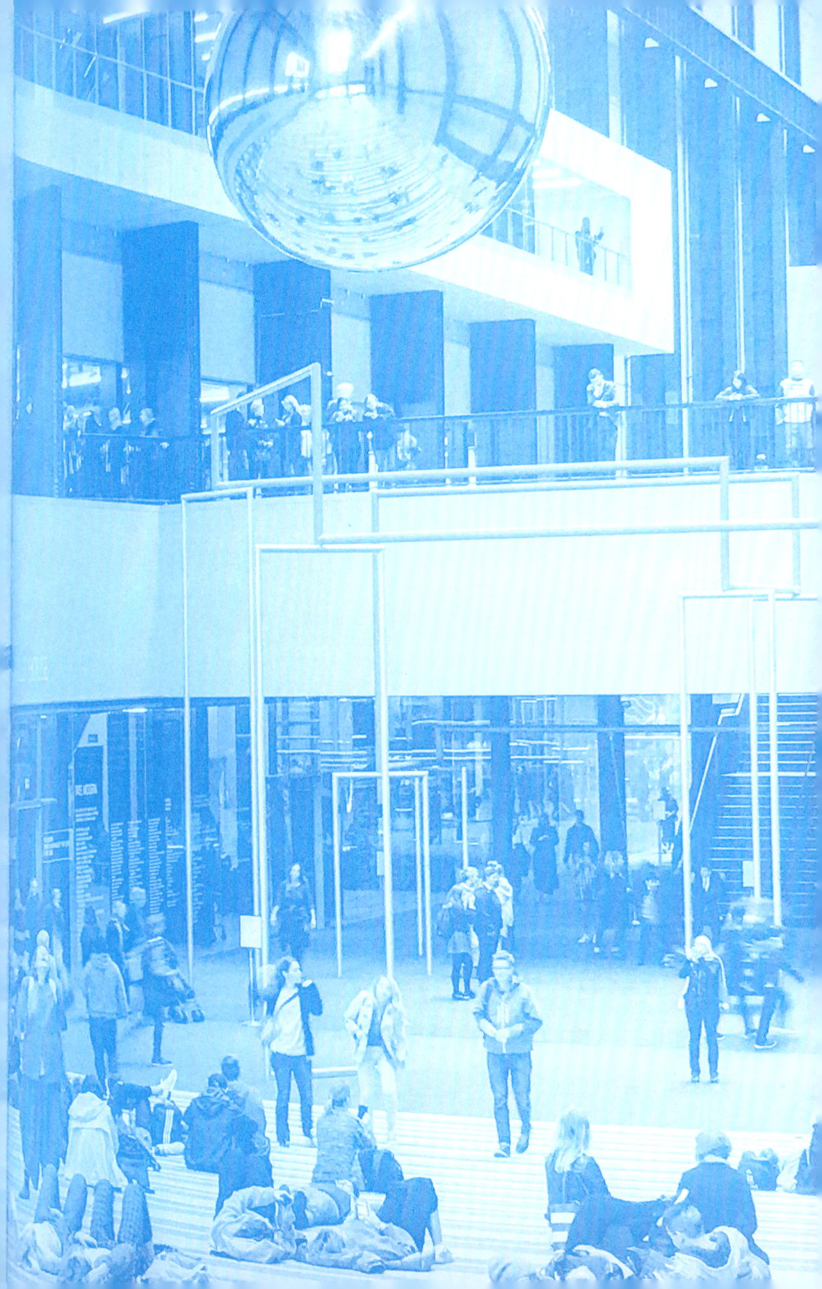

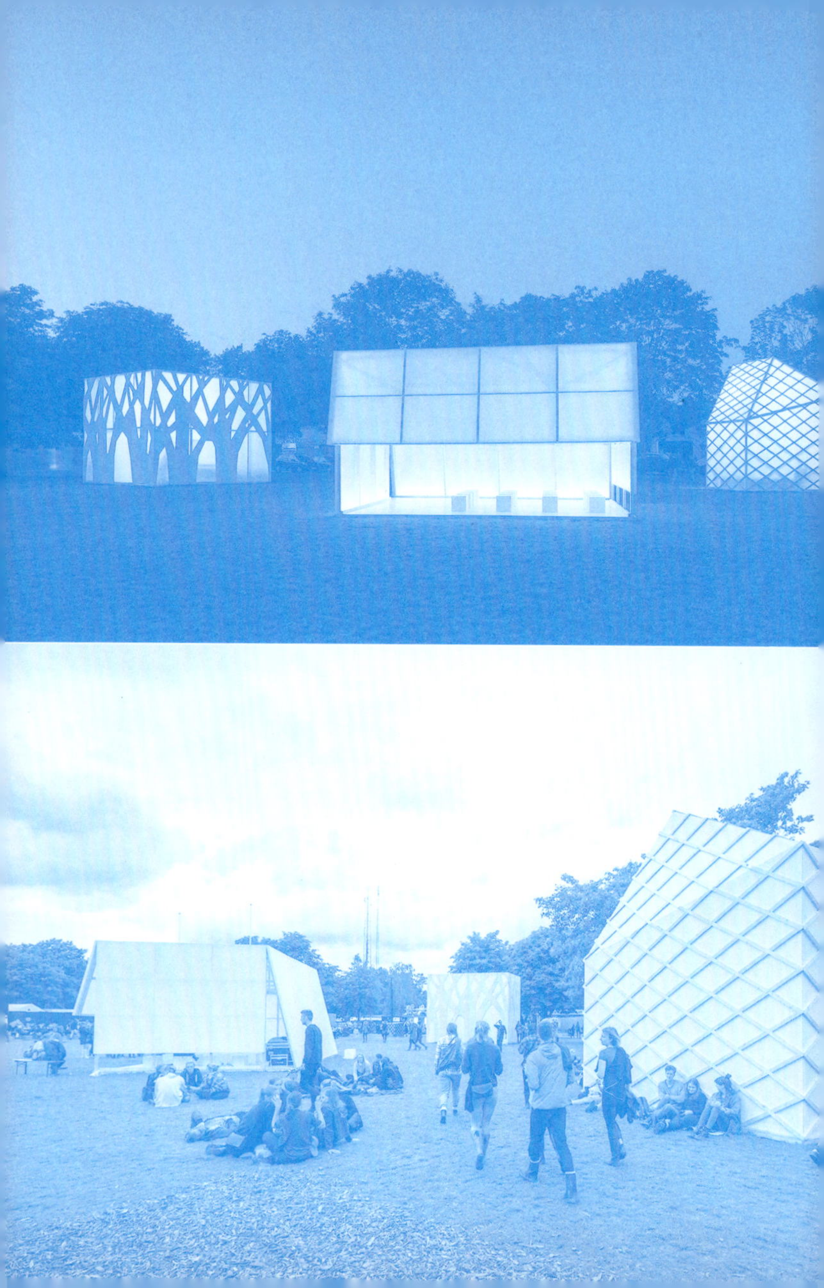

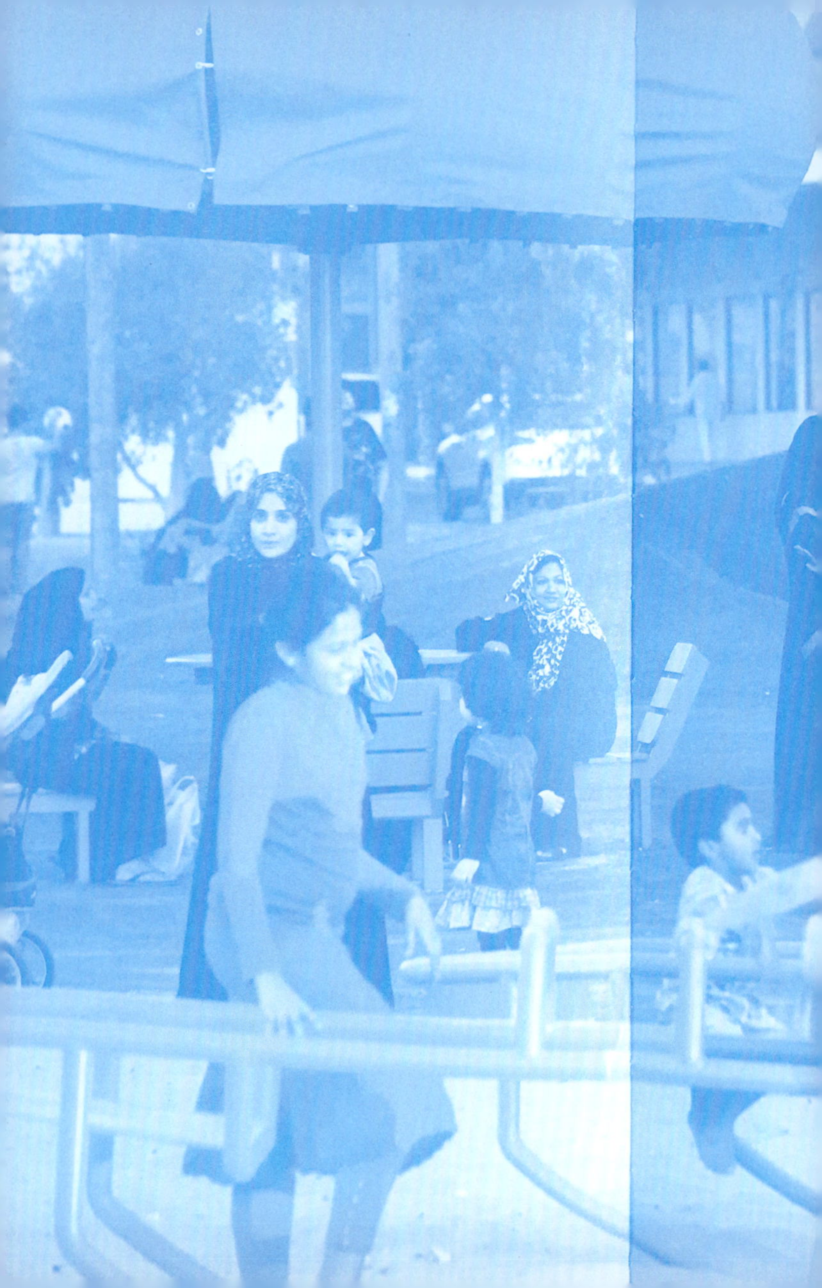

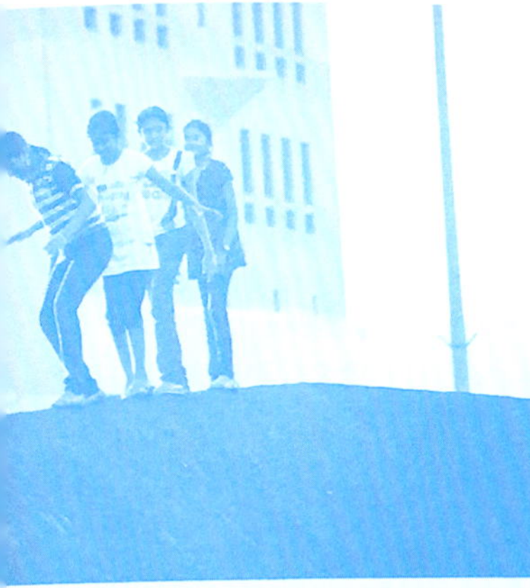
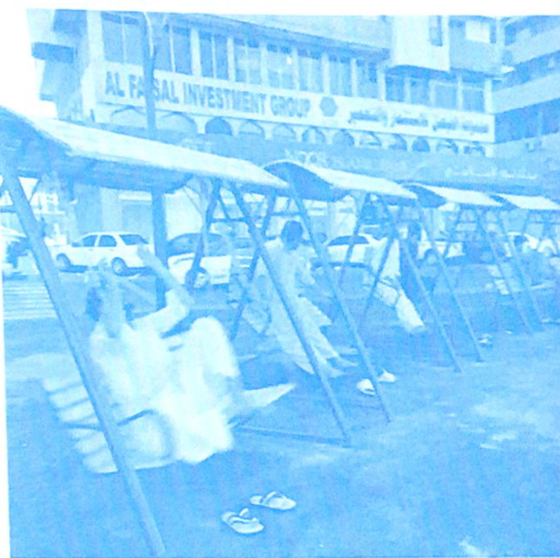
AL FAISAL INVESTMENT GROUP
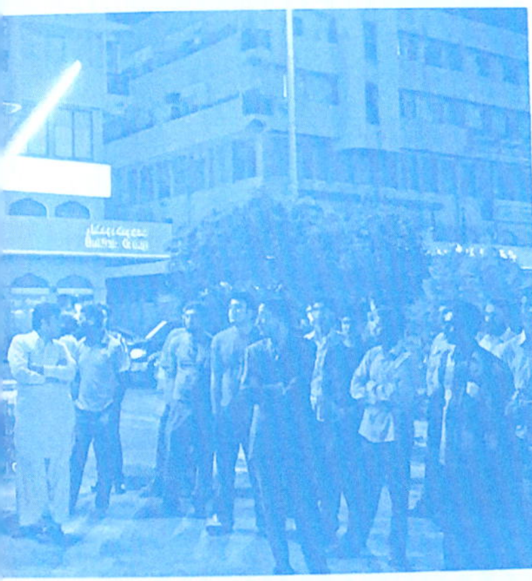
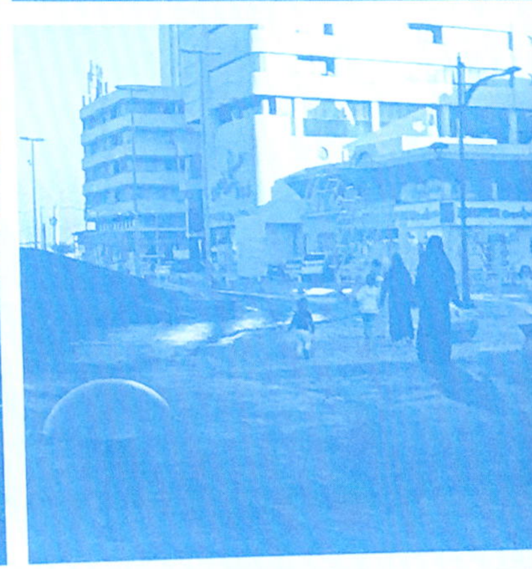
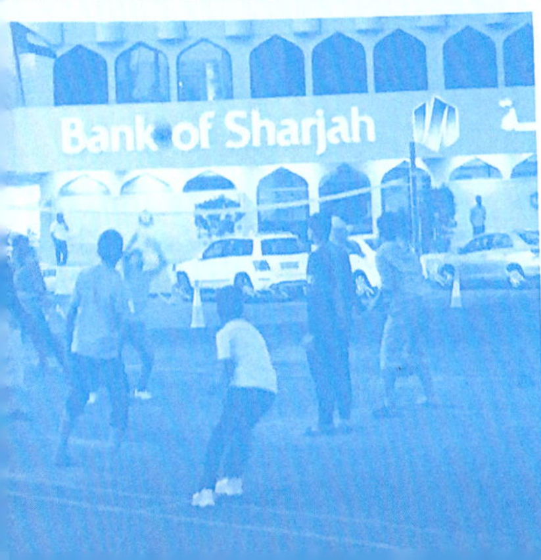
Bank of Sharjah
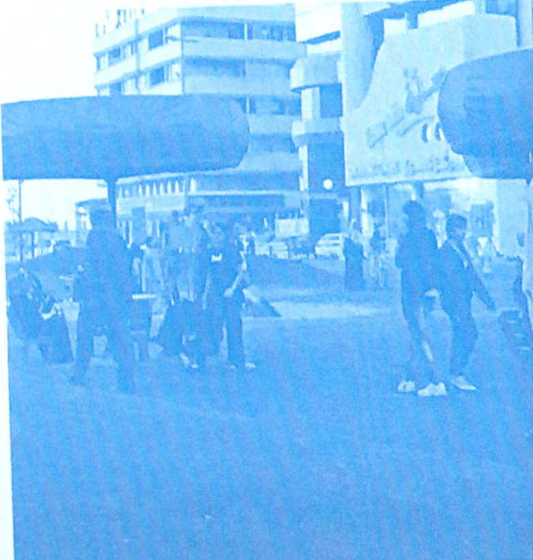

Tell us about your memory of a public object from your home town/ city or country. Please note the following:
- The object should have a function
- Functions for inspiration are: Light (Light pole, light sign, etc..) Seating/ relaxation: Bench, table, platform, pavilion...
- Leisure: Games, playground, sports for kids and/or adults
- Vegetation: Plants, trees, cactus etc...

Attach photo here or email to sharmeen@sharjahart.org

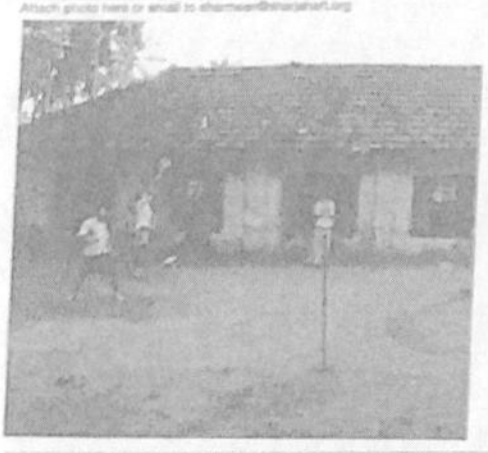

We are making a park on Bank Street. We want you to be involved in selecting what is in the park. When you submit an object, we will try to get it here and put it in the park on Bank Street for you, your family and the public. It is a great opportunity for you to share your memory and an object from your home country.

Please submit:
- Few sentences about your memory

I have many About This Play Ground and my Friends

I used to Play here with my Friend

- A photograph of the object (attach with this form)
- Your name: Pooja
- Your hometown: Kannur Kerala India
- Your contact: 055 832 2440

Tell us about your memory of a public object from your home town/ city or country. Please note the following:
- The object should have a function
- Functions for inspiration are: Light (Light pole, light sign, etc..) Seating/ relaxation: Bench, table, platform, pavilion...
- Leisure: Games, playground, sports for kids and/or adults
- Vegetation: Plants, trees, cactus etc...

Attach photo here or email to sharmeen@sharjahart.org

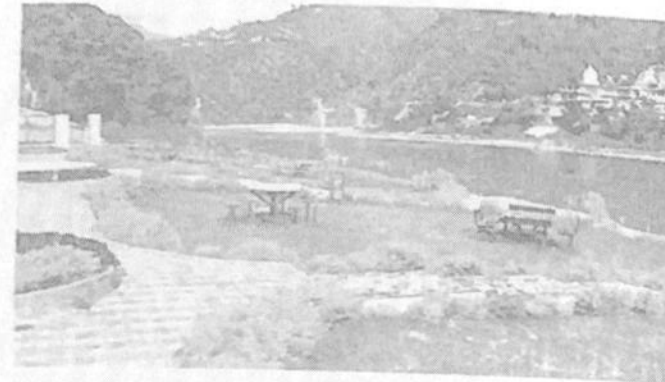

We are making a park on Bank Street. We want you to be involved in selecting what is in the park. When you submit an object, we will try to get it here and put it in the park on Bank Street for you, your family and the public. It is a great opportunity for you to share your memory and an object from your home country.

Please submit:
- Few sentences about your memory

The colorful seats are all different.

- A photograph of the object (attach with this form)
- Your name: Habib Akhtar
- Your hometown: Pakistan Azad Kashmir - Kotli.
- Your contact: 055 7400394

Tell us about your memory of a public object from your home town/ city or country. Please note the following:
- The object should have a function
- Functions for inspiration are: Light (Light pole, light sign, etc..) Seating/ relaxation: Bench, table, platform, pavilion...
- Leisure: Games, playground, sports for kids and/or adults
- Vegetation: Plants, trees, cactus etc...

Attach photo here or email to sharmeen@sharjahart.org

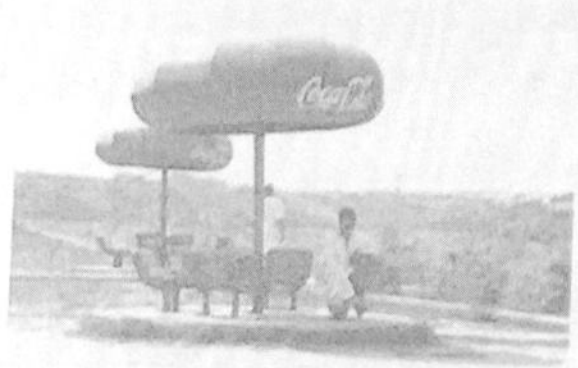

We are making a park on Bank Street. We want you to be involved in selecting what is in the park. When you submit an object, we will try to get it here and put it in the park on Bank Street for you, your family and the public. It is a great opportunity for you to share your memory and an object from your home country.

Please submit:
- Few sentences about your memory

Mirpur → these coca-cola seats are very striking because of the color and the shape and provide for very comfortable seats and shading.

- A photograph of the object (attach with this form)
- Your name: Zaib Iqbal
- Your hometown: Pakistan Azad Kashmir
- Your contact: 0343 6818678

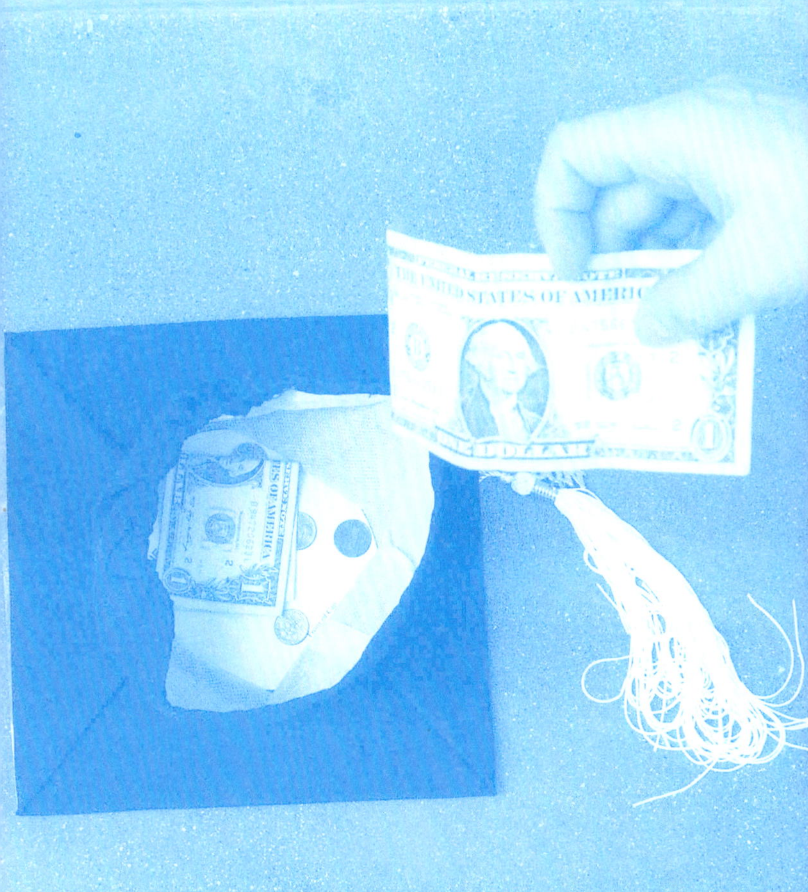

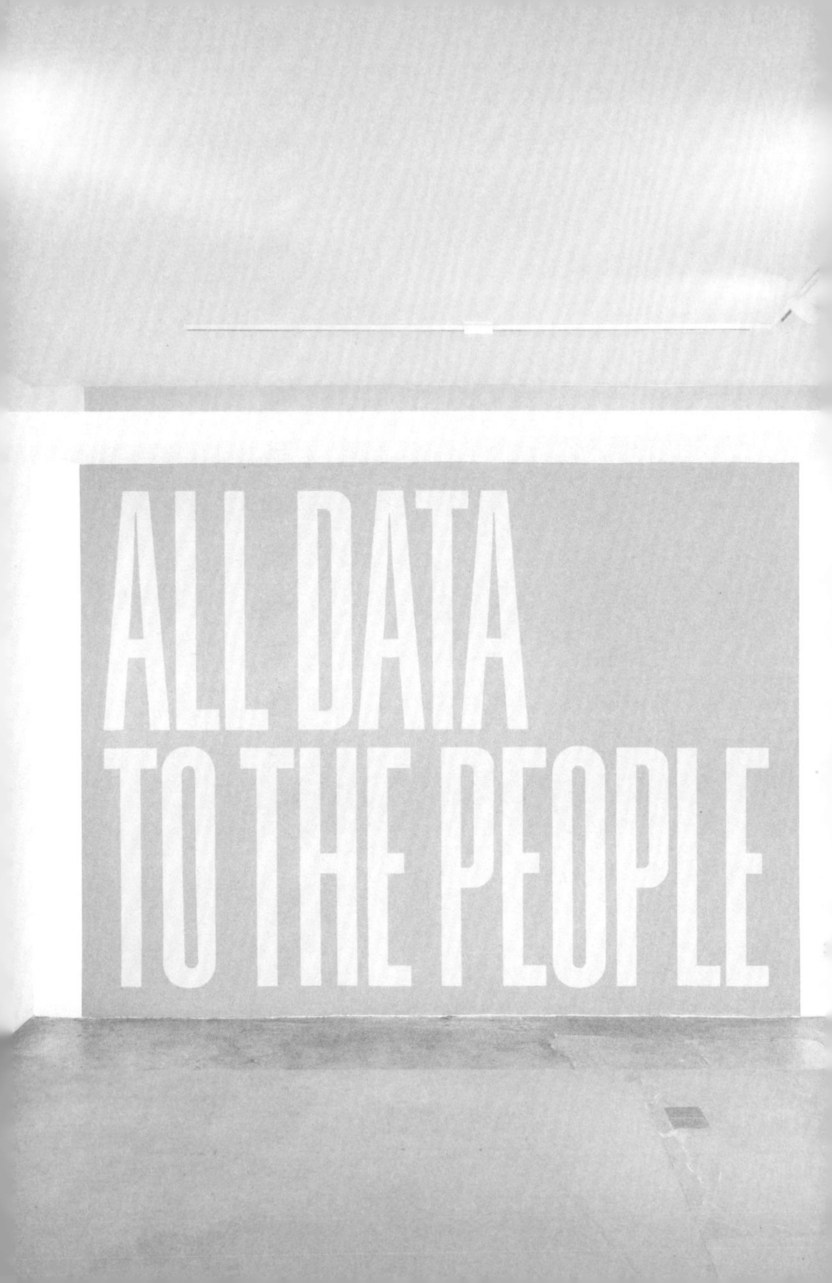

ALL DATA
TO THE PEOPLE

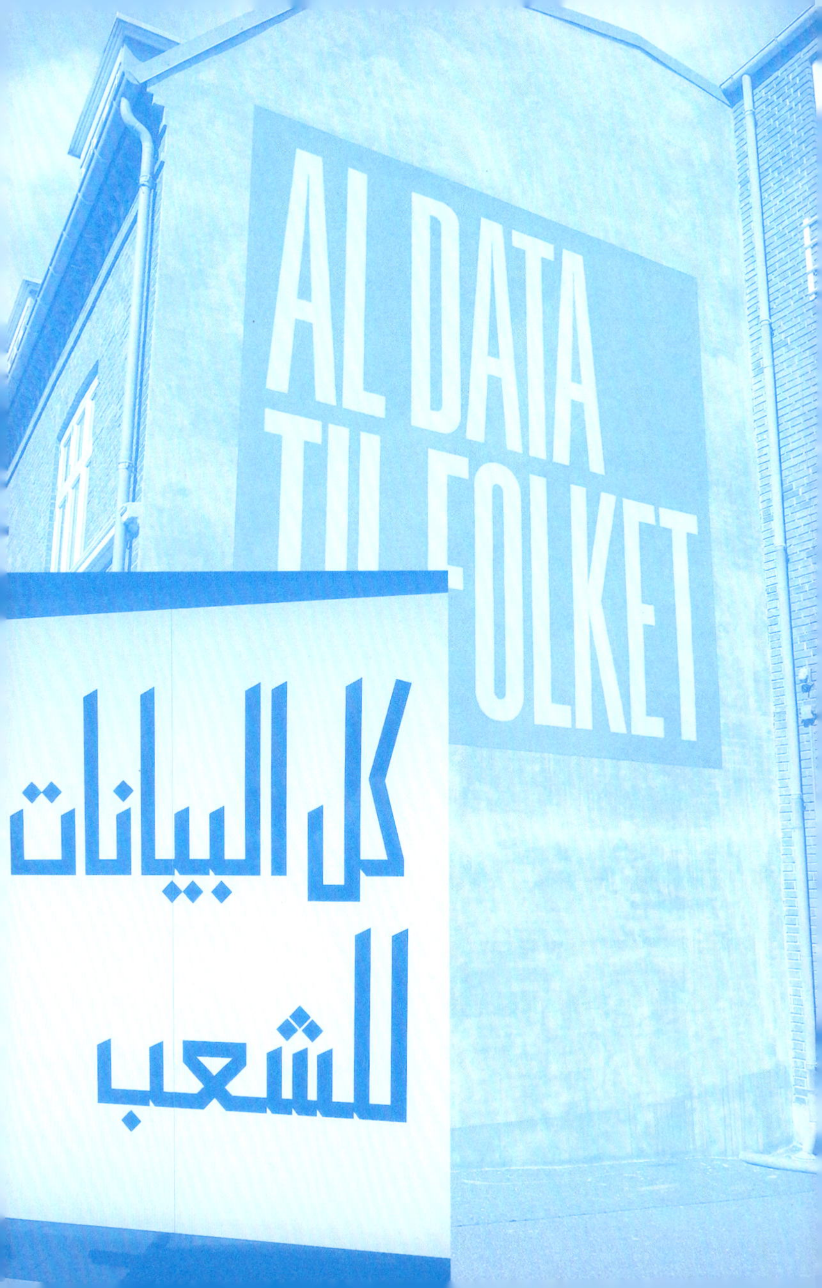

AL DATA
TIL FOLKET
كل البيانات
للشعب

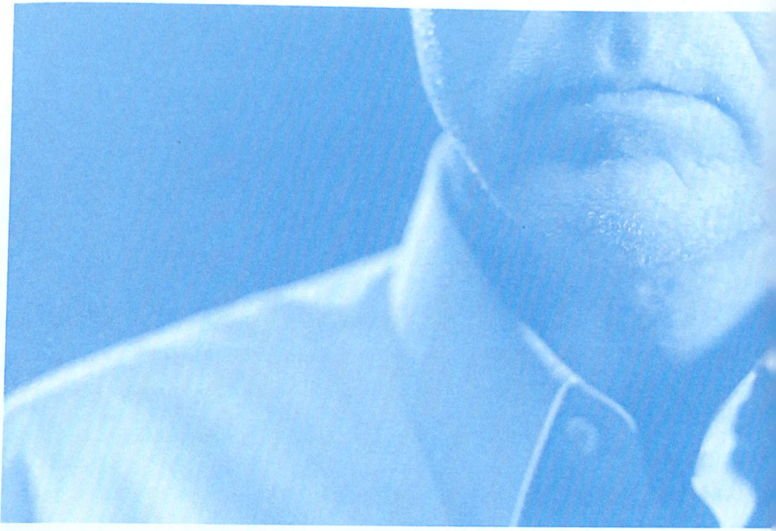

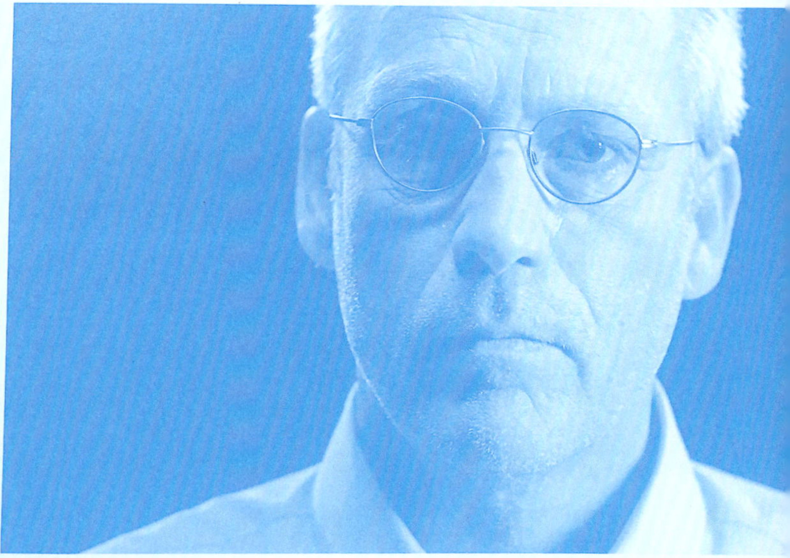

SUPERFLEX

LOCATION: EARLSFORT TERRACE

BJØRNSTJERNE REUTER CHRISTIANSEN
BORN 1969 IN COPENHAGEN (DNK)
JAKOB FENGER BORN 1968 IN ROSKILDE (DNK)
RASMUS NIELSEN BORN 1969 IN HJØRRING (DNK)
SUPERFLEX ESTABLISHED IN 1993
LIVE AND WORK IN COPENHAGEN (DNK)

'The Financial Crisis (Session I-IV)' is a new film work in which Superflex address the financial crisis from a therapeutic perspective. The viewer will be guided through his/her worst nightmares to reveal the crisis without as if it were a psychosis within. In four sessions, the visitor will experience the fascination of speculation and the power of fear, the experience of loss and personal disaster, and finally the anxiety and frustration of losing control—and come out feeling fresh, comfortable and happy! Superflex describe their practice as an exercise in providing 'tools' to affect or inf[luen]ence their social or economic context. Previc[ous] projects include paying visitors to enter th[e] exhibition, the development and marketing [of] a new beverage—'Free Beer'—and the p[ro]duction of a self-sufficient, portable bio[gas] unit to provide energy for a family in Afr[ica]. Recent solo shows include 'Free Sol Lew[itt]' Van Abbe Museum, Eindhoven, (2010) [and] 'Flooded McDonald's' at South Lon[don] Gallery (2009). Superflex also participate[d] the 2011 Singapore Biennial.

KINDLY SUPPORT

STATENS
KUNSTR[...]

Superflex

(gegr. 1993, DK, Kopenhagen)
Supercopy | Haacke Hermès, 2015, Seidentuch,
elektrischer Ventilator, 290 × 290 cm.
Investment Bank Flowerpots, 2015, Architekturmodelle
mit Pflanzen, unterschiedl. Abmessungen

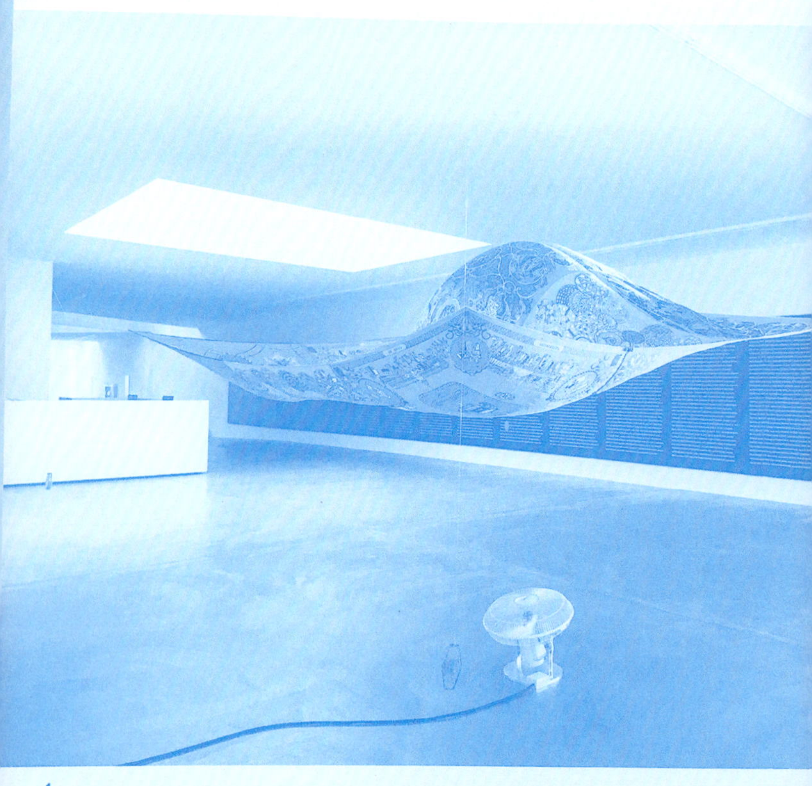

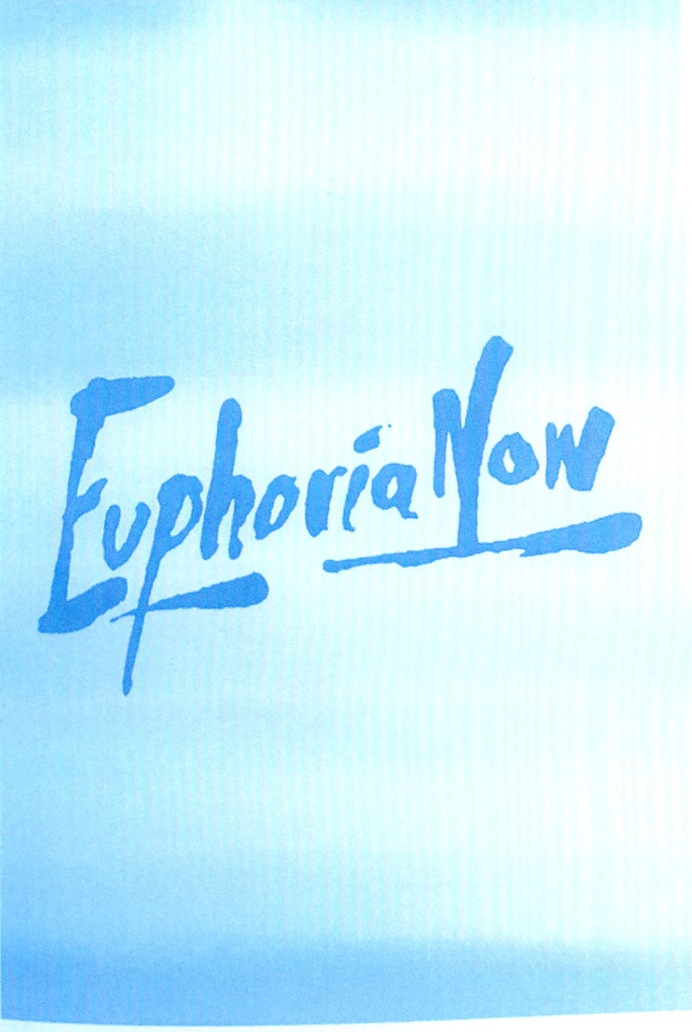

Euphoria Now / Pound Sterling
The colours of the carpet designed for *One Two Three Swing!* is derived from British bank notes, initially realized as the painting series Euphoria Now!, based on colour schemes of global currencies. The conceptual starting-point for the series is the to induce hypnagogic hallucination by observation of its flickering light, and supposedly encourage artistic production. Directly referring to the colours of currencies, SUPERFLEX transfers the concept of the 'dreamachine' into contemporary society's greatest hypnagogic hallucination of all: money.

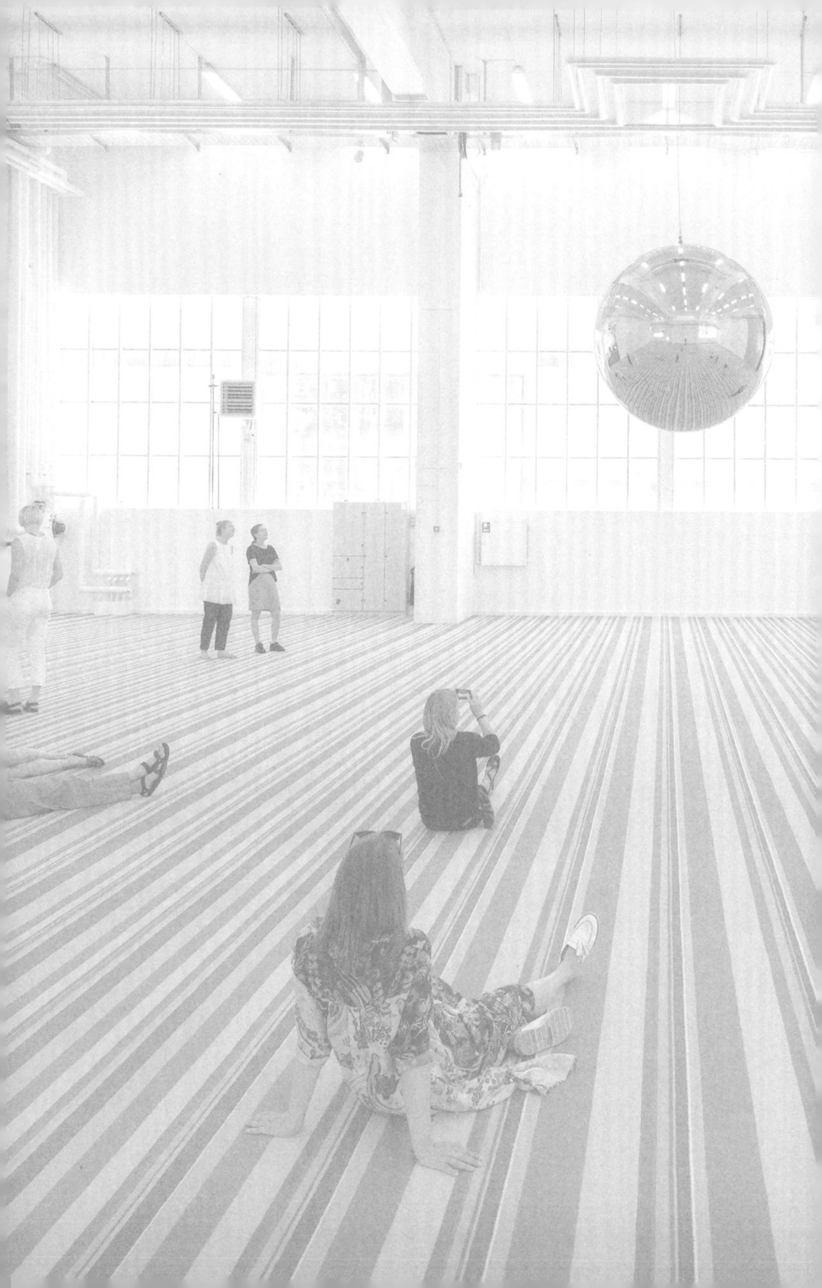

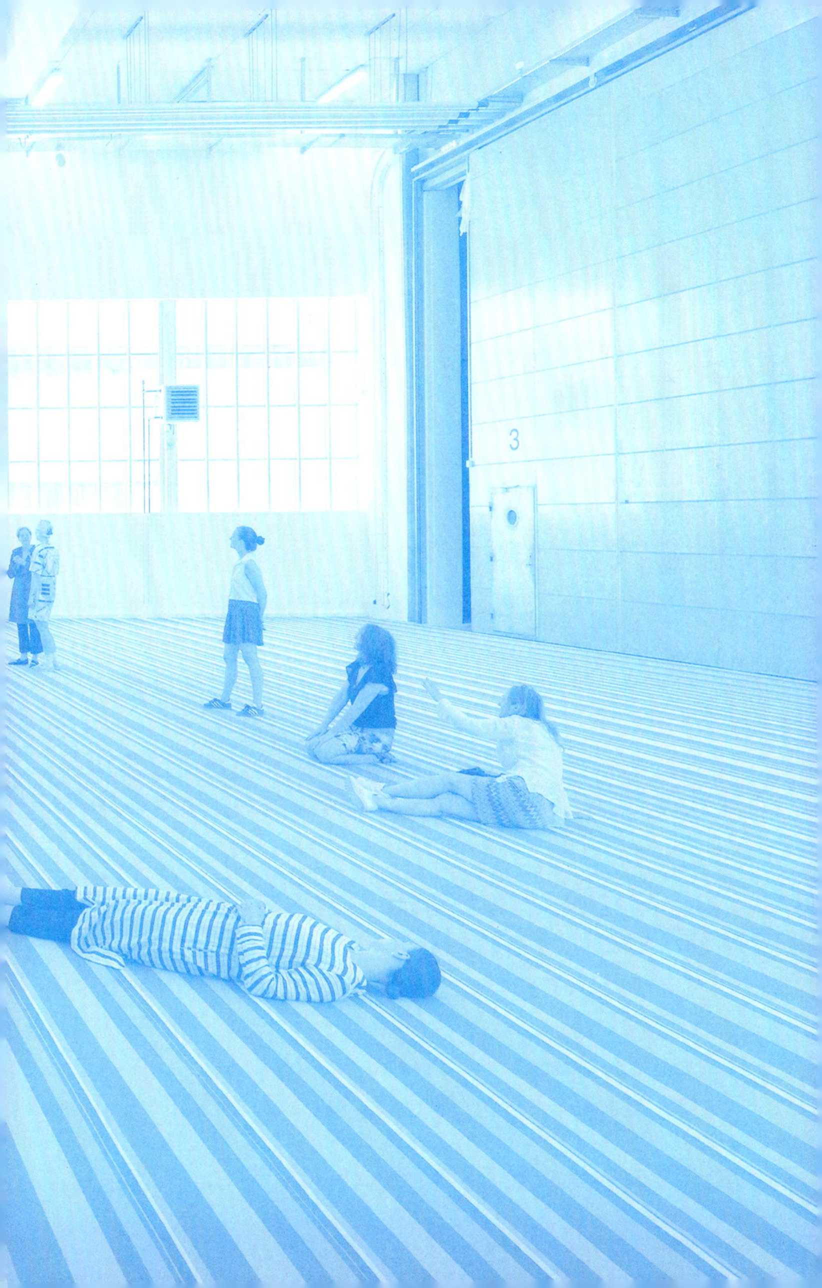

Title:
Bankrupt Banks/
XXXX Bank acquired by
XXXXXX,XX date and
XXXX year
Material:
Cotton fabric,acrylic pain
Size: 200x215cm
Edition: Each unique

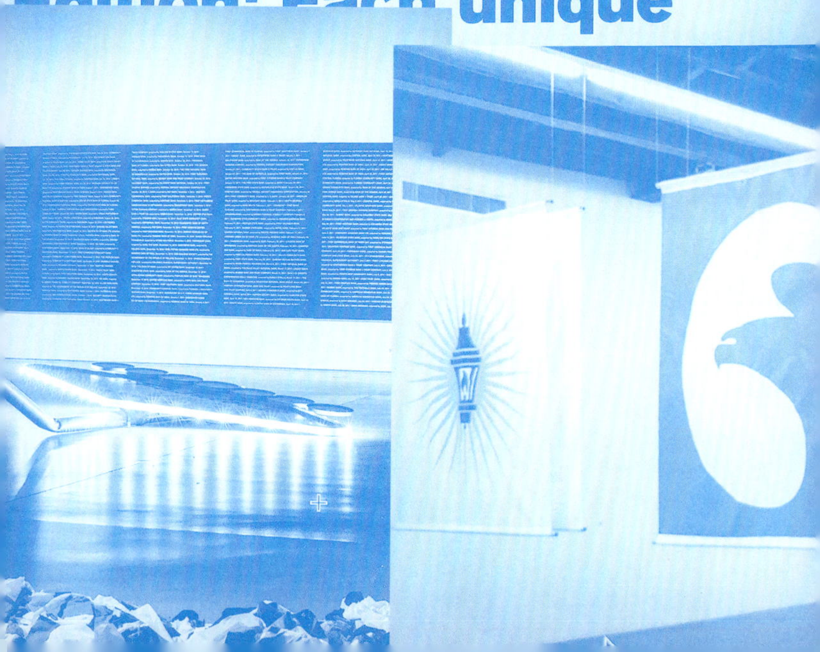

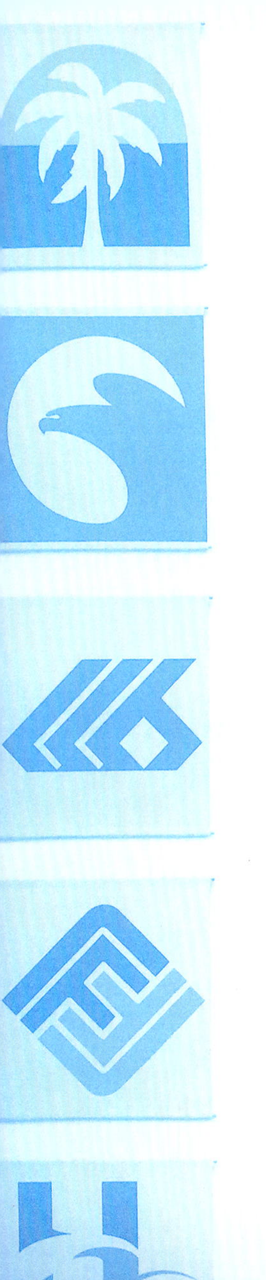

Bankrupt Banks / BankUnited FSB Acquired by BankUnited, May 21st, 2009, 2012

Acrylic paint on cotton
215 × 200 cm

Exhibitions: 2012: *Bankrupt Banks*, Peter Blum Gallery, New York. 2013: *The Corrupt the Speculative Machine*, Fundacion Jumex, Mexico City.

Note: Hand-painted banner depicting the logo of a bankrupt bank.

Bankrupt Banks / Colonial Bank Acquired by BB&T, August 14th, 2009, 2012

Acrylic paint on cotton
215 × 200 cm

Exhibitions: 2012: *Bankrupt Banks*, Peter Blum Gallery, New York. 2013: *The Corrupt the Speculative Machine*, Fundacion Jumex, Mexico City.

Note: Hand-painted banner depicting the logo of a bankrupt bank.

Bankrupt Banks / United Commercial Bank Acquired by East West Bank, November

Acrylic paint on cotton
215 × 200 cm

Exhibitions: 2012: *Bankrupt Banks*, Peter Blum Gallery, New York. 2013: *The Corrupt the Speculative Machine*, Fundacion Jumex, Mexico City.

Note: Hand-painted banner depicting the logo of a bankrupt bank.

Bankrupt Banks / First Federal Bank of California Acquired by OneWest Bank, Dece 2009, 2012

Acrylic paint on cotton
215 × 200 cm

Exhibitions: 2012: *Bankrupt Banks*, Peter Blum Gallery, New York. 2013: *The Corrupt the Speculative Machine*, Fundacion Jumex, Mexico City.

Note: Hand-painted banner depicting the logo of a bankrupt bank.

Bankrupt Banks / Horizon Bank Acquired by Washington Federal Savings and Loan January 8th, 2010,, 2012

Acrylic paint on cotton
215 × 200 cm

Exhibitions: 2012: *Bankrupt Banks*, Peter Blum Gallery, New York. 2013: *The Corrupt

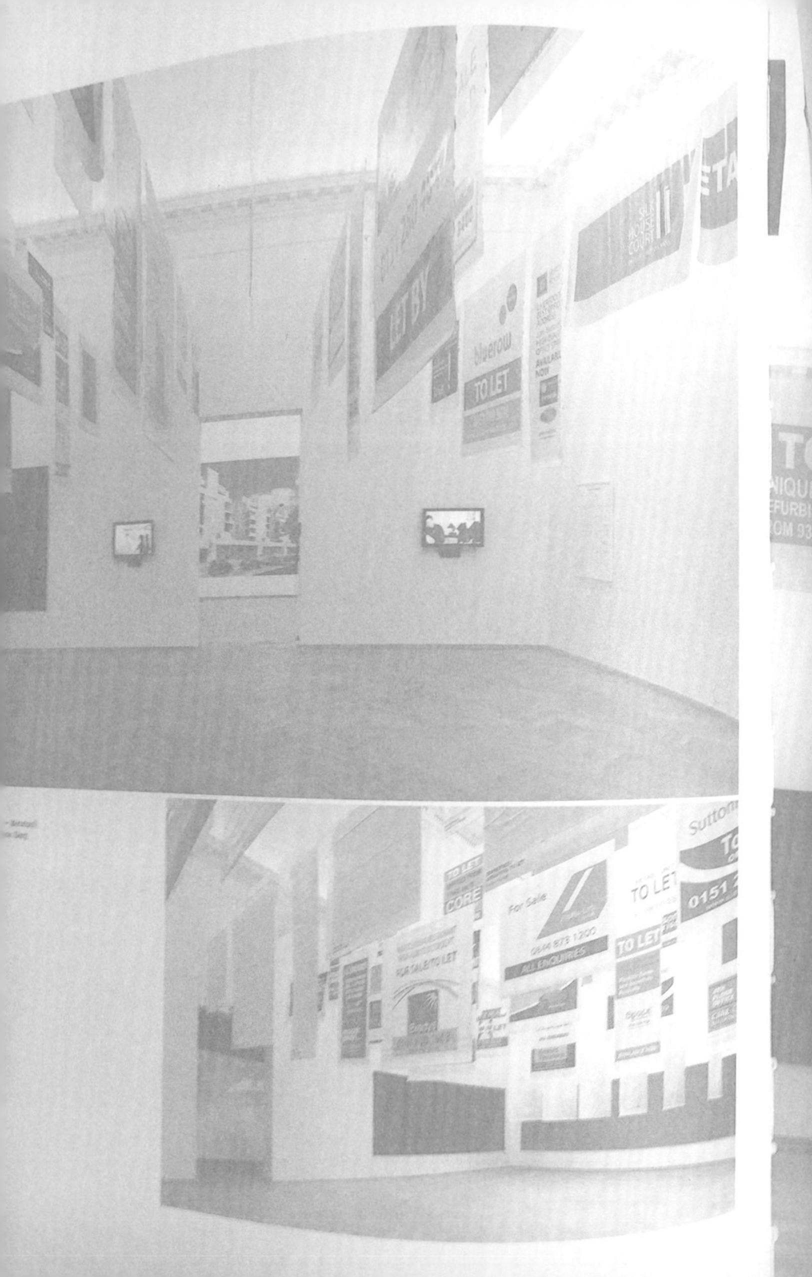

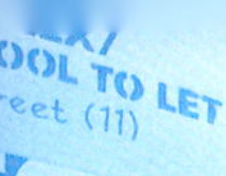
OOL TO LET
reet (11)

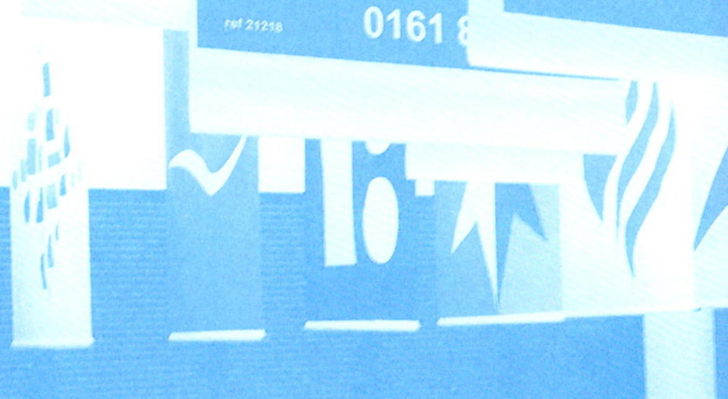
TO LET
ALITY OFFICES
H CAR PARKING
SQFT - 37,671 sqft
Matthews & Goodman
0151 236 8732
JONES LANG LASALLE
0151 236 7336
TO LET
0161 795 9999
018 096 9534
CUDDL
TO
0151 706
www.cuddly-b
TO LET
Potential Restaurant
Bar Opportunity
Lower Ground Floor Extending to
5,000 sq ft
www.colliers.com/uk/leisure
ref 21218
0161 8
ALL ENQUIR
FORMER BANK
HALL & OFFIC
WITH COVER
CAR PARKIN
23,111 SQFT
(2147 SQ M)
mason owen...
0151 242 3000
www.masonowen.com
SUPE
LIVER

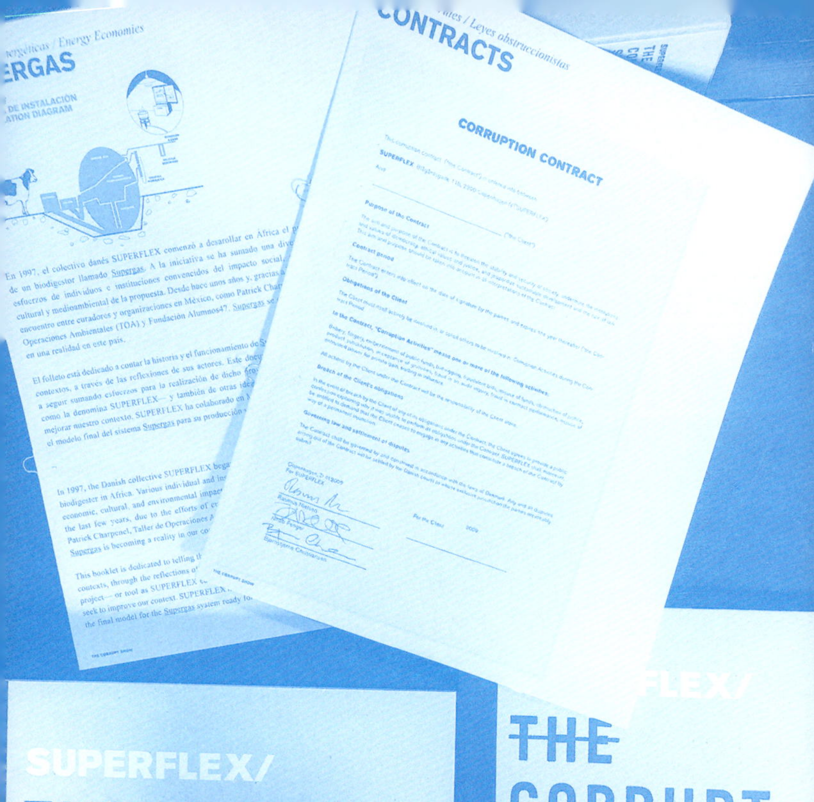

Energéticas / Energy Economics
SUPERGAS
DE INSTALACIÓN
ATION DIAGRAM
CONTRACTS
CORRUPTION CONTRACT
Purpose of the Contract
Contract period
Obligations of the Client
In the Contract, "Corruption Activities"
Breach of the Client's obligations
Governing law and settlement of disputes
SUPERFLEX/
THE
CORRUPT
SHOW
AND
THE
SPECULATIVE
MACHINE

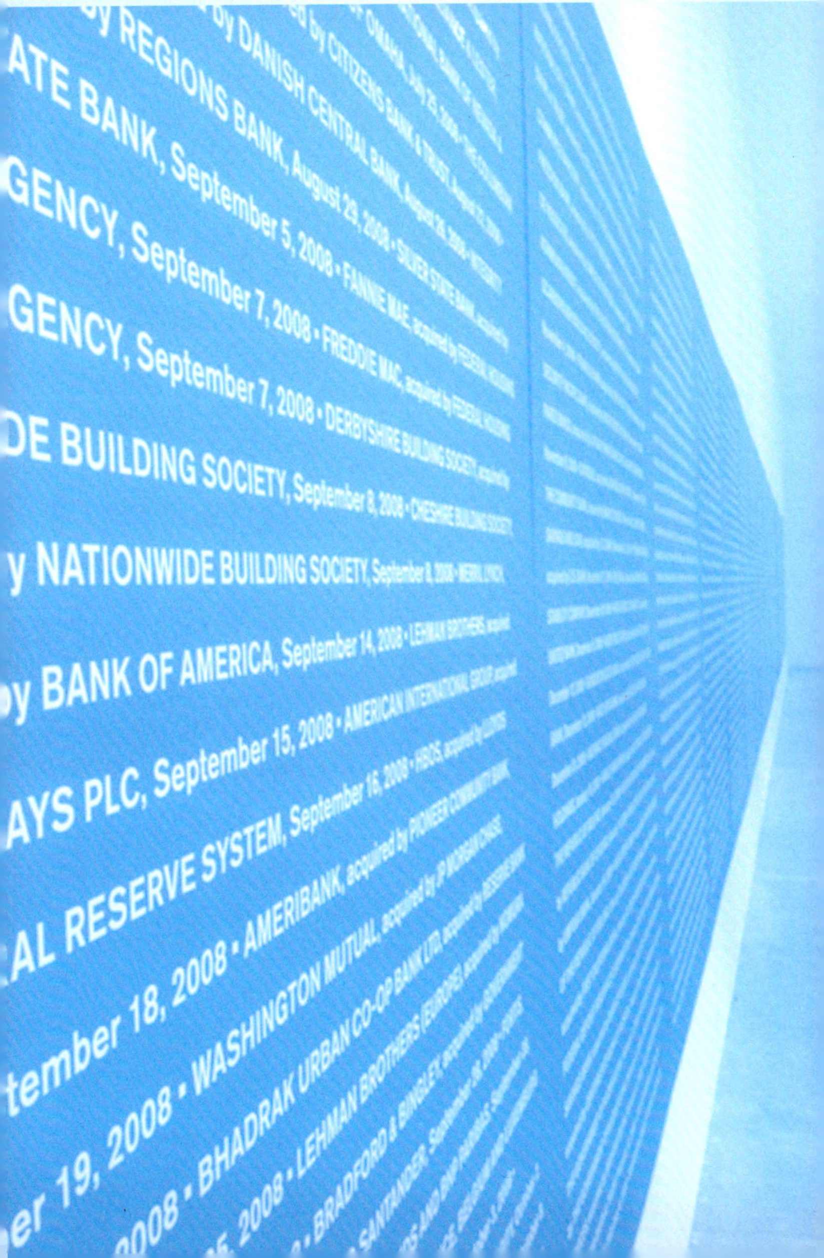

by REGIONS BANK, August 29, 2008 · by DANISH CENTRAL BANK & TRUST · by CITIZENS BANK

ATE BANK, September 5, 2008 · FANNIE MAE,

GENCY, September 7, 2008 · FREDDIE MAC, acquired by FEDERAL HOUSING

GENCY, September 7, 2008 · DERBYSHIRE BUILDING SOCIETY,

DE BUILDING SOCIETY, September 8, 2008 · CHESHIRE BUILDING SOCIETY

y NATIONWIDE BUILDING SOCIETY, September 8, 2008 · MERRILL LYNCH,

by BANK OF AMERICA, September 14, 2008 · LEHMAN BROTHERS,

AYS PLC, September 15, 2008 · AMERICAN INTERNATIONAL GROUP,

AL RESERVE SYSTEM, September 16, 2008 · HBOS, acquired by

tember 18, 2008 · AMERIBANK, acquired by PIONEER COMMUNITY BANK

er 19, 2008 · WASHINGTON MUTUAL, acquired by JP MORGAN CHASE

008 · BHADRAK URBAN CO-OP BANK LTD · LEHMAN BROTHERS (EUROPE)

2008 · BRADFORD & BINGLEY, acquired by · SANTANDER

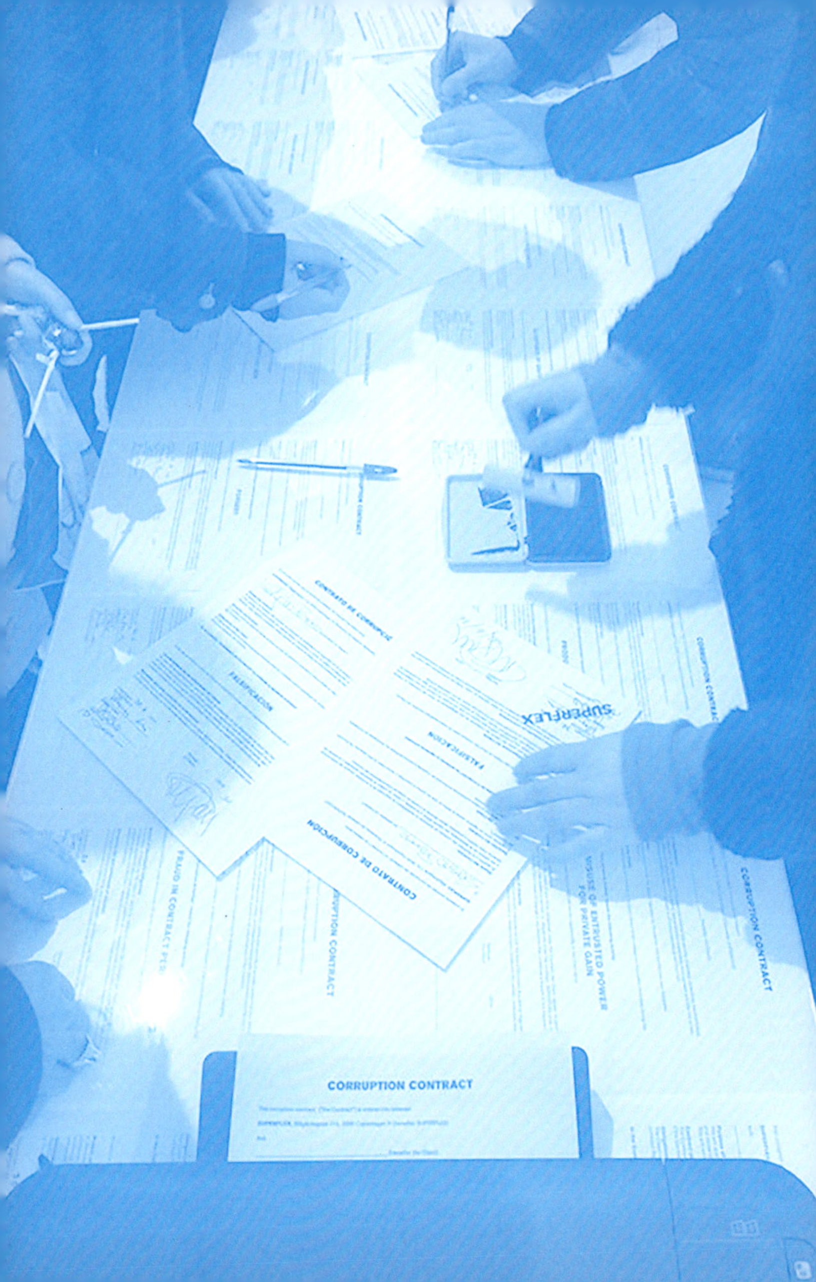
CONTRATO DE CORRUPÇÃO
FALSIFICACION
SUPERFLEX
FALSIFICACION
CONTRATO DE CORRUPCION
CORRUPTION CONTRACT
FRAUD IN CONTRACT (FIC)
MISUSE OF ENTRUSTED POWER FOR PRIVATE GAIN
CORRUPTION CONTRACT
CORRUPTION CONTRACT

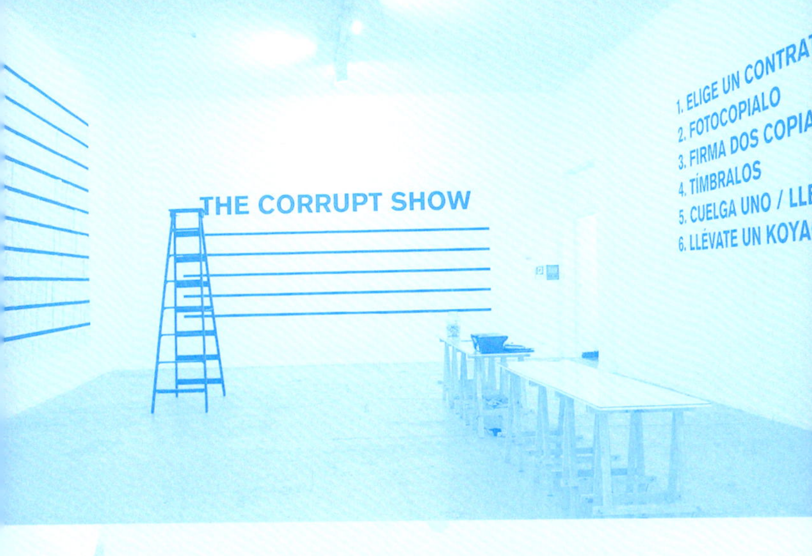

CONTRATO DE CORRUPCIÓN

El presente contrato de corrupción (en adelante "el Contrato") se celebra entre

SUPERFLEX, Blågårdsgade 11b, 2200 Copenhagen N, Dinamarca, (en adelante "SUPERFLEX")

y

Fernando Balcells _______ (en adelante "el Cliente")

Objeto del Contrato
El objetivo y la finalidad del contrato es amenazar la estabilidad y la seguridad de la sociedad, socavar las instituciones y los valores de la democracia, los valores éticos y la justicia, y poner en peligro el desarrollo sostenible y el estado de derecho. Este objetivo y propósito deben tenerse en cuenta en todas las interpretaciones del contrato.

Duración del Contrato
El contrato entra en vigencia desde la fecha en que las partes lo suscriben y vence hasta un año después ("la Duración del Contrato").

Obligations of the Client
El Cliente debe estar por si mismo activamente involucrado en, o solicitar a otros a participar en, Actividades de Corrupción durante la Duración del Contrato.

En el contrato, "Actividades de Corrupción" se entiende la siguiente actividad:

MAL USO DEL PODER PARA BENEFICIO PROPIO

Todas las acciones por parte del Cliente en virtud del Contrato serán de responsabilidad exclusiva del Cliente.

Incumplimiento de las obligaciones del Cliente
En caso de incumplimiento por parte del Cliente de cualquiera de sus obligaciones en virtud del Contrato, el Cliente se compromete a proporcionar una confesión pública que explica por qué era incapaz de cumplir con sus obligaciones bajo este Contrato de Corrupción. SUPERFLEX tendrá, además, el derecho a exigir que el cliente deje de participar en cualquier actividad que constituya un incumplimiento del Contrato por medio de una resolución judicial.

Normativa aplicable y solución de controversias
El Contrato regirá e será interpretado de acuerdo a las leyes vigentes en Chile. Todas las controversias que surjan del Contrato serán resueltas por los tribunales daneses a cuya jurisdicción exclusiva las partes se someten irrevocablemente.

Copenhagen, 30/6/2016
Per SUPERFLEX

Santiago, 1 Julio/2016
el Cliente

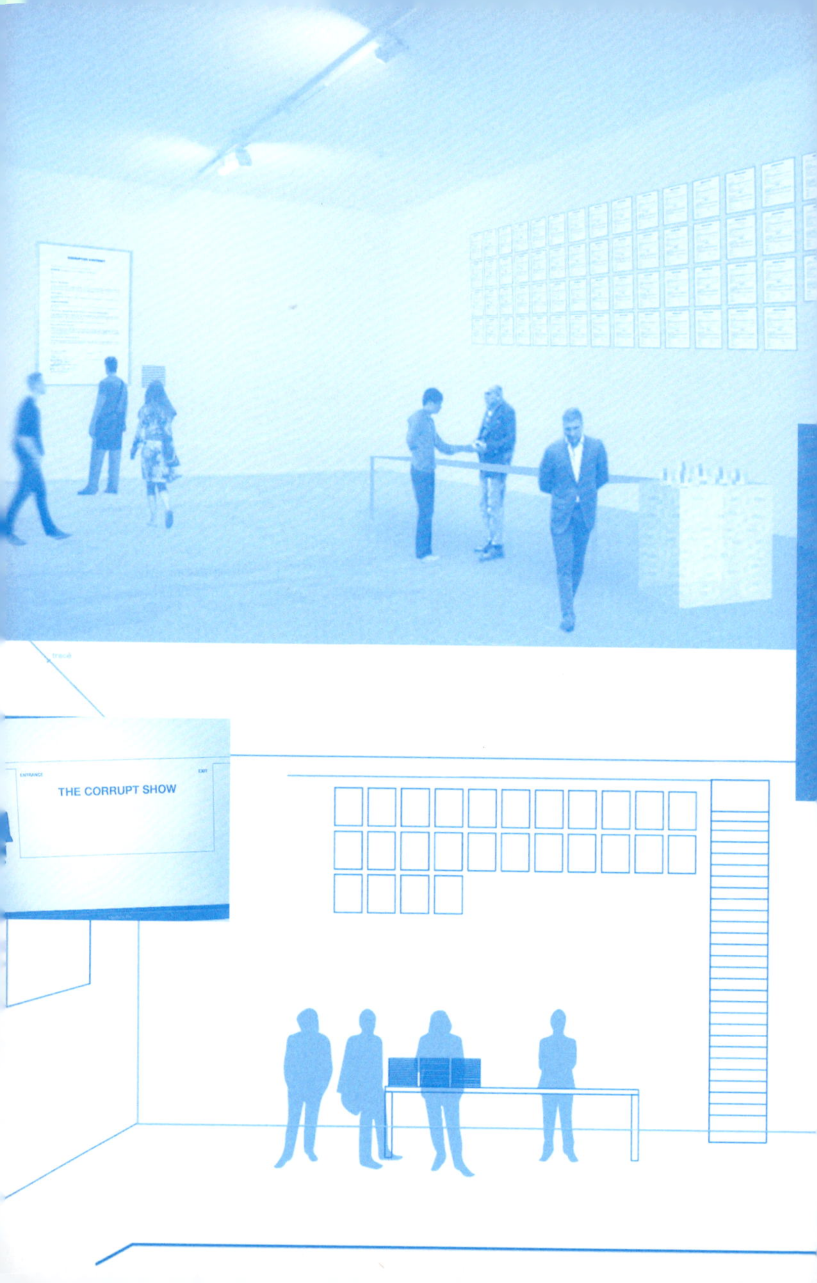
THE CORRUPT SHOW
ENTRANCE
EXIT

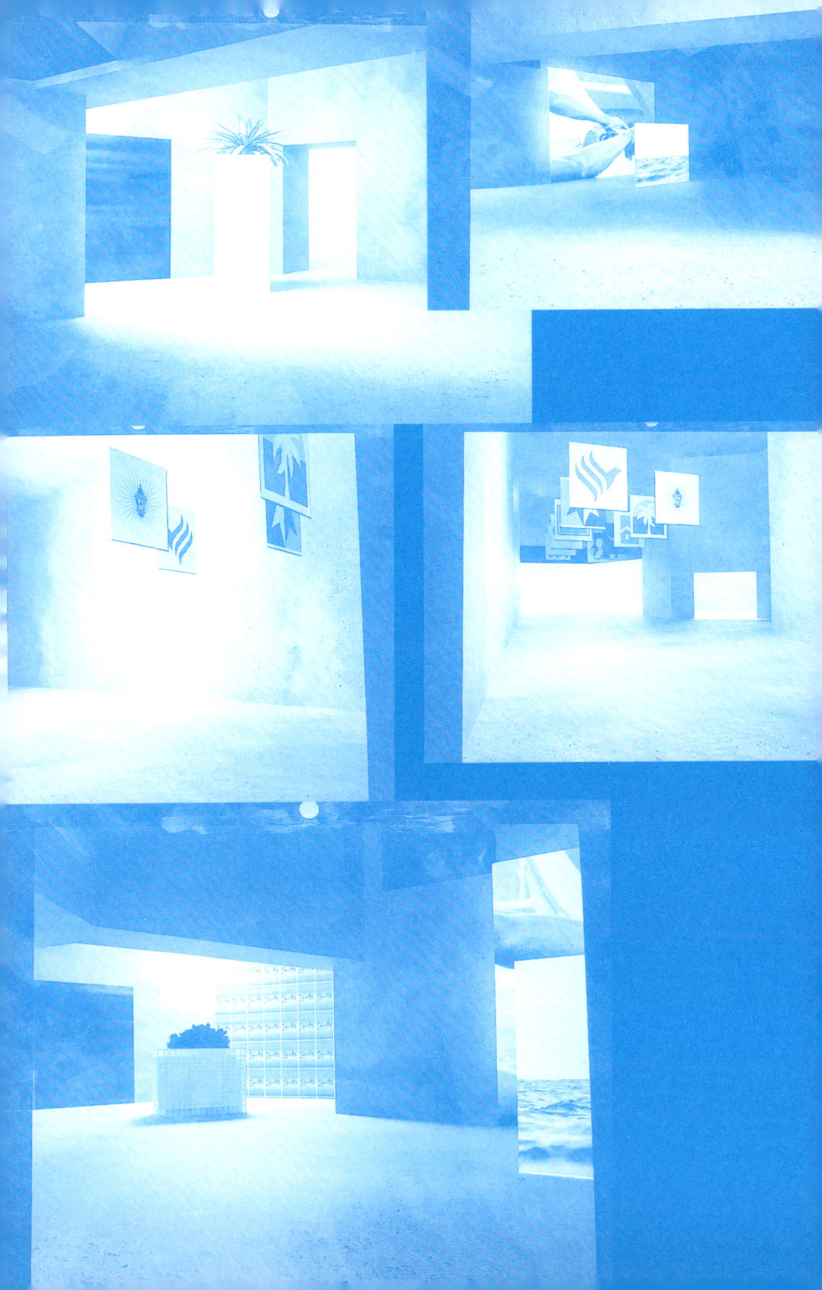

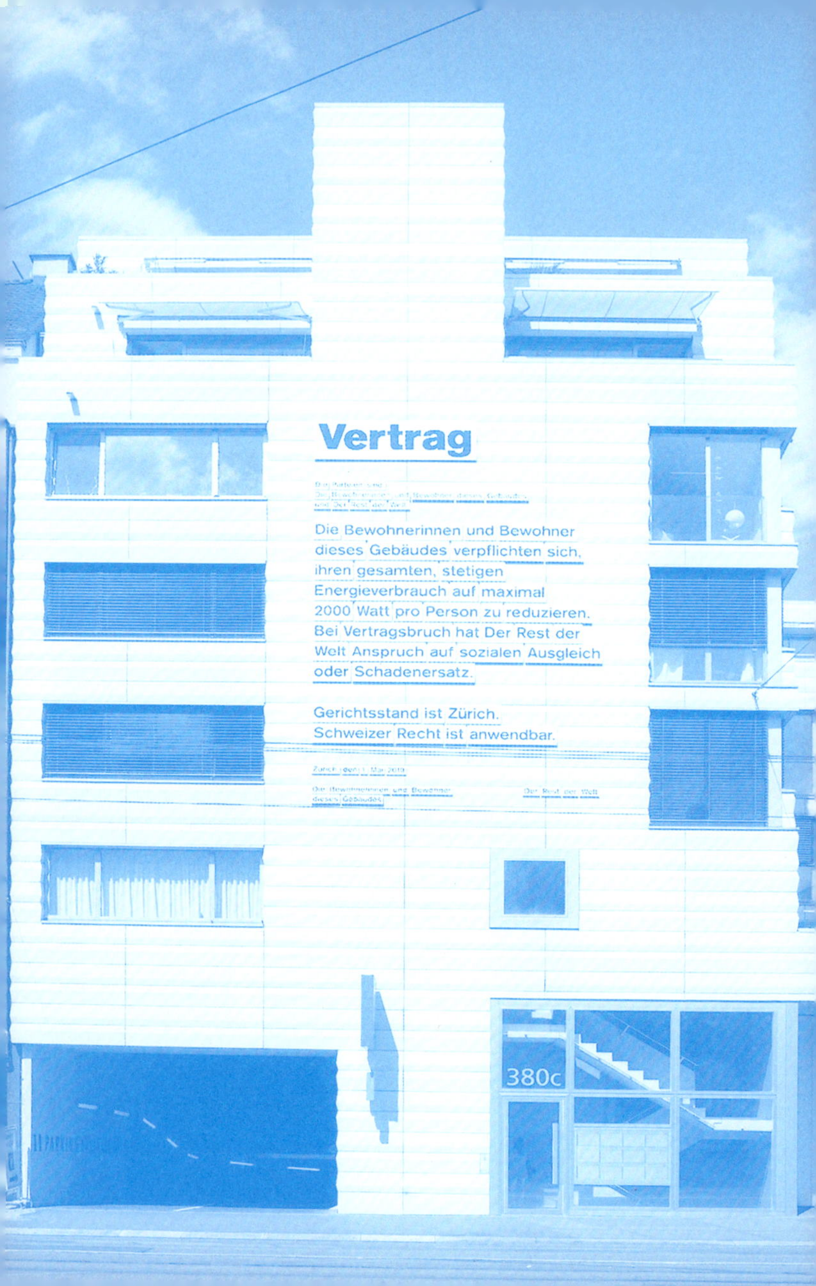

Vertrag

Die Bewohnerinnen und Bewohner
dieses Gebäudes verpflichten sich,
ihren gesamten, stetigen
Energieverbrauch auf maximal
2000 Watt pro Person zu reduzieren.
Bei Vertragsbruch hat Der Rest der
Welt Anspruch auf sozialen Ausgleich
oder Schadenersatz.

Gerichtsstand ist Zürich.
Schweizer Recht ist anwendbar.

380c

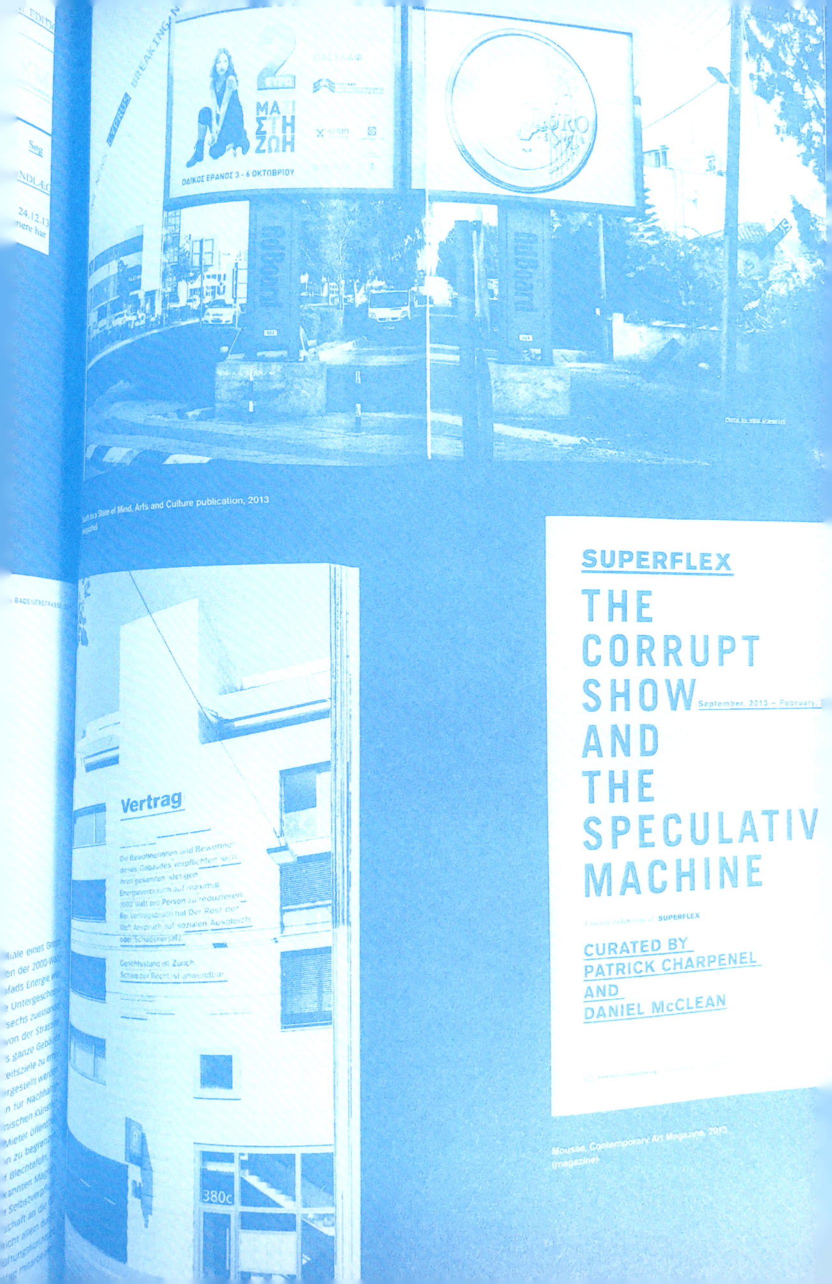

...ism is a State of Mind, Arts and Culture publication, 2013
(magazine)

Mousse, Contemporary Art Magazine, 2013
(magazine)

CONTRACT

Parties to this contract (hereafter The Contract) are:

SUPERFLEX
Blågårdsgade 11b, DK-2200 Copenhagen, (hereafter "SUPERFLEX")
And

Katerina Gregos (Curator of the Danish Pavilion) and The Danish Arts Agency
H.C. Andersens Boulevard 2, DK-1553 Copenhagen (hereafter "The Client")

The Client is obliged under The Contract within the period from the date of signing of The Contract until the end the 54rd. Venice Biennial to refrain in written or oral form [i.e. communication] from directly or indirectly using the following words or combinations of words or any translation hereof:

- **Freedom of Speech**
- **Freedom of Expression**
- **Denmark or any Nation**
- **Danish or any Nationality**

Subject to The Contract is The Client, including management, staff – directly or indirectly – in addition to full-time, part-time employees and short-term employees.

In the event of breach of The Contract by The Client, SUPERFLEX shall have the right to damages and compensation (including for violations of rights) and the right to seek injunction [i.e. against the party in breach of The Contract] for any such violation or breach of The Contract.

Any claims [i.e. claims, disputes, suits or demands] between the parties of The Contract will be arbitrated under Danish law and brought before an ordinary court of law in Denmark.

Copenhagen, 10. Aug 2010
For SUPERFLEX

Jakob Fenger

Rasmus Nielsen

Bjørnstjerne Chrstiansen

Copenhagen,   2010

Katerina Gregos

For The Danish Arts Agency

Anette Østerby

SUPERFLEX

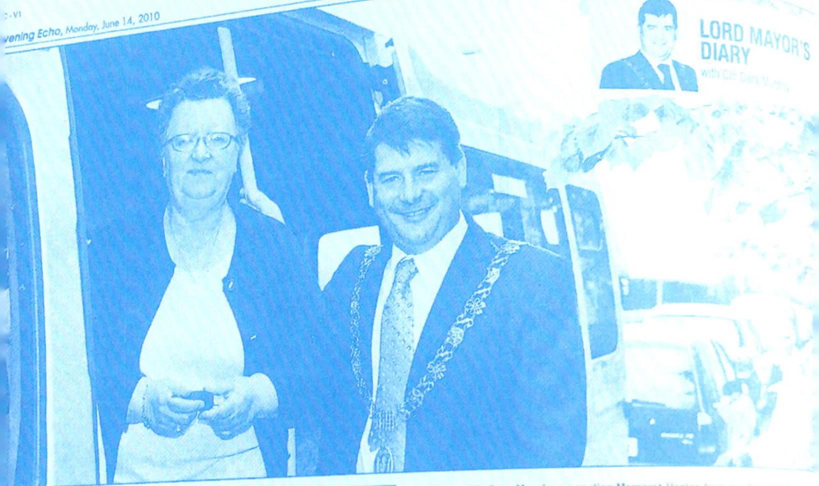

LORD MAYOR'S DIARY
with Cllr Dara Murphy

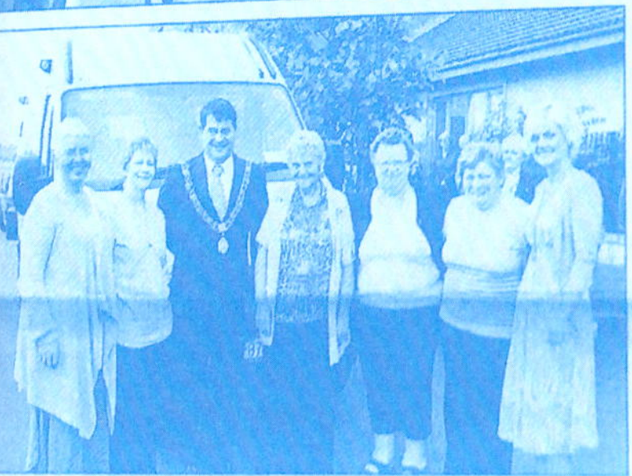

Lord Mayor Cllr Dara Murphy presenting Margaret Hanlon from the St Brendan's Centre, Coolamber Drive, The Glen, with the keys to the new community bus. Noreen Glynn, centre co-ordinator, Rita Cashman, Cllr Murphy, and centre Margaret Hanlon and Peggy O'Shea with Lady Mayoress Tanya Murphy.

Access all areas as seniors get the b

THE Glen community are celebrating after getting a new community bus.

The 17-seater community bus was funded through the RAPID Programme and the Health Service Executive.

The bus is available at a low cost to those groups who wouldn't be able to afford a commercial bus — including schools, youth and training groups and older people's groups.

It is primarily focused on groups from The Glen but also used by communities in Mayfield and Blackpool.

The bus is wheelchair accessible and is driven by volunteer drivers, the community warden, and staff from the various groups.

The vehicle was officially launched by Lord Mayor Cllr Dara Murphy at St Brendan's Day Centre, Coolamber Drive, The Glen.

Rita Cashman of St Brendan's Senior Citizens said: "Our older groups have been waiting a very long time for this facility and are

Cork Lord Mayor officially bans use of word recession

THE word 'recession' will be banned in Cork for one day this week — and that's an official decree.

Lord Mayor Cllr Dara Murphy is to issue a decree on behalf of the citizens of Cork to refrain from using the word 'recession' for one whole day this Thursday.

The feelgood initiative is part of the Cork Midsummer Festival which has joined forces with the Cork-based National Sculpture Factory.

They in turn have commissioned the internationally renowned Danish art group Superflex to create a art piece titled Today We Don't Use the Word Recession.

David Dobz O'Brien, programmes manager with the National Sculpture Factory, said not using the word recession for a day allows people to have fun with the word — or be reflective about it.

"The word recession brings people down and we just want to lift the spirits of the city," said David.

"We're now trying to get as many people, companies and groups as possible not to use the word. We'll also be having games to try and catch people out who might use it. It would be great for just one day if the word recession didn't exist, but that doesn't take away from those who've been affected by it.

"This project strives to achieve a collective moment that uplifts us from the doom and gloom in a very subtle yet playful way," he added.

For further information contact www.nationalsculpturefactory.com.

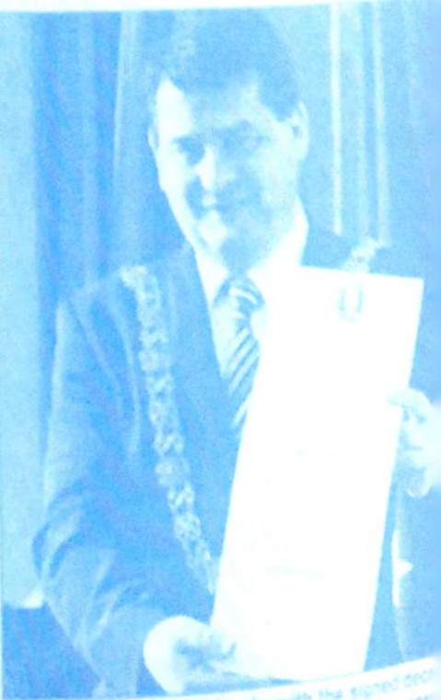

Lord Mayor Cllr Dara Murphy with the signed decree on the citizens of Cork not to use the word recession. June 17.

◇ Flooded McDonald's

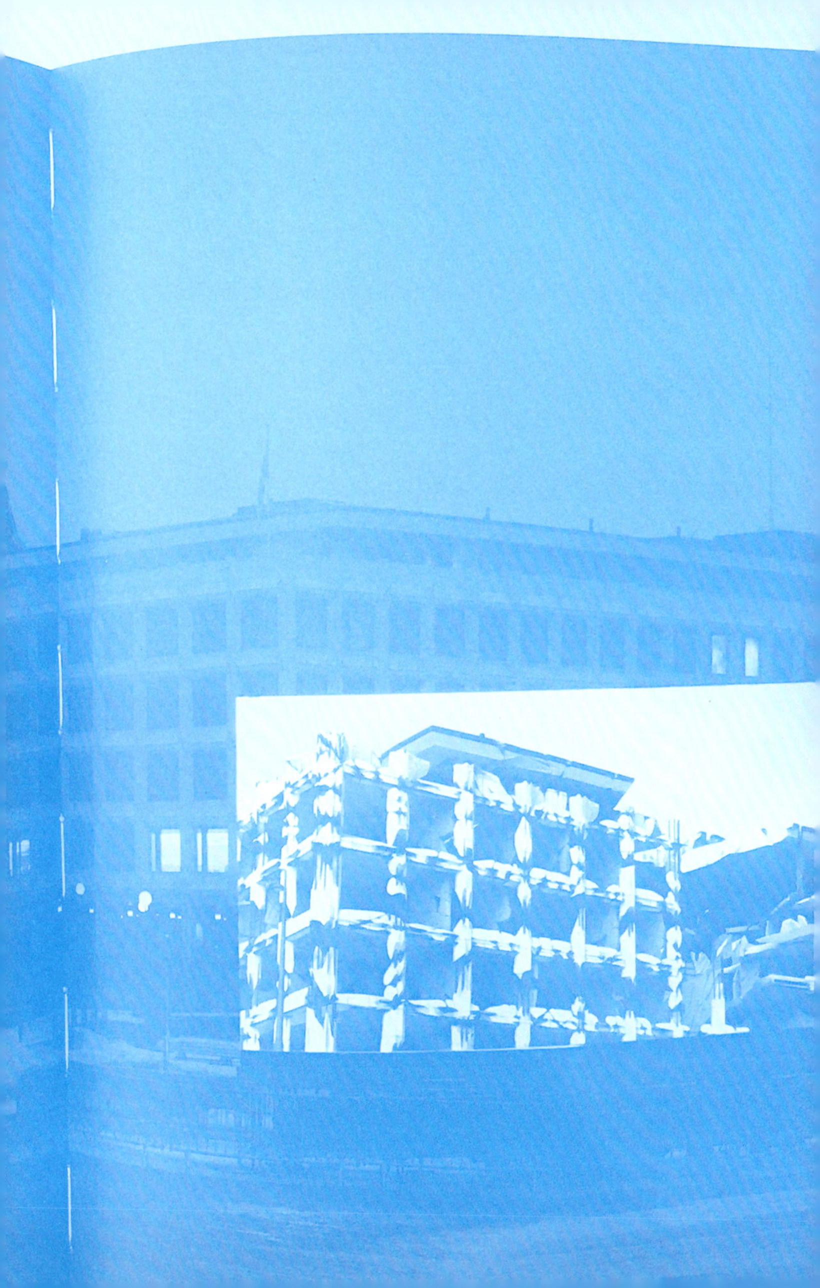

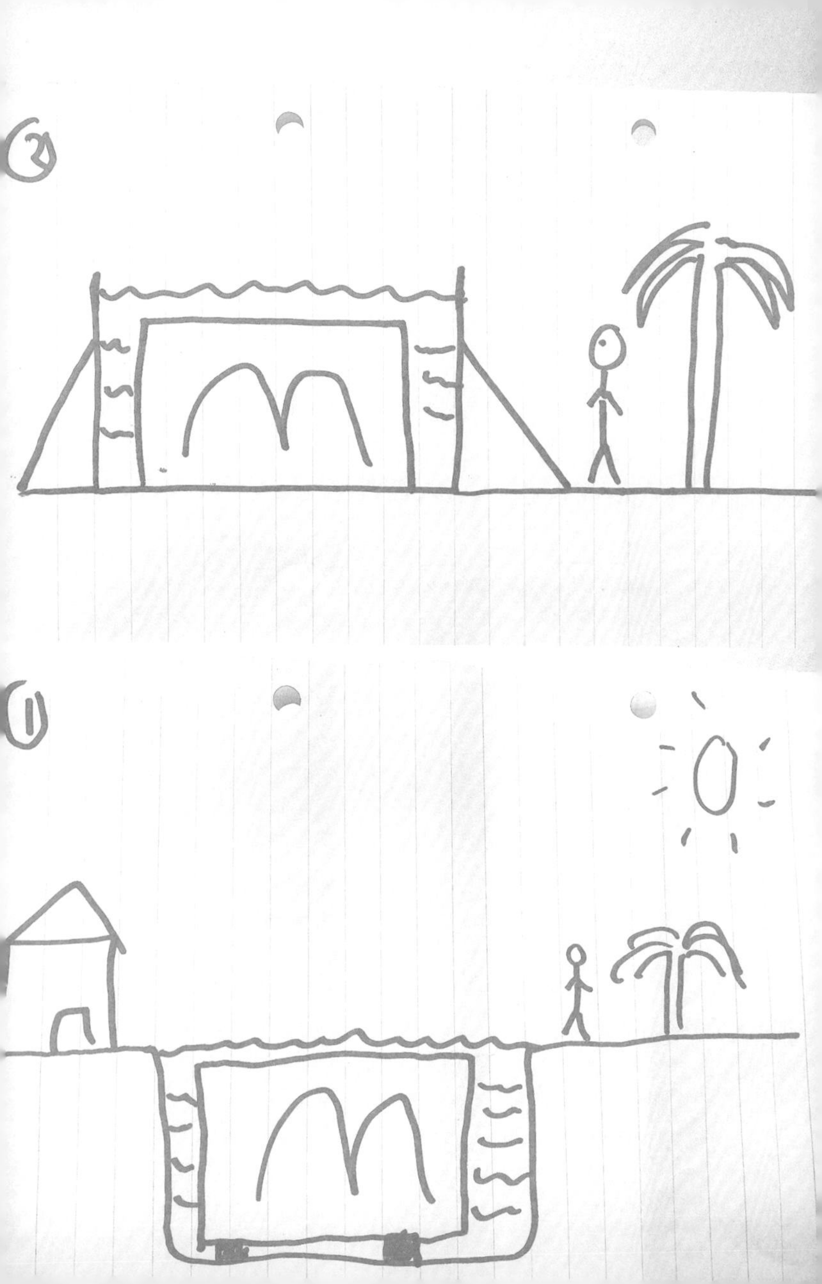

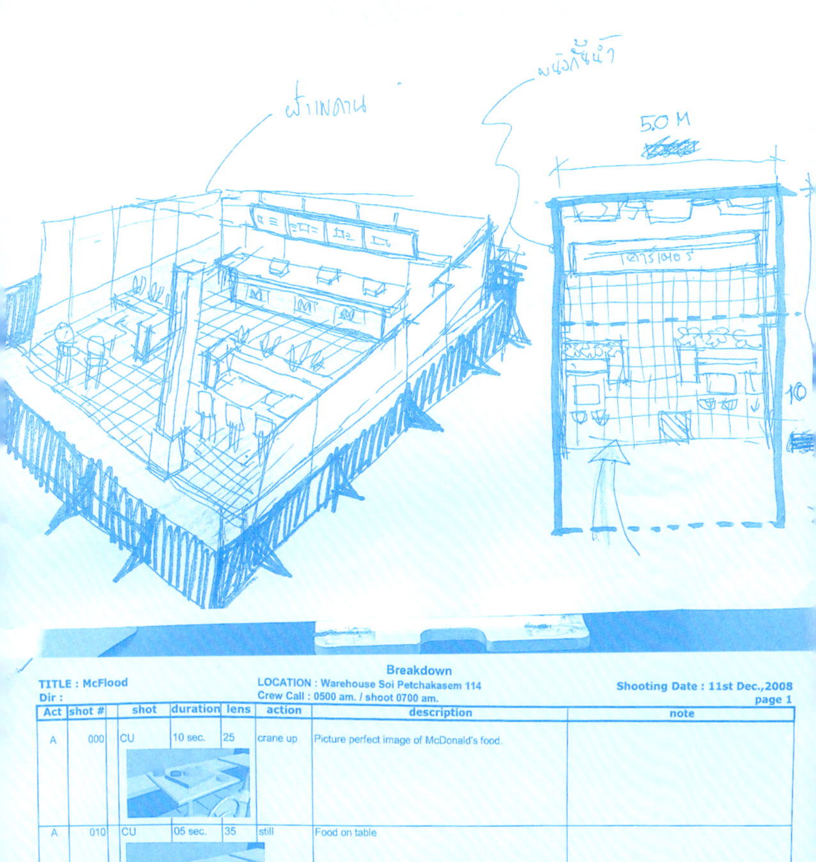

Breakdown

TITLE : McFlood
Dir :
LOCATION : Warehouse Soi Petchakasem 114
Crew Call : 0500 am. / shoot 0700 am.
Shooting Date : 11st Dec.,2008
page 1

Act	shot #	shot	duration	lens	action	description	note
A	000	CU	10 sec.	25	crane up	Picture perfect image of McDonald's food.	
A	010	CU	05 sec.	35	still	Food on table	
A	001	LS	25 sec	25	crane down	LS crane down to reveal McD logo	
A	019	LS	25 sec	25	still	High cam, low angle from top corner of McD	
A	004	LS	30 sec.	35	track R	Track along edge of set	

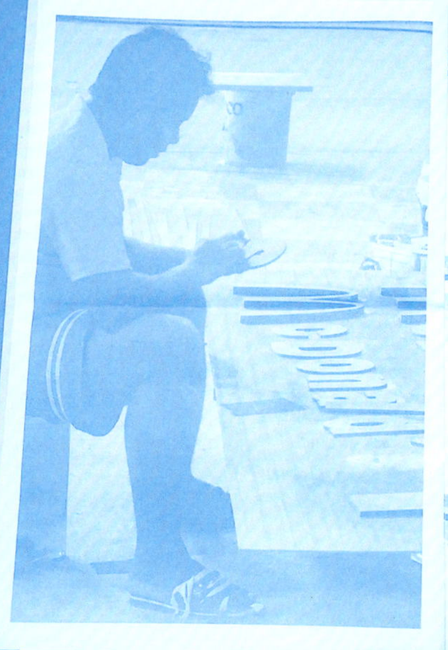
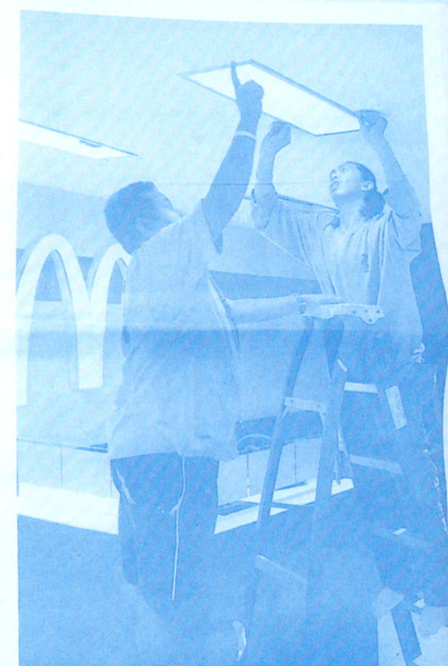
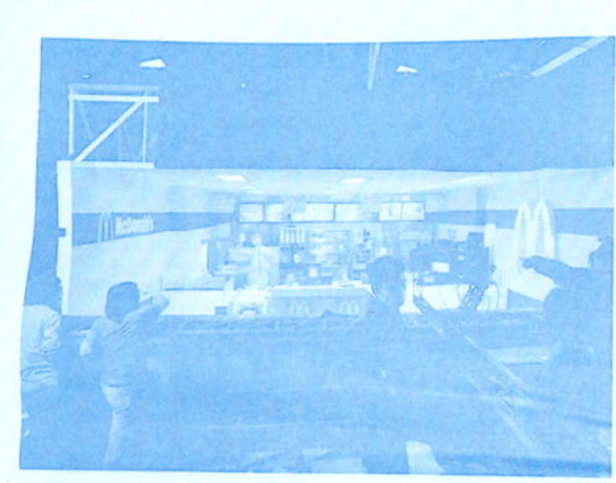
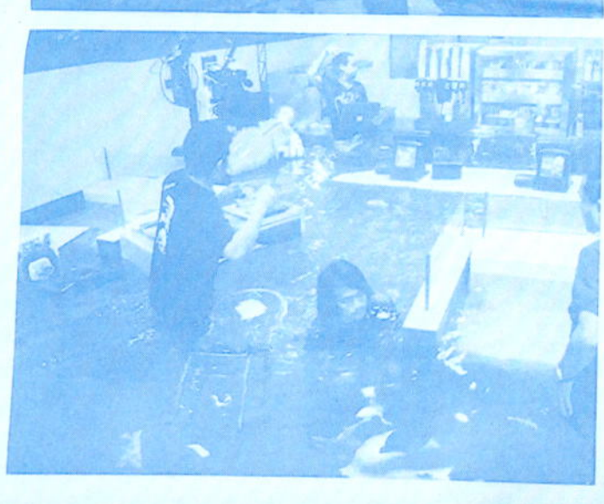
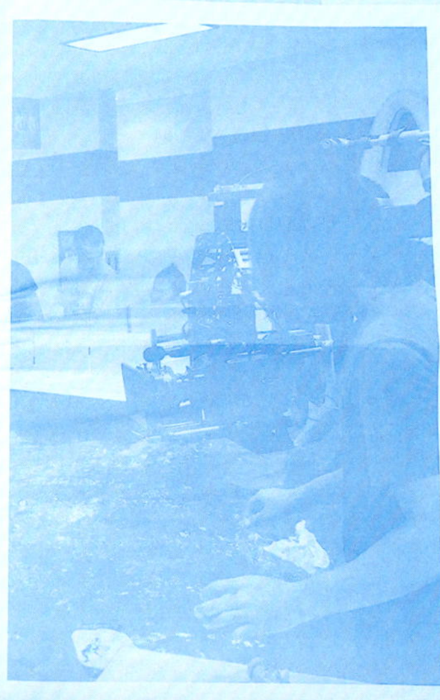

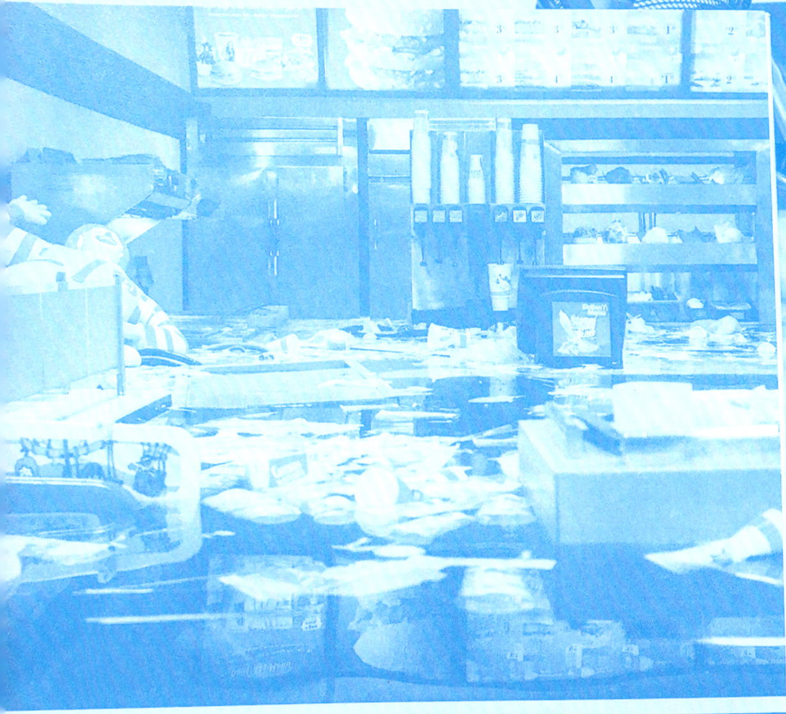

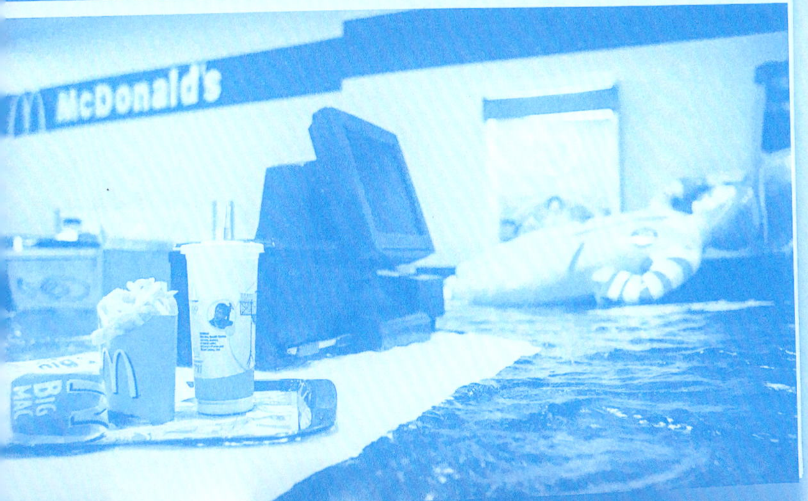

McDonald's
BIG MAC

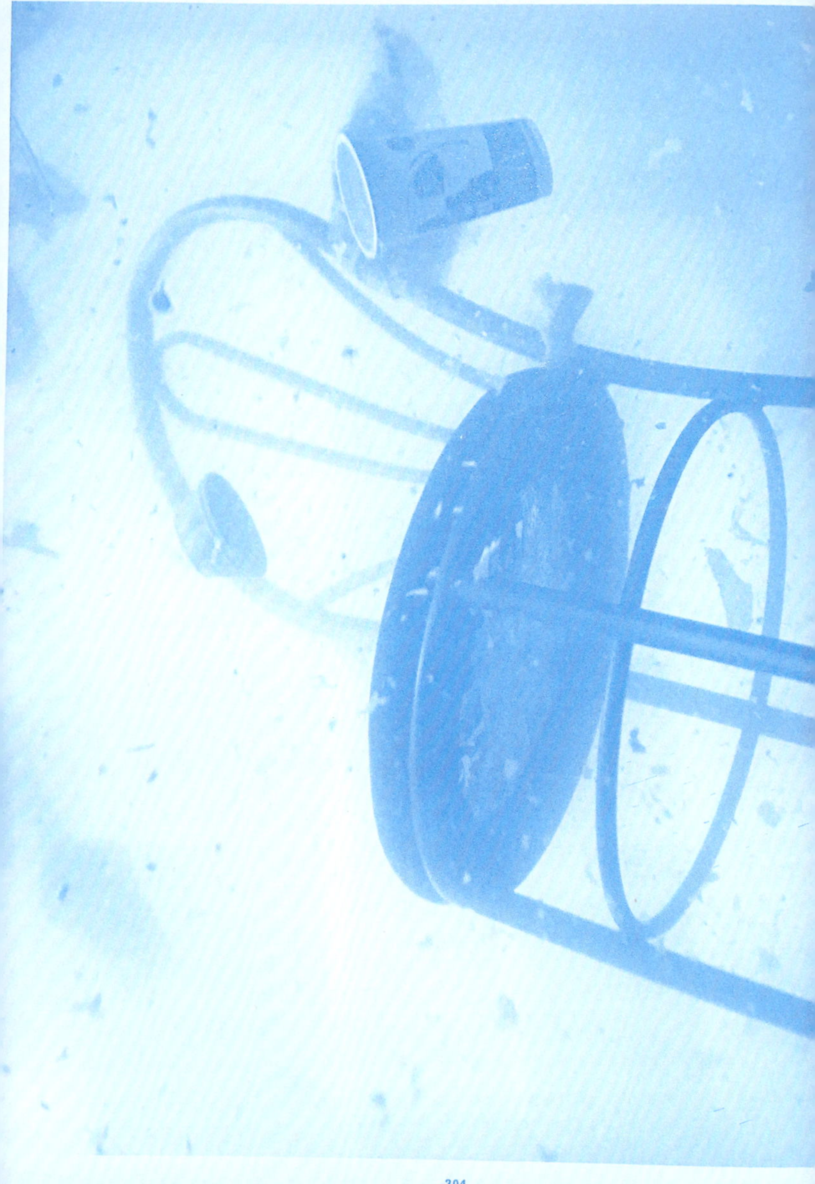

Fast-flood restaurant

McDonald's submerged for a movie

thelondonpaper

Weird News: The South London Gallery is showcasing the work of a group that have flooded a McDonald's restaurant in the name of art

Friday 16 January 2009

The London Paper, 2009
(newspaper)

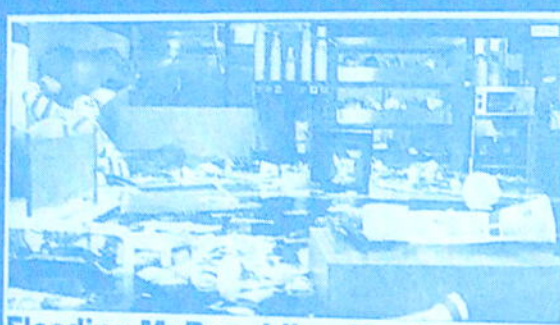

SLP – South London Press, 2009
(newspaper)

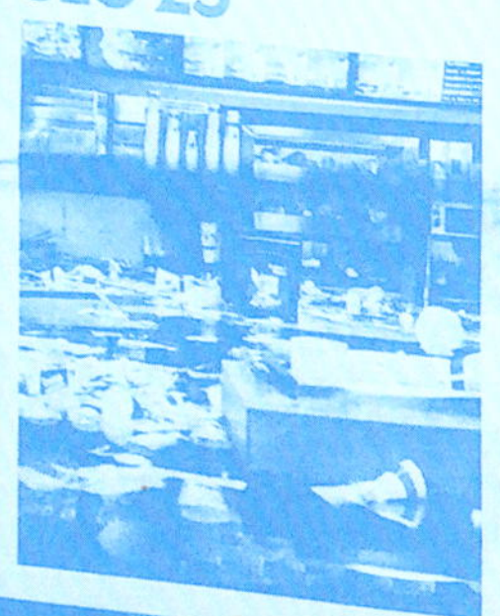

South London Gallery, 2009
(catalogue)

A sinking star to suit our times

EXHIBITION

SUPERFLEX: FLOODED MCDONALD'S

SOUTH LONDON GALLERY, SE25

AS the apparent meltdown of global capitalism continues apace, with news this week that enfeebled British banks require yet more handouts from the Government, there could be few more timely works of art than *Flooded McDonald's*, a new film by Danish artists' collective Superflex.

On show in the South London Gallery, the film presents a life-size replica of the interior of a McDonald's burger bar, which, over the course of 20 minutes, inexorably floods. Water seeps beneath the door and gradually inundates the restaurant, which is empty, as though the diners have all fled. Slowly, the murky liquid becomes clogged with all the detritus of their abandoned meals: semi-chewed Chicken McNuggets and gnawed-at hamburgers, straws, French fries, packets of barbecue sauce.

On the surface, plastic trays ride the deluge like forlorn surf boards. Electrical tills spark and smoke as the water rises. A bright yellow sign with the words "Caution: Wet Floor" (oh, the irony!) is tossed about in the swell.

A large, waving figure of Ronald McDonald, the fast-food chain's clown mascot, is lifted aloft: he twirls like a mechanical ballerina atop a wind-up music box, before slopping into the morass and floating aimlessly, like a gormless holidaymaker on a Lilo. A neon sign of the chain's famous golden arches logo flickers and goes out.

The set was meticulously created from scratch, without the blessing of McDonald's, over two weeks in a swimming pool in a Bangkok studio, before 80,000 litres of water were pumped in, and the results filmed over two days. The footage is redolent of disaster movies and apocalyptic news stories, calling to mind images of flood-struck New Orleans in the wake of Hurricane Katrina, and, as Ronald totters and falls, the well-known moment in 2003 when US troops helped Iraqis to pull down a massive metal statue of Saddam Hussein in Baghdad's main square.

The piece is obviously about the impotence of the West to cope with the threats of climate change, but it also lodges a strong anti-capitalist protest, which feels justified given that the mismanagement of bloated corporations precipitated today's economic disaster.

It's a haunting, thought-provoking, brilliantly realised work that – crucially – refrains from being preachy. Days after seeing it, I have yet to forget Ronald McDonald's sinister face, with his fixed rictus grin, shock of red hair, and corpse-white skin. In the film, with one hand aloft, he is presented as an icon of the West, the modern-day counterpart of rousing imperial statuary from ancient Rome. What a chilling comment on our times that is.

Until March 1. Information: 020 7703 6120.

RATING ★ ★ ★ ★

Alastair Sooke

SUPERFLEX

COPENHAGUE, DANEMARK + BRÉSIL

THE FINANCIAL CRISIS (SESSION I-IV), 2009
INSTALLATION FILMIQUE, 12 MIN, VERSION ORIGINALE ANGLAISE, COULEUR /
SINGLE-CHANNEL FILM PROJECTION, 12 MIN, ENGLISH, COLOR
COURTOISIE DE / *COURTESY OF SUPERFLEX + NILS STAERK GALLERY, COPENHAGUE/COPENHAGEN;*
CRÉÉ POUR / *CREATED FOR FRIEZE ART FAIR 2009, LONDRES / LONDON*

LOST MONEY, 2009

INSTALLATION : 2000 PIÈCES DE MONNAIE ALTÉRÉES, BOULONS, ÉD. DE 3 + 1 EA,
CHAQUE ÉDITION UNIQUE / *INSTALLATION: 2000 COINS WELDED WITH BOLTS, ED. OF 3 +
1 AP EACH UNIQUE*
COURTOISIE DE / *COURTESY OF SUPERFLEX + NILS STAERK GALLERY, COPENHAGUE, DANEMARK / COPENHAGEN,
DENMARK*

Fondé en 1993, SUPERFLEX (Bjørnstjerne Reuter Christiansen, Jakob Fenger, Rasmus Nielsen) vit et travaille au Danemark et au Brésil. Le travail du collectif fut récemment présenté dans le cadre d'expositions individuelles à Nils Staerk Gallery, Copenhague, Danemark, 2009; South London Gallery, Londres, Royaume Unis, 2009; Kunsthalle Basel, Bâle, Suisse, 2005; Schirn Kunsthalle, Frankfort, Allemagne, 2004; Museum of Contemporary Art Kiasma, Helsinki, Finlande, 2003; Rooseum Malmo, Suède, 2002; Kunstverein Wolfsburg, Allemagne, 1999. De plus, ils participèrent à plusieurs expositions collectives d'envergure, incluant Louisiana Museum, Denmark, 2009; MOCA Miami, 2009; Prospect.1, Nouvelle Orléans, 2008; Taipei Biennial, Taiwan, 2008; Van Abbemuseum, Pays Bas, 2007; Moscow Biennale of Contemporary Art, Russie, 2007; Sao Paulo Biennale, Brésil, 2006; et CCA Wattis, San Francisco, 2006. SUPERFLEX fut récipiendaire du prix George Maciunas prize en 2009.
/
Formed in 1993, **SUPERFLEX** (Bjørnstjerne Reuter Christiansen, Jakob Fenger, Rasmus Nielsen) work and live in Denmark and Brazil. Their work has been featured in solo exhibitions at Nils Staerk Gallery, Copenhagen, Denmark, 2009; South London Gallery, London, UK, 2009; Kunsthalle Basel, Switzerland, 2005; Schirn Kunsthalle, Frankfurt, Germany, 2004; Museum of Contemporary Art Kiasma, Helsinki, Finland, 2003; Rooseum Malmo, Sweden, 2002; Kunstverein Wolfsburg, Germany, 1999. Group exhibitions include shows at the Louisiana Museum, Denmark, 2009; MOCA Miami, 2009; Prospect.1, New Orleans, 2008; Taipei Biennial, Taiwan, 2008; Van Abbemuseum, The Netherlands, 2007; Moscow Biennale of Contemporary Art, Russia, 2007; Sao Paulo Biennale, Brazil, 2006; and the CCA Wattis, San Francisco, 2006. SUPERFLEX was awarded the George Maciunas prize in 2009.

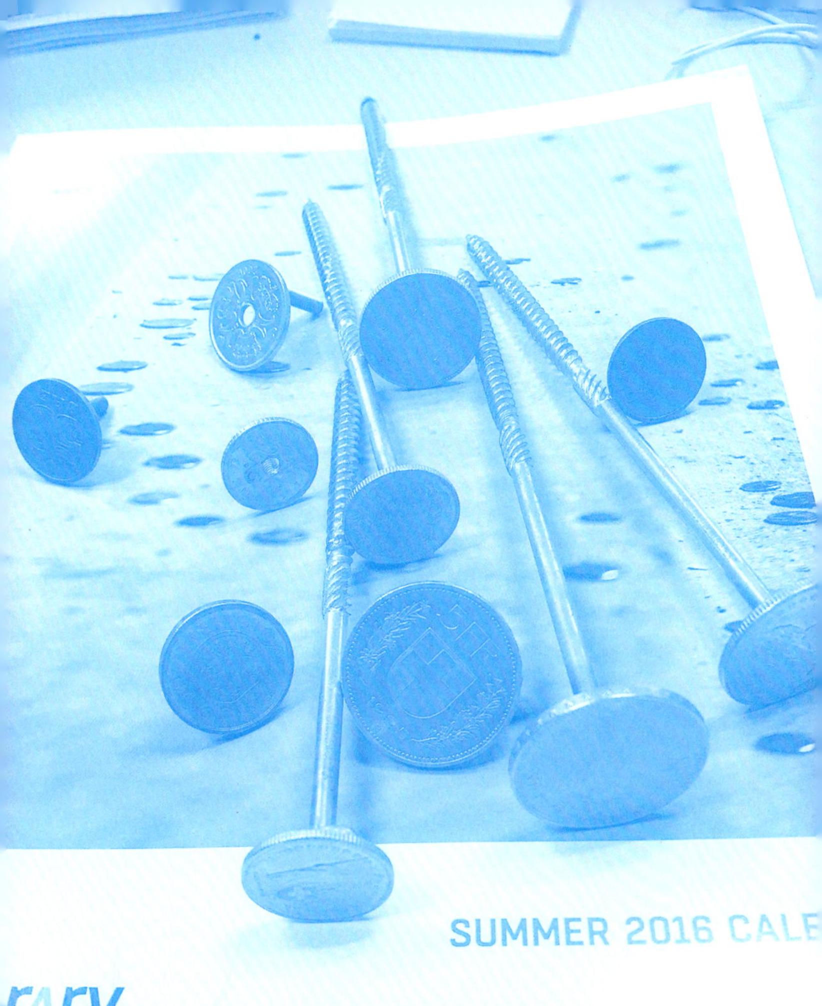
SUMMER 2016 CALE
rary

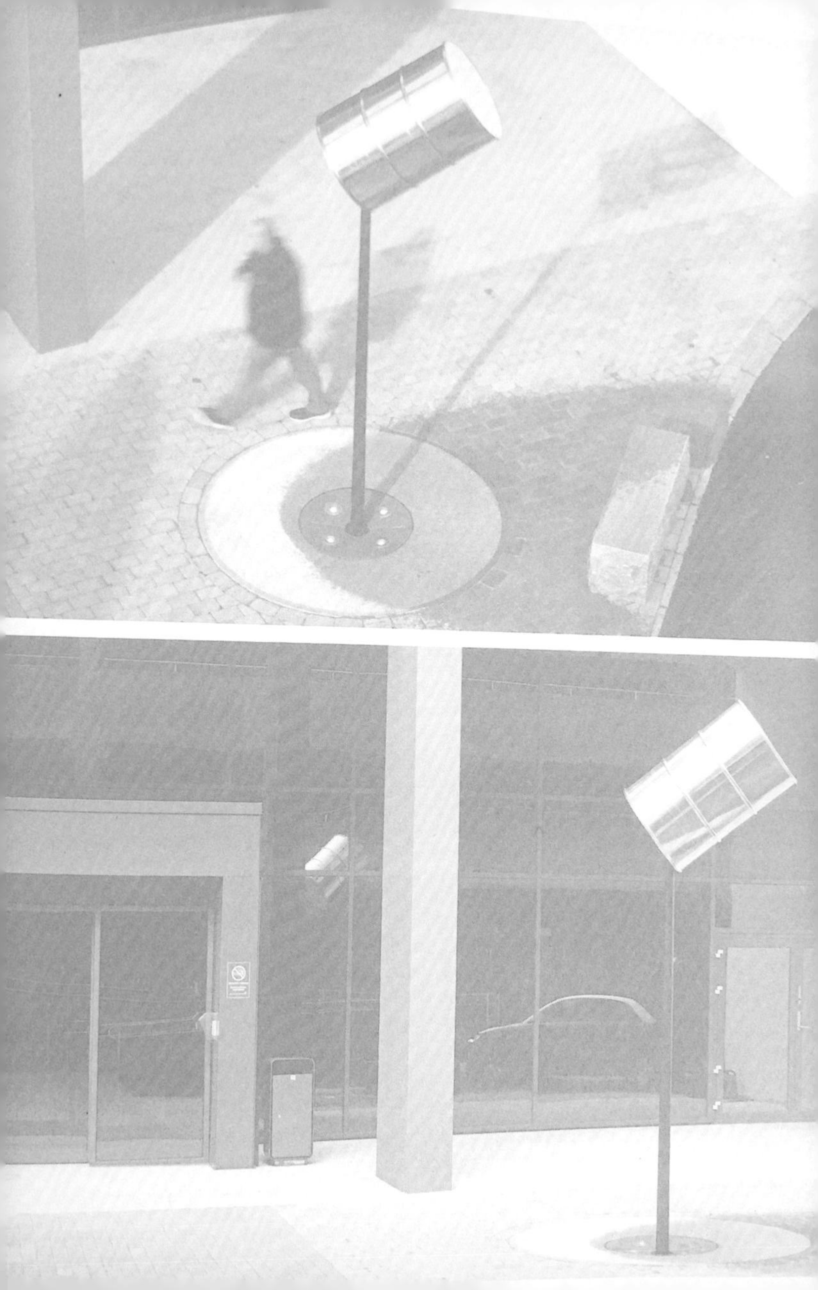

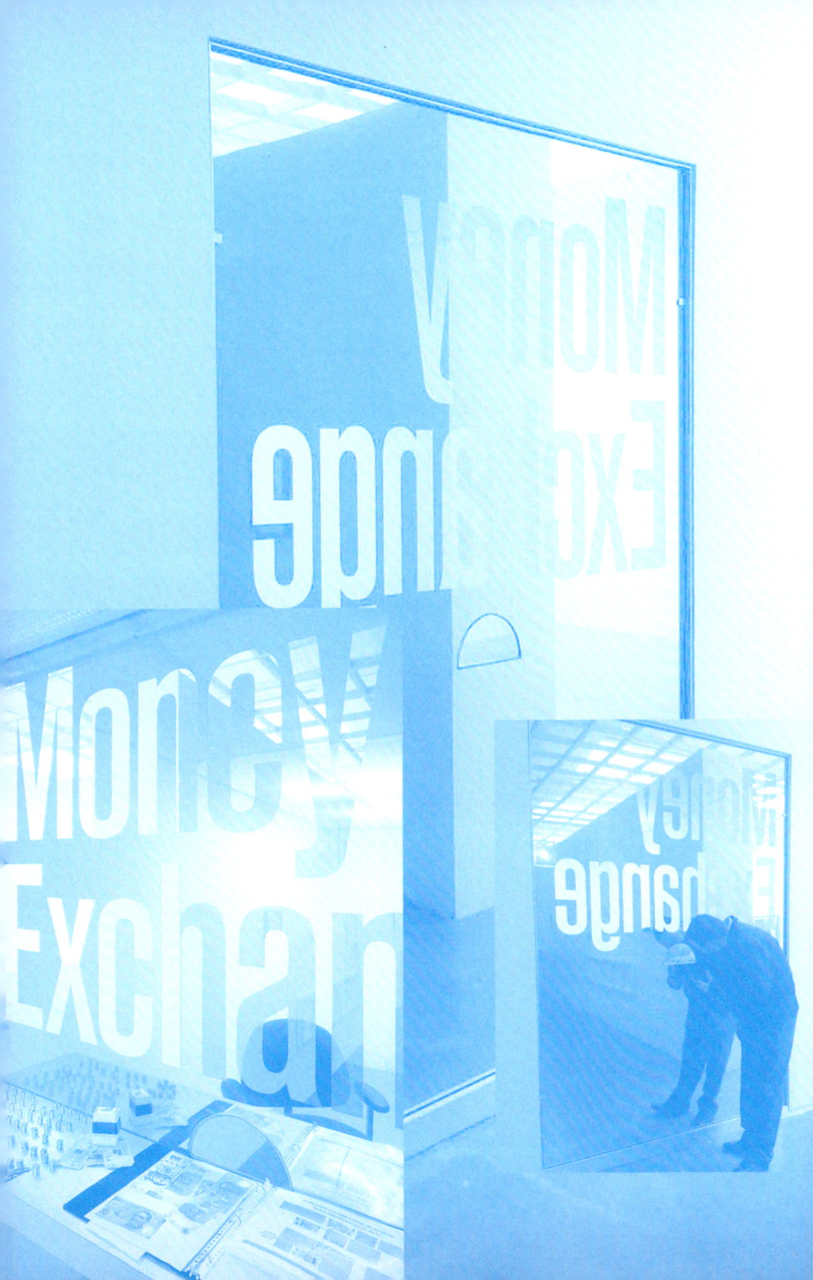

CONTRACT

TODAY WE DON'T USE THE WORD DOLLAR(S)

The Parties to this contract (in the hereafter The Contract) are:

SUPERFLEX, Blågårdsgade 11b, 2200 Copenhagen N (hereafter SUPERFLEX)

And **The ANZ Bank, Newton Branch**, 312 Karangahape Road, Newton, Auckland, (hereafter The Bank)

The Bank is obliged under The Contract within the period between 9am – 4.30pm 27th May, 2009 regarding all affairs relating to The Bank to refrain written or oral form of communication from directly or indirectly using the w "Dollar(s)".

The Contract shall apply to all the staff of The Bank – management and st directly or indirectly – in addition to full-time and part-time employees and short-term employees.

In the event of breach of The Contract by a member of the staff of The Bar the staff member involved shall immediately pay a forfeit penalty of One D (NZ$1) into The Bank Branch Staff Social Fund.

The Contract is legally binding upon the Parties for the period between 9ar 4.30pm, 27th May 2009.

For SUPERFLEX
Emma Bugden, Director, Artspace

For the ANZ Bank, Newton Bra
Lisa Burns, Branch Manager

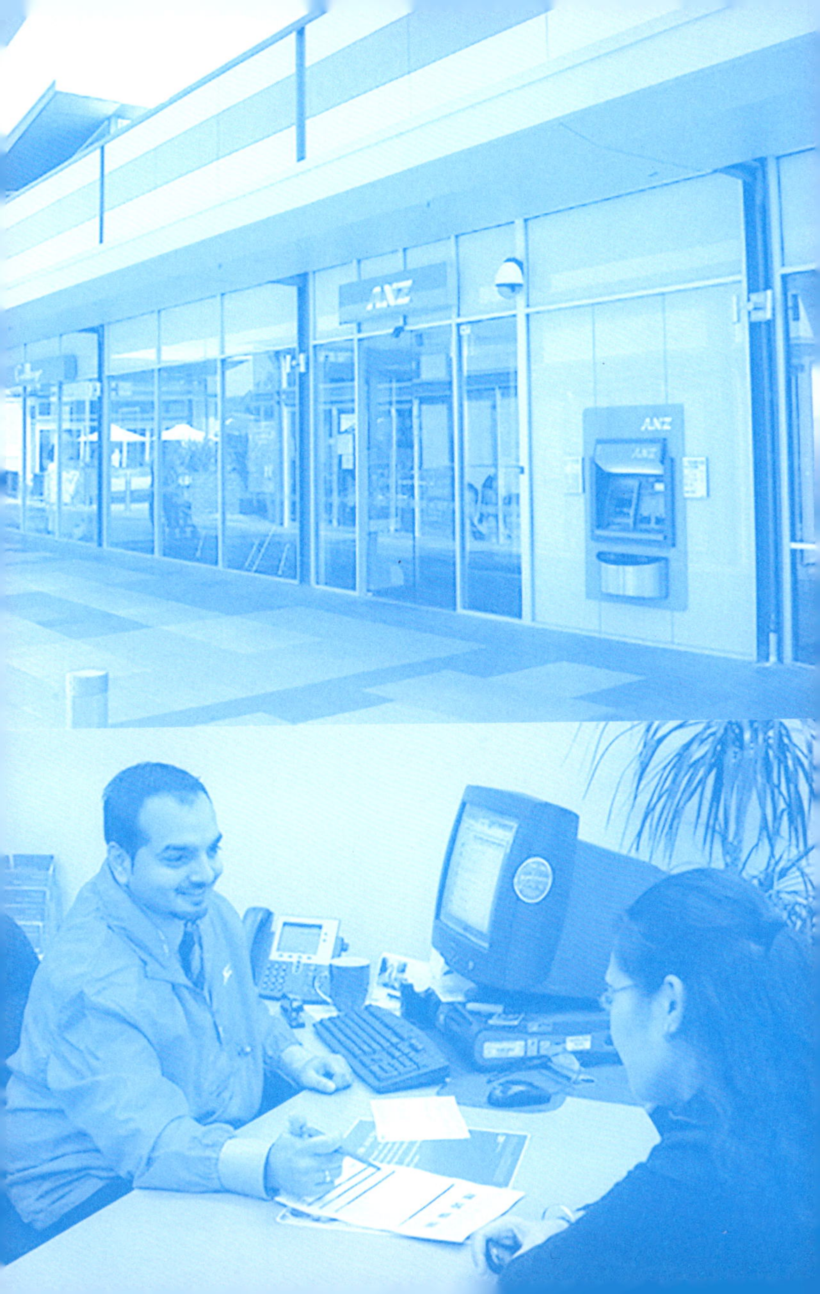

C.R.E.A.M.

Cash
rules
everything
around
me
C.R.E.A.M.
Get
the
money
Euro
euro
bill,
y'all

Superflex, 2017

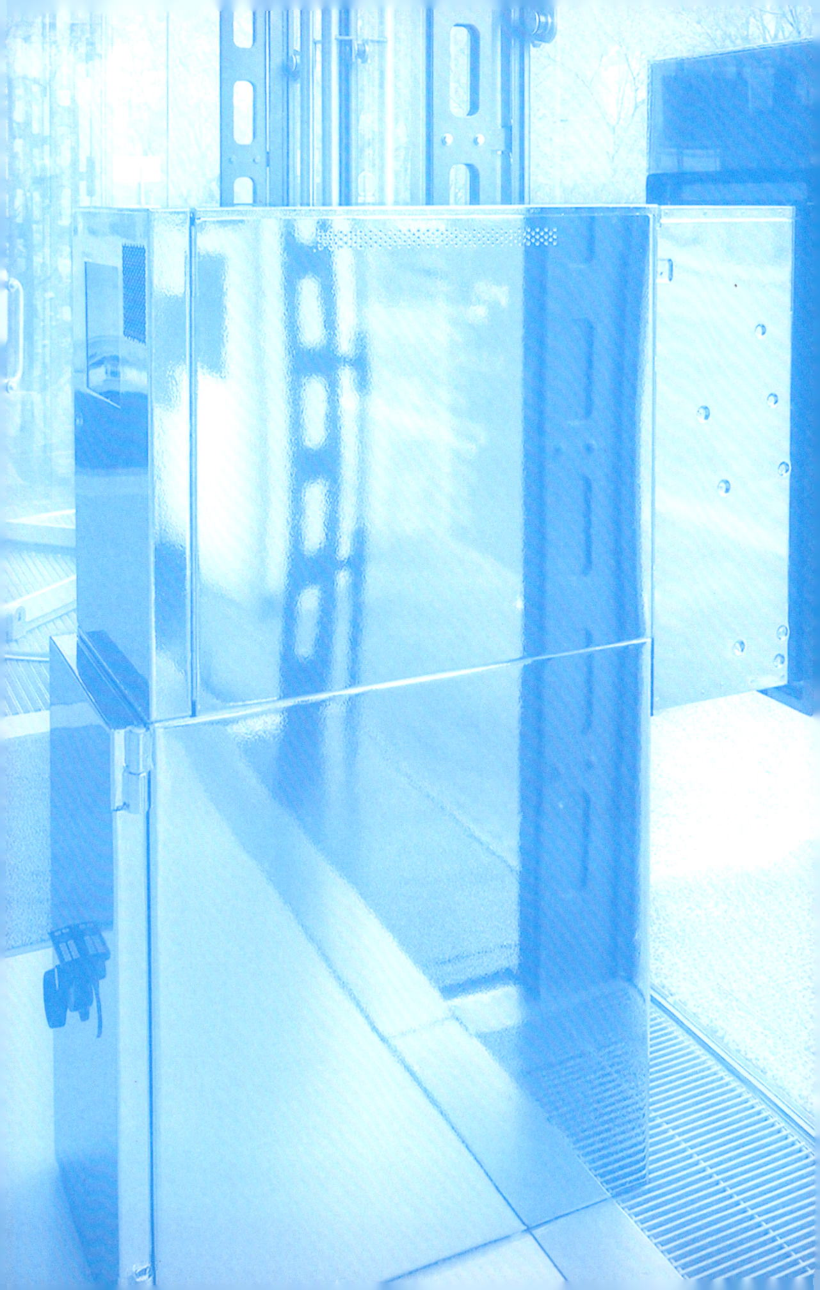

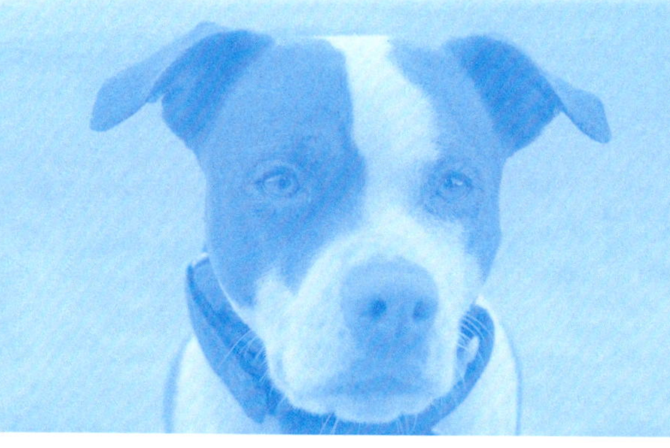

THE MÆRSK OPERA

A SUPERFLEX FILM

Director SUPERFLEX
Composer Anders Monrad
Librettists Nikolaj Heltoft & SUPERFLEX
Editors Copenhagen Brains & Ritika M. Puttianna Coleman
Opera producer Jesper Lützhøft

Supported by Danish Arts Foundation

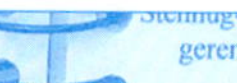

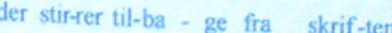

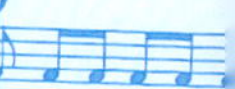

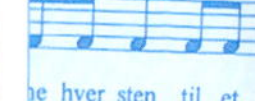

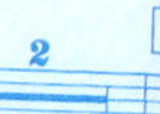

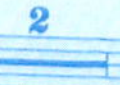

...eraen: Prolog - Vocal Score

Musik: Anders Monrad
Libretto: Nikolaj Heltoft & SUPERFLEX

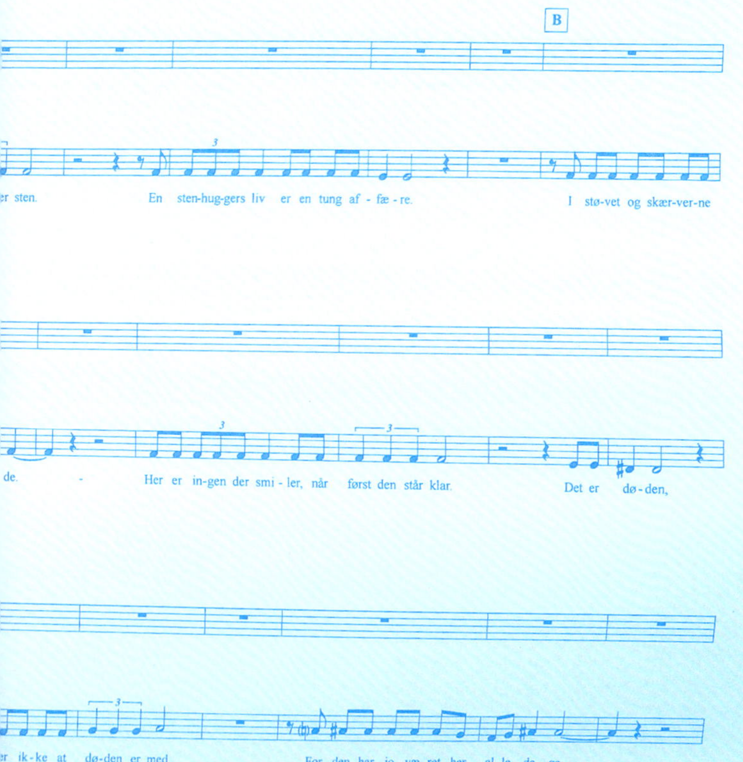

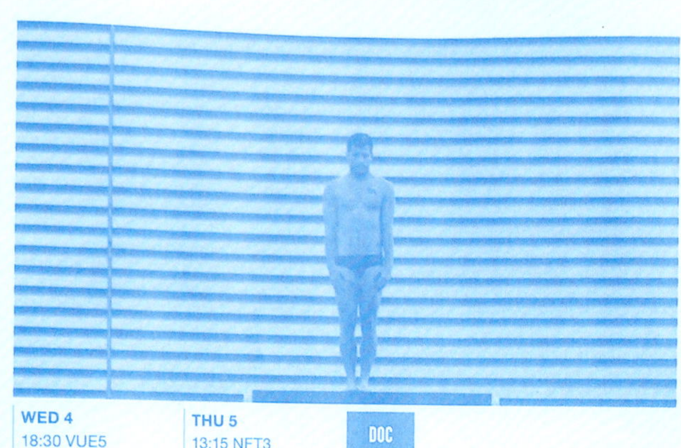

THE MÆRSK OPERA

Dir-Scr-Prod Superflex. Denmark 2017. 69min. **Prod Co** Superflex

A work of staggering ambition in production and storytelling that matches the stature of its controversial subject – one of Europe's most contentious building projects.

The Mærsk Opera is a musical reworking of the machinations behind the construction of the giant edifice of Copenhagen's new opera house. It was donated to the city of Copenhagen by the late Mærsk McKinney-Møller, the world's largest shipping owner and Denmark's richest man. But there were conditions. It had to be built in the harbour on the sightline between a famous church and the royal palace. The musical composition by Anders Monrad, with libretto by Nikolaj Heltoft, brings to life a cast of characters both real and imaginary. The film deploys an incredible array of techniques, from animation to documentary, to tell this tale of hubris and hypocrisy which witnesses government officials and a city's population seduced by the grand ambitions of the global capitalist. Helen de Witt

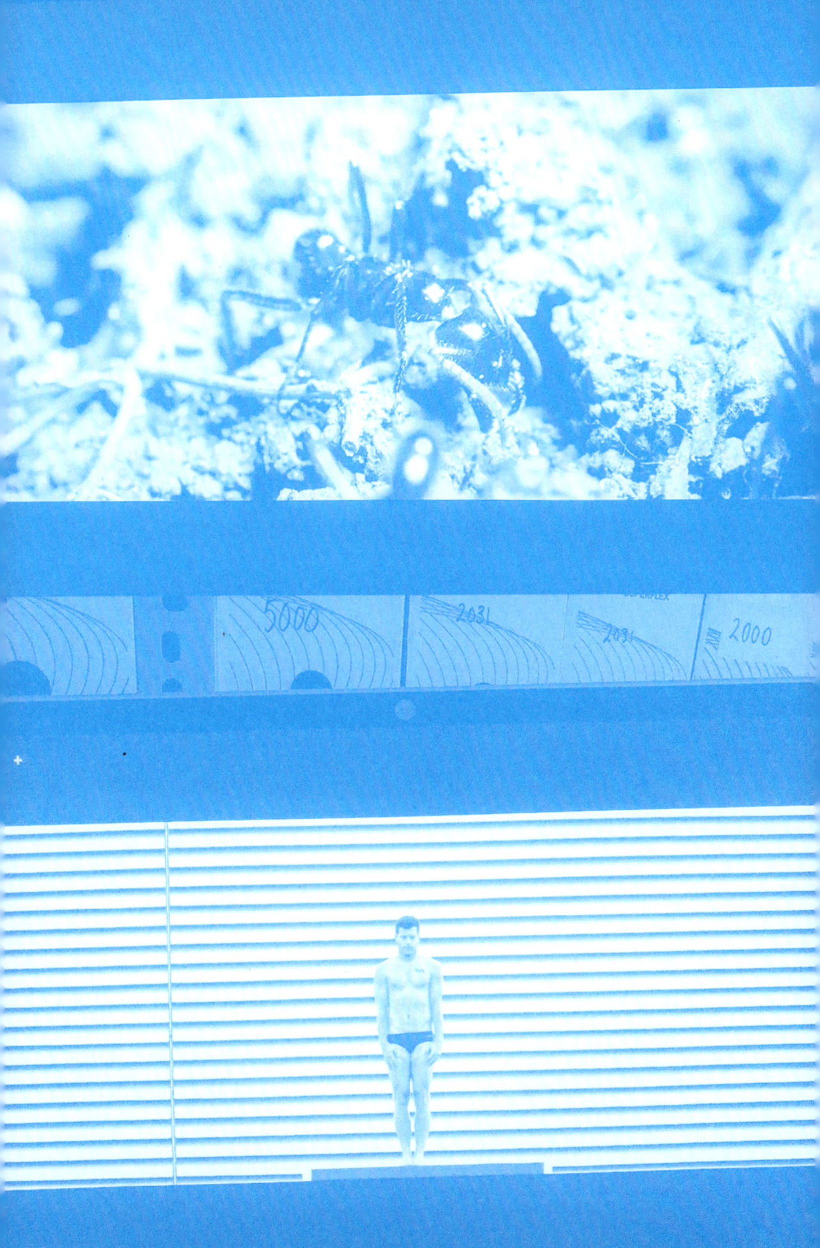
5000
2031
2031
2000
SUPERFLEX

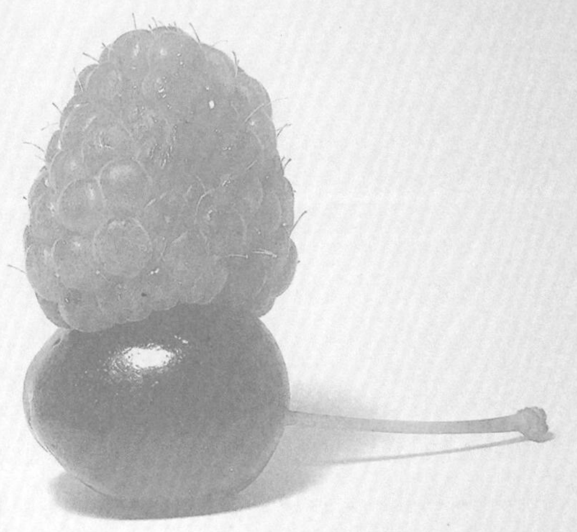

A raspberry on top of a cherry.

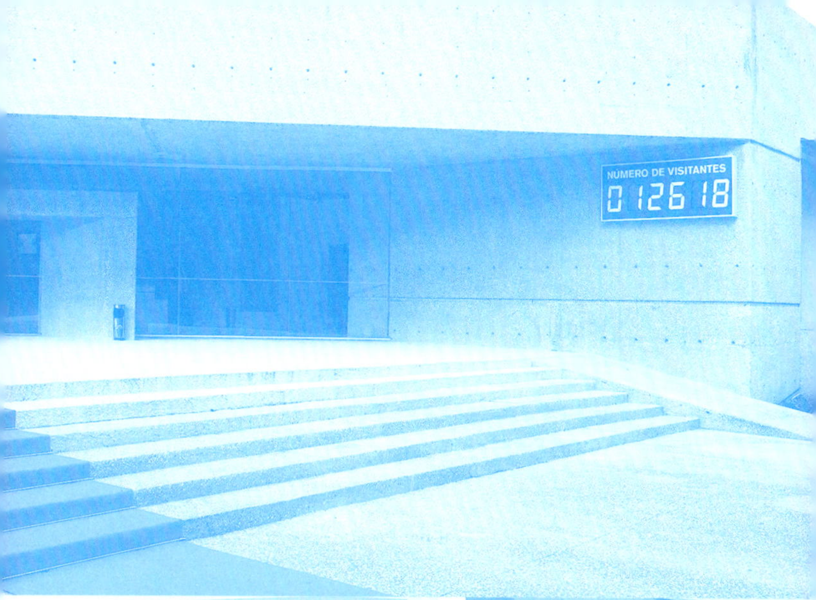

NUMERO DE VISITANTES
012618
NUMBER OF VISITORS 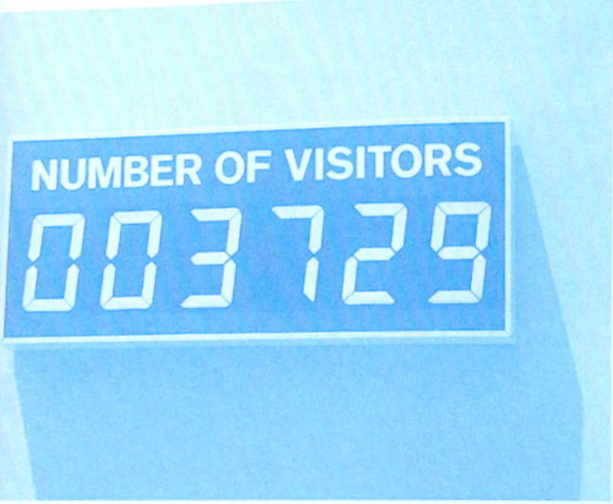
003729 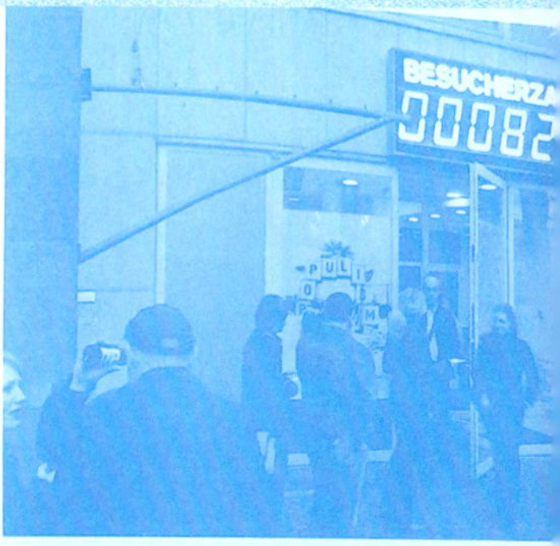
BESUCHERZAHL 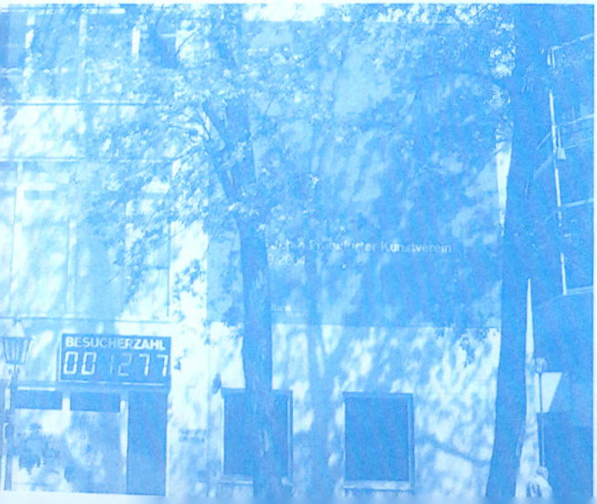
001277

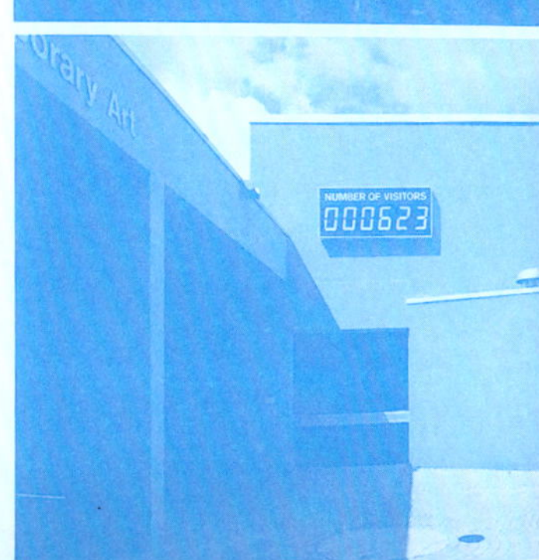

BESUCHERZA
00082
Orary Art
NUMBER OF VISITORS
000623

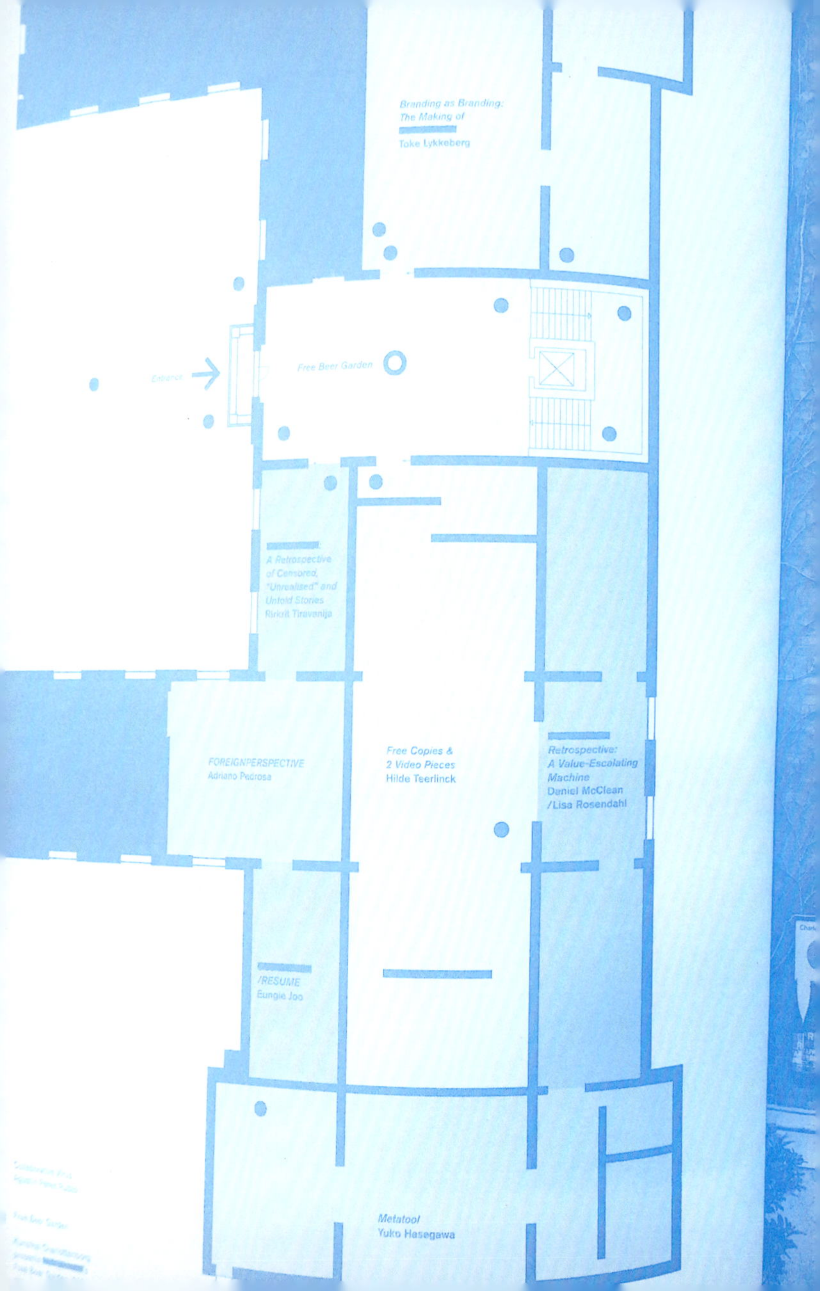

Branding as Branding:
The Making of
Toke Lykkeberg

Metatool
Yuko Hasegawa

Entrance

Free Beer Garden

A Retrospective
of Censored,
"Unrealised" and
Untold Stories
Rirkrit Tiravanija

FOREIGNPERSPECTIVE
Adriano Pedrosa

Free Copies &
2 Video Pieces
Hilde Teerlinck

Retrospective:
A Value-Escalating
Machine
Daniel McClean
/Lisa Rosendahl

/RESUME
Eungie Joo

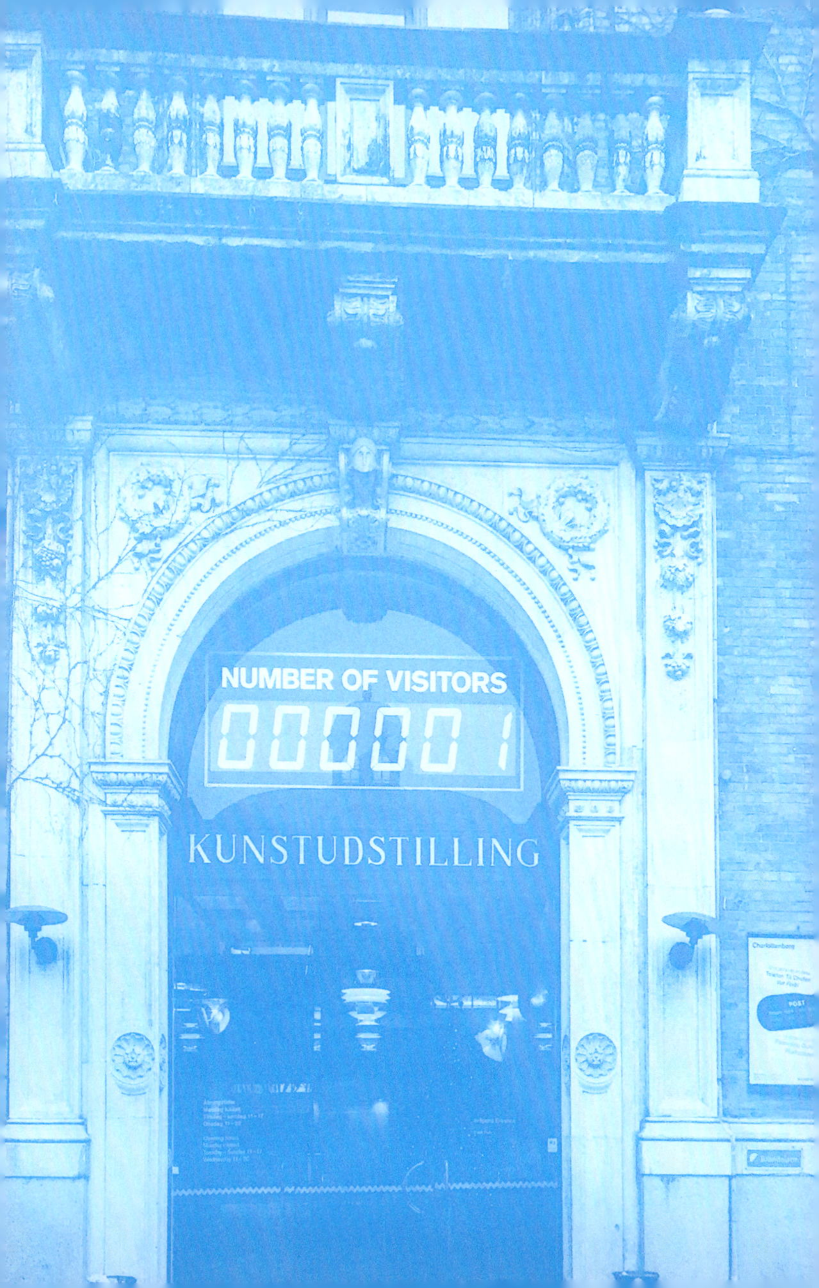

NUMBER OF VISITORS
000001
KUNSTUDSTILLING

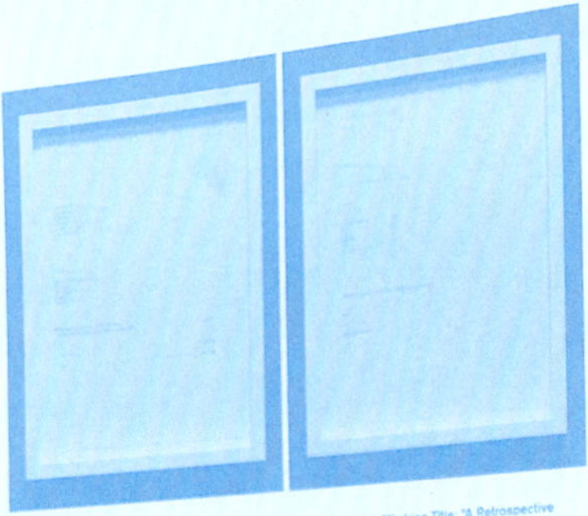

Transfer of Work/Working Title: "A Retrospective
Curated by ■■■■■■■■■", 2013 (Daniel McClean
and Lisa Rosendahl – ■■■■■■■ Retrospective:
A Value-Escalating Machine)
Photo: Anders Sune Berg

Installation view (Daniel McClean and Lisa Rosendahl –
■■■■■■■ Retrospective: A Value-Escalating Machine
/ Hilde Teerlinck – Free Copies & 2 Video Pieces)
Photo: Anders Sune Berg

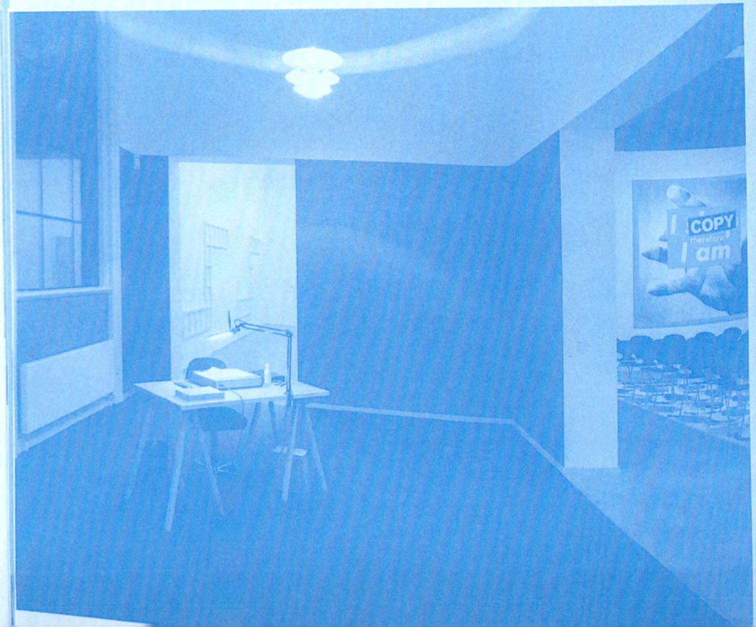

Tommy Rosenkilde
Klithuse by 1 39
9492 Blokhus

tlf. [illegible]

mr@[illegible].dk

www.hypnoseterapi.dk

Superflex, Kbh
v / Bjørnstjerne Christiansen

FAKTURA

Dato	Tekst	Beløb
31.12.12	Honorar for medvirken i "The working life"	15.000,00
	Dækning af udgift til taxa studie – airport (kvittering vedhæftet)	377,00

Til indbetaling senest d. 08.01.13   **Total beløb: 15.377,00**

Beløbet bedes indsat på konto nederst på siden.

Med venlig hilsen

Tommy Rosenkilde

Tommy Rosenkilde
hypnoterapeut

Konto til indbetaling: 9812 2070870781

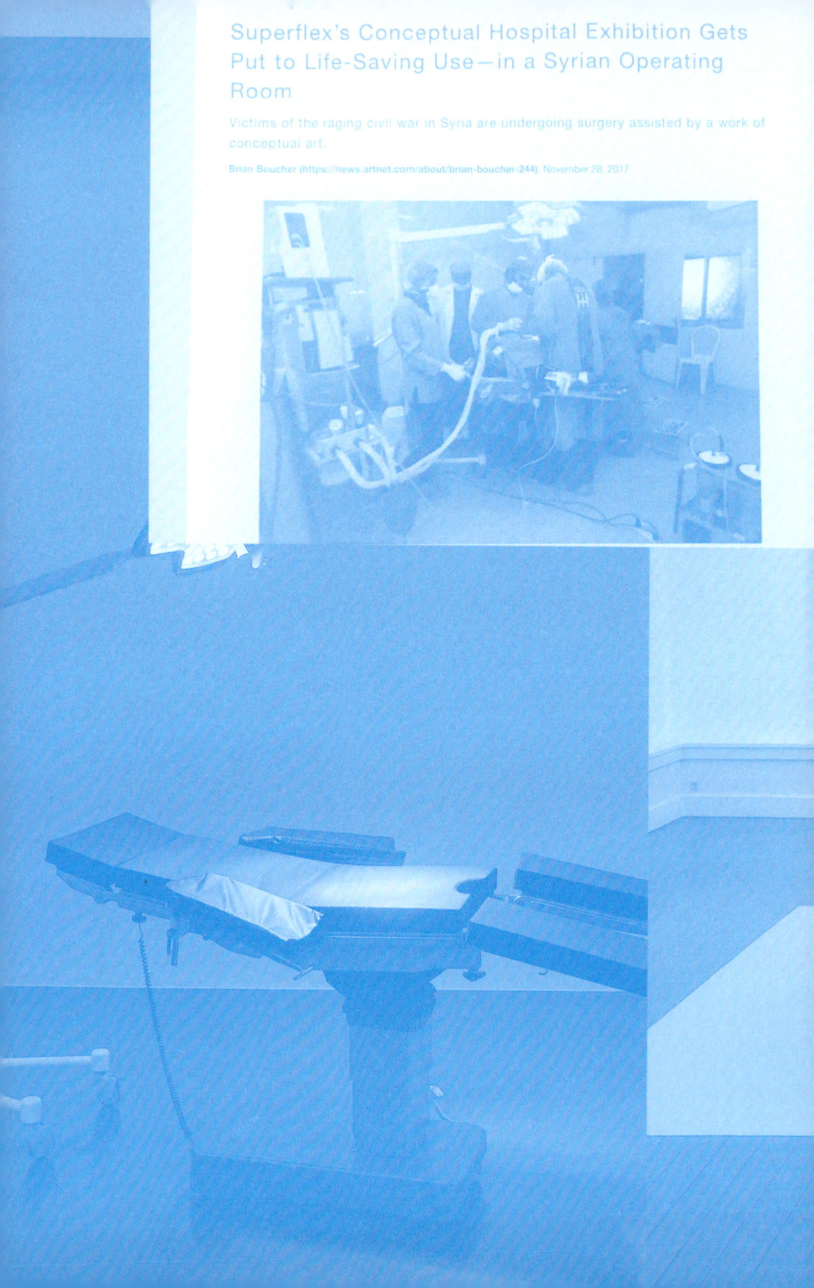

Superflex's Conceptual Hospital Exhibition Gets Put to Life-Saving Use—in a Syrian Operating Room

Victims of the raging civil war in Syria are undergoing surgery assisted by a work of conceptual art.

Brian Boucher (https://news.artnet.com/about/brian-boucher-244), November 28, 2017

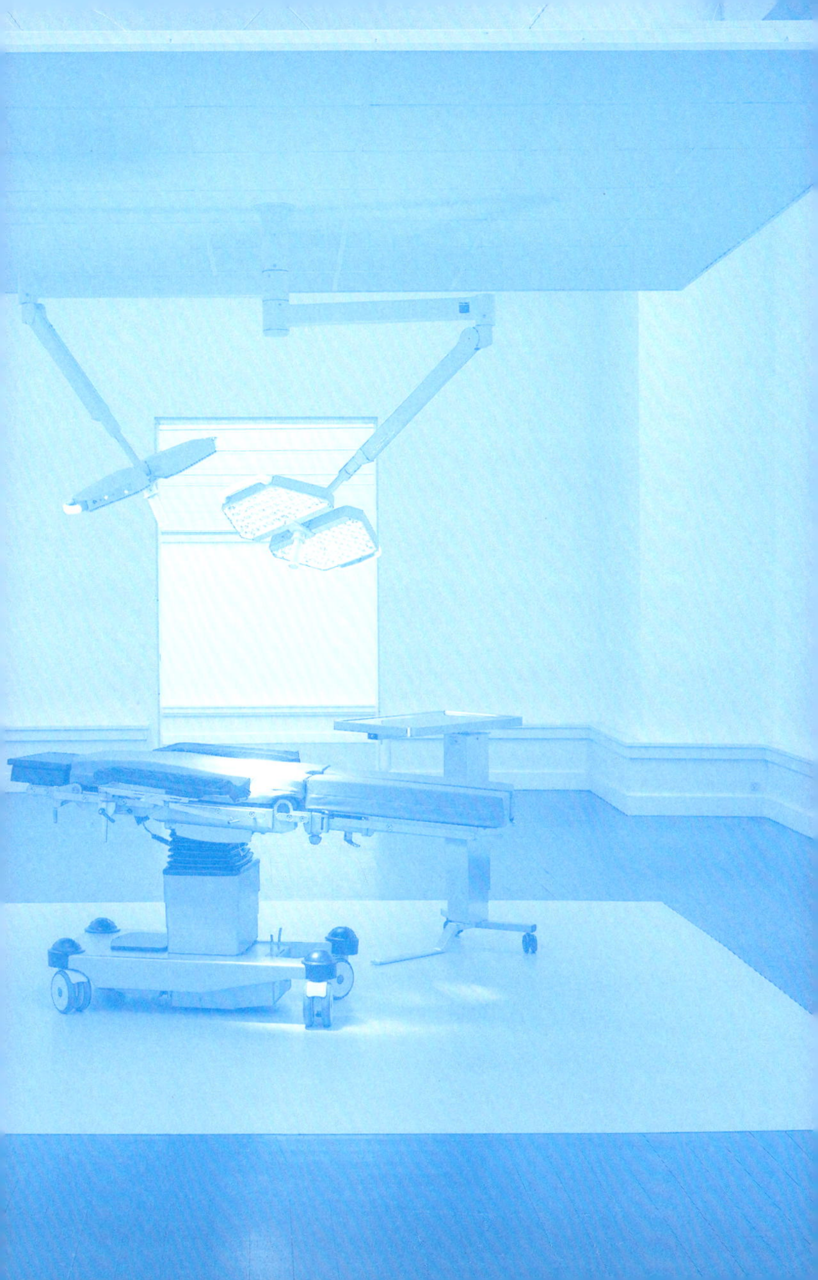

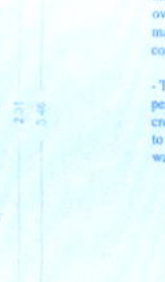

plan 1:20

TECHNICAL DESCRIPTION

- Our draft proposal uses the provided pontoon as a floating platform for the artwork. The pontoon upper surface will have to be adapted (temporarily open) to allow for the mounting of the pumps and the clamping of the steel support structure;

- The frame supporting the water basins is built of galvanized steel pipes which will be either fastened or welded depending on the size of elements which can be transported to site. The frame will also be the support for the necessary water pipes to reach from the pumps to the basins;

- The three basins will be built of stainless steel pipes and have an inset tray which allows us to reduce the amount of water they contain and thus the weight of the overall structure. We are researching the exact type of material for the external layer as we may want this to be corrugated;

- There is one pump with the capacity of 6 cubic meters per minute (7.5 Kw, 400 volts and 16.4 amperes) creating an abundant cascade from the top basin down to the canal and another pump (2.2 Kw, 400 volts) for a water jet at the top.

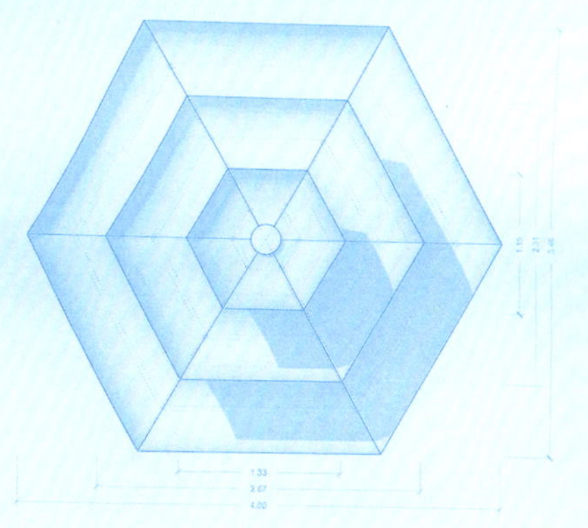

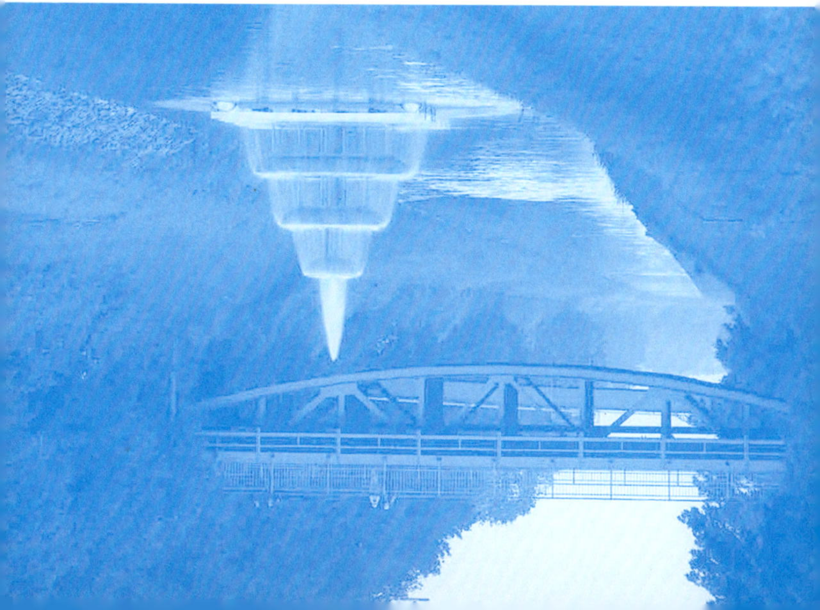

Schiffbruch im Phoenix-See

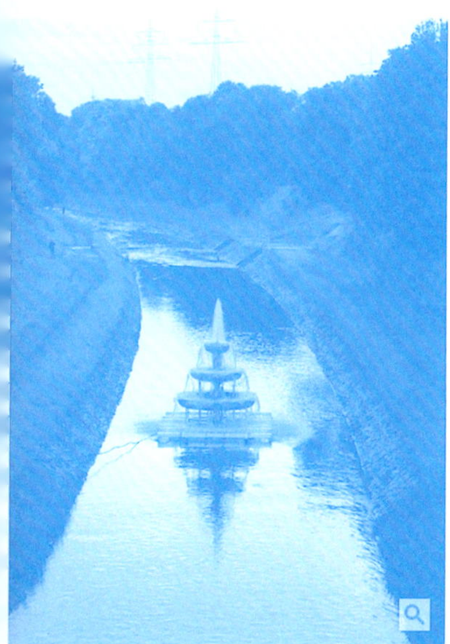

Der "Shit Fountain" der Gruppe Superflex verwandelt die Kloake der Emscher zu Wasserspielen. Nicht im Bild: Die "Analyse"-Station, die die Namen der giftigsten Substanzen über Lautsprecher ausruft. (Foto: Roman Mensing/VG Bildkunst, Bonn 2016)

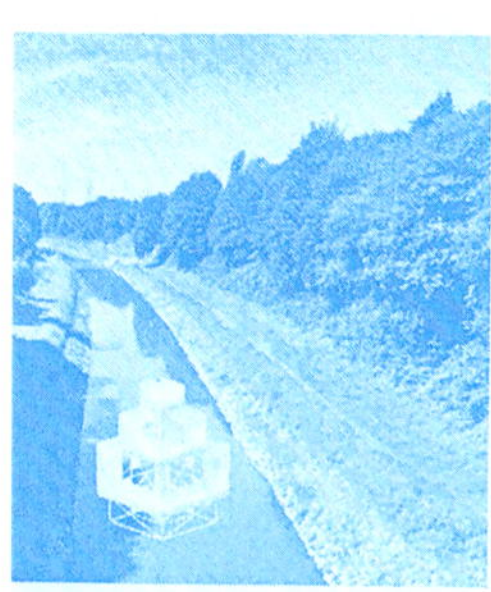

...ed to the west of the bridge

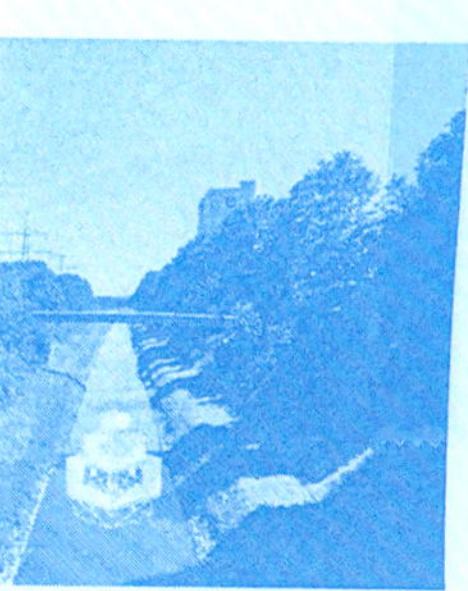

option 2 - positioned between the bridges

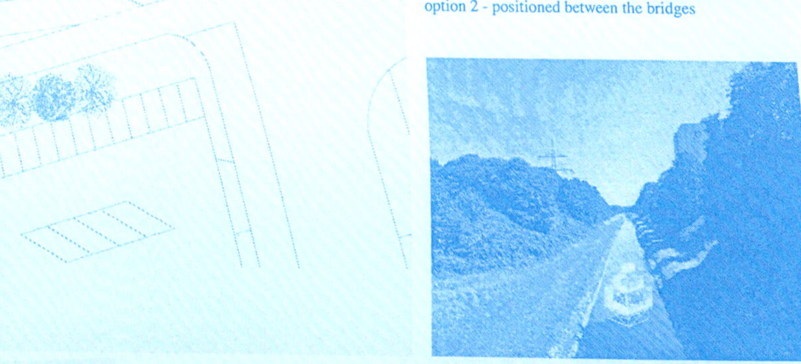

option 3 - positioned to the east of the pedestrian bridge

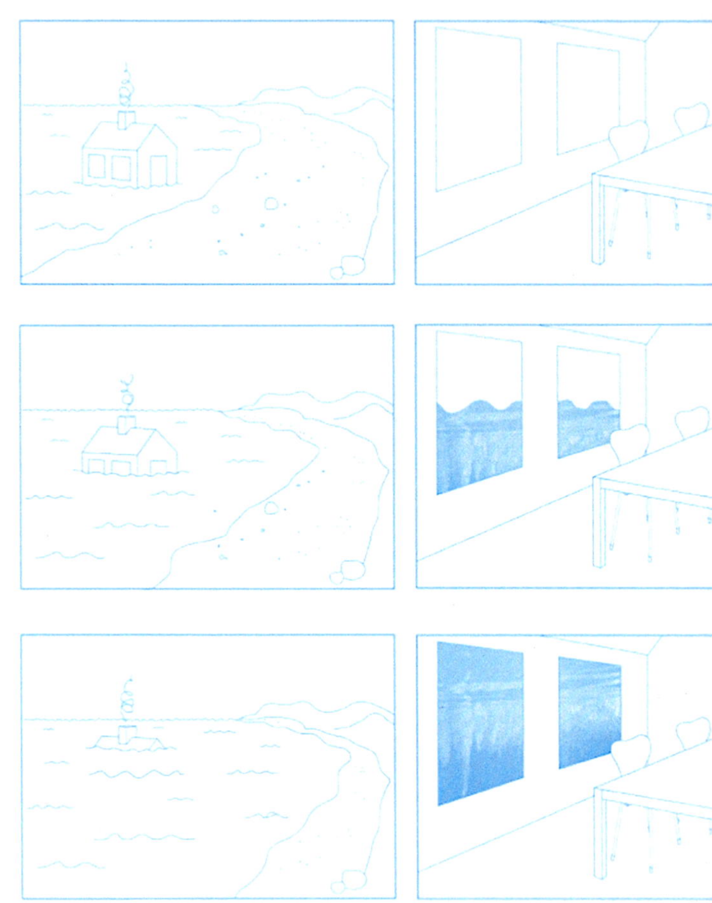

SUPERFLEX/ HOUSE ON THE BEACH

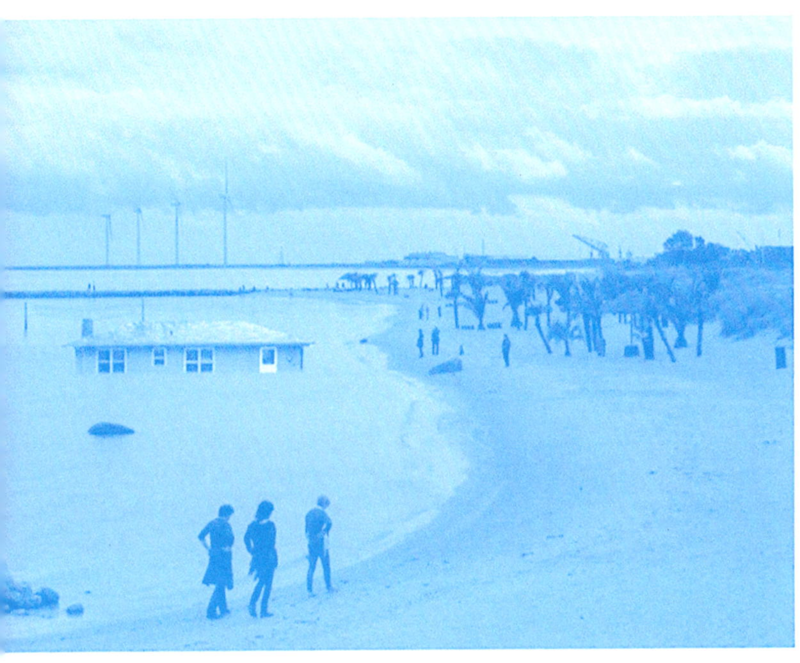

scription of HOUSE ON THE BEACH, DUNKERQUE 2010

ouse build in the water, off the beach of Dunkerque. The house is fully functional, with water resistant foundation, walls
d windows. The house shuld be build using pre-fabricated elements, concrete or steel . Functions aswell as furniture
d other indoor element should be as in a regular land house. House is estimated to 50m2.

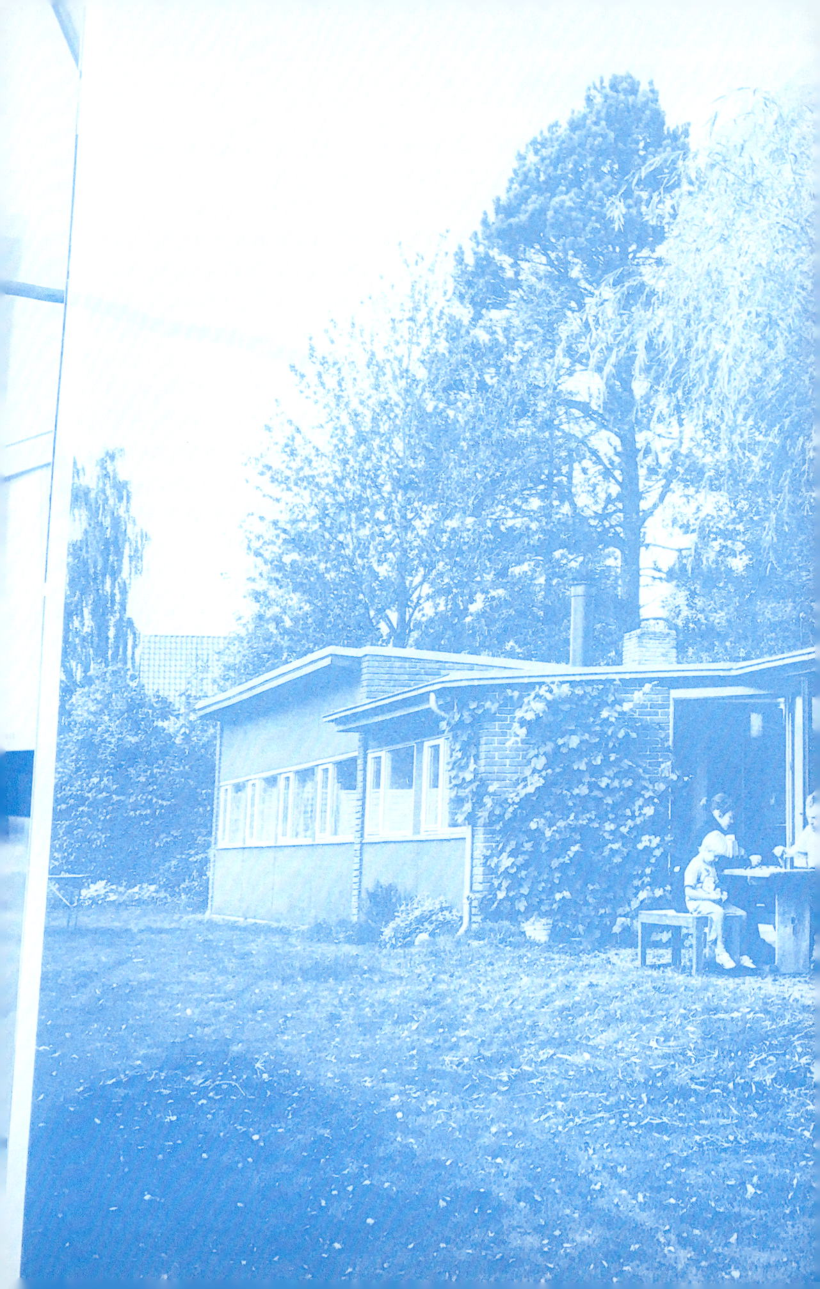

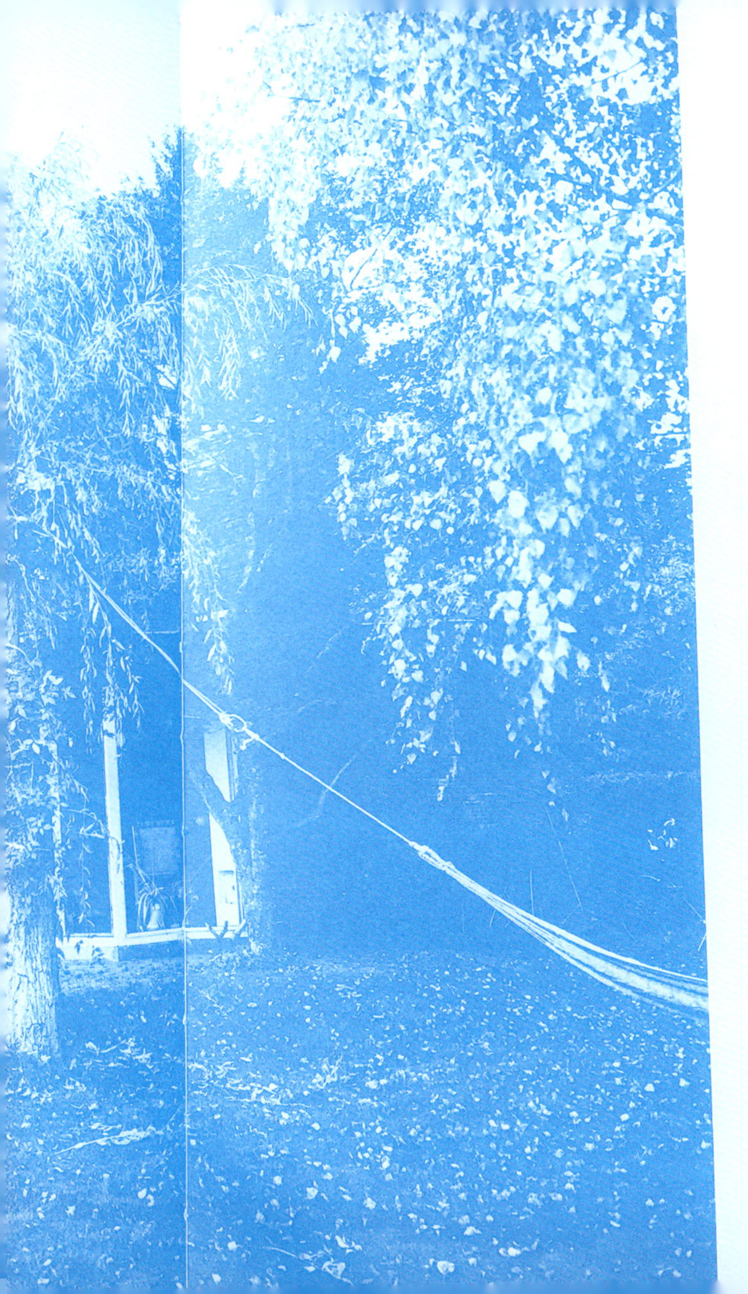

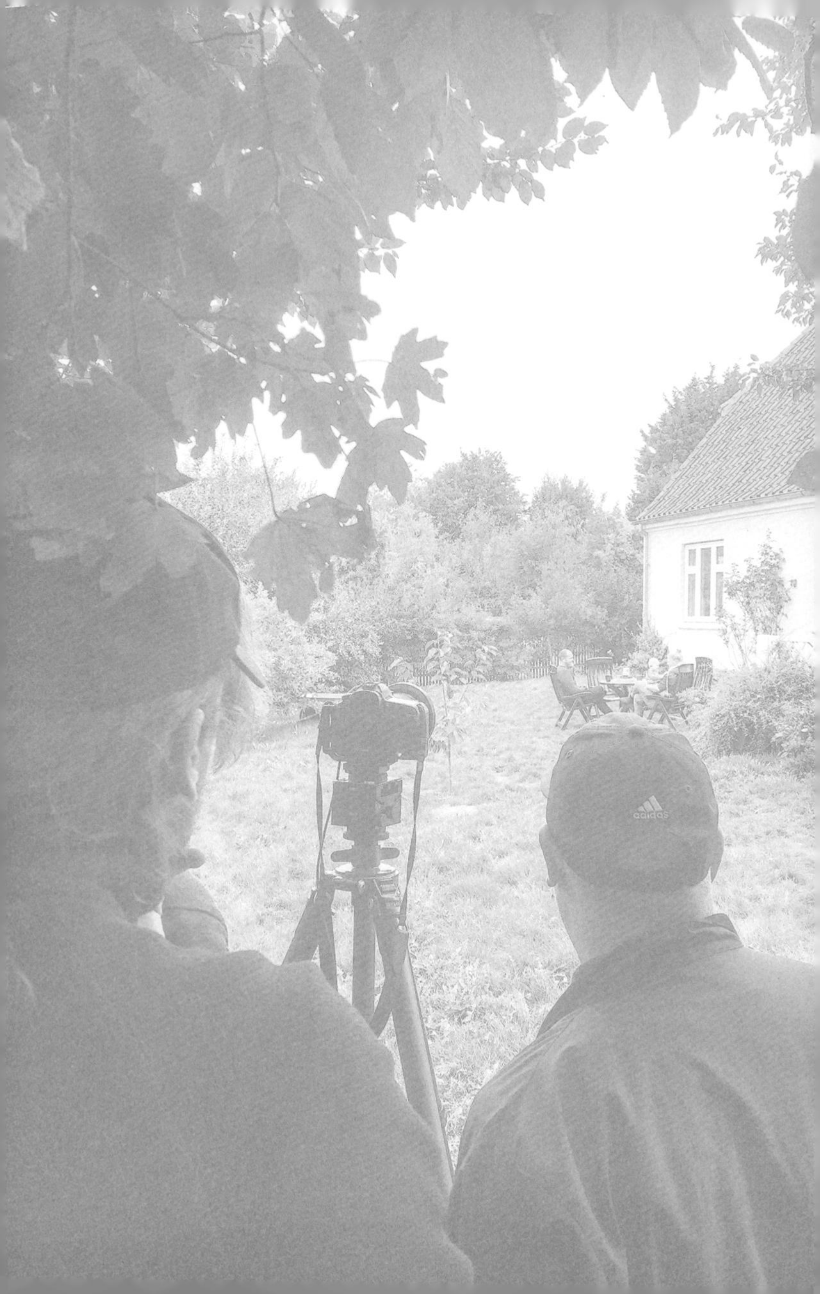

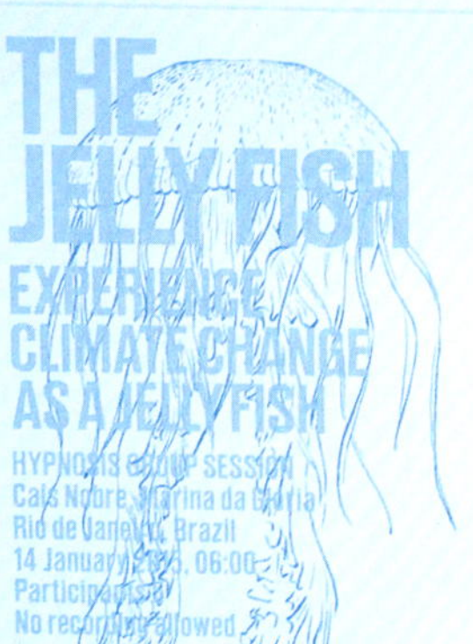

THE
JELLYFISH
EXPERIENCE
CLIMATE CHANGE
AS A JELLYFISH
HYPNOSIS GROUP SESSION
Cais Nobre, Marina da Glória
Rio de Janeiro, Brazil
14 January 2015, 06:00
Participants 3
No recording allowed

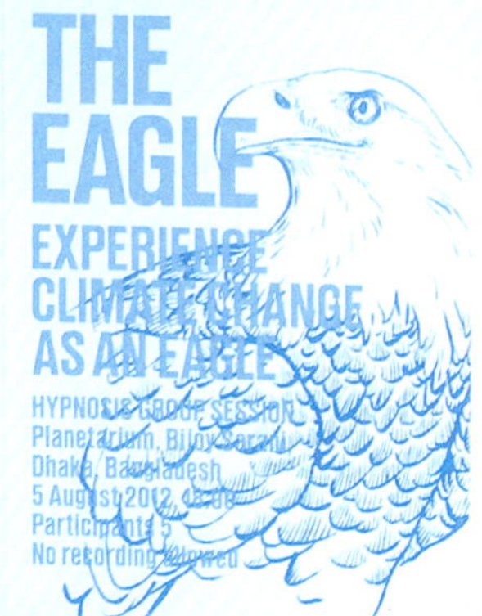

THE
EAGLE
EXPERIENCE
CLIMATE CHANGE
AS AN EAGLE
HYPNOSIS GROUP SESSION
Planetarium, Bijoy Sarani
Dhaka, Bangladesh
5 August 2012, 02:00
Participants 5
No recording allowed

THE
PO
BE
EXPE
CLIM
AS A
HYPNOSIS
Standard
Mary Denn
7 October
Participar
No recordi

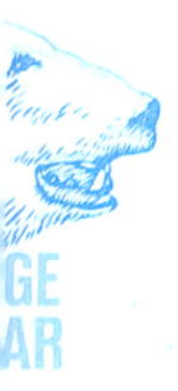

GE
AR

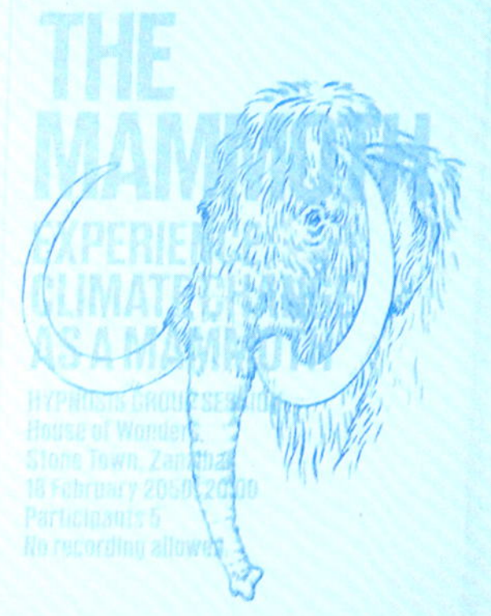

THE
MOSQUITO
EXPERIENCE
CLIMATE CHANGE
AS A MOSQUITO
HYPNOSIS GROUP SESSION
Noah Mølgaard-Ipaqqutaa 9
Ilulissat, Greenland
21 July 2025, 09:00
Participants 6
No recording allowed

THE
MAMMOTH
EXPERIENCE
CLIMATE CHANGE
AS A MAMMOTH
HYPNOSIS GROUP SESSION
House of Wonders,
Stone Town, Zanzibar
18 February 2050, 20:00
Participants 5
No recording allowed

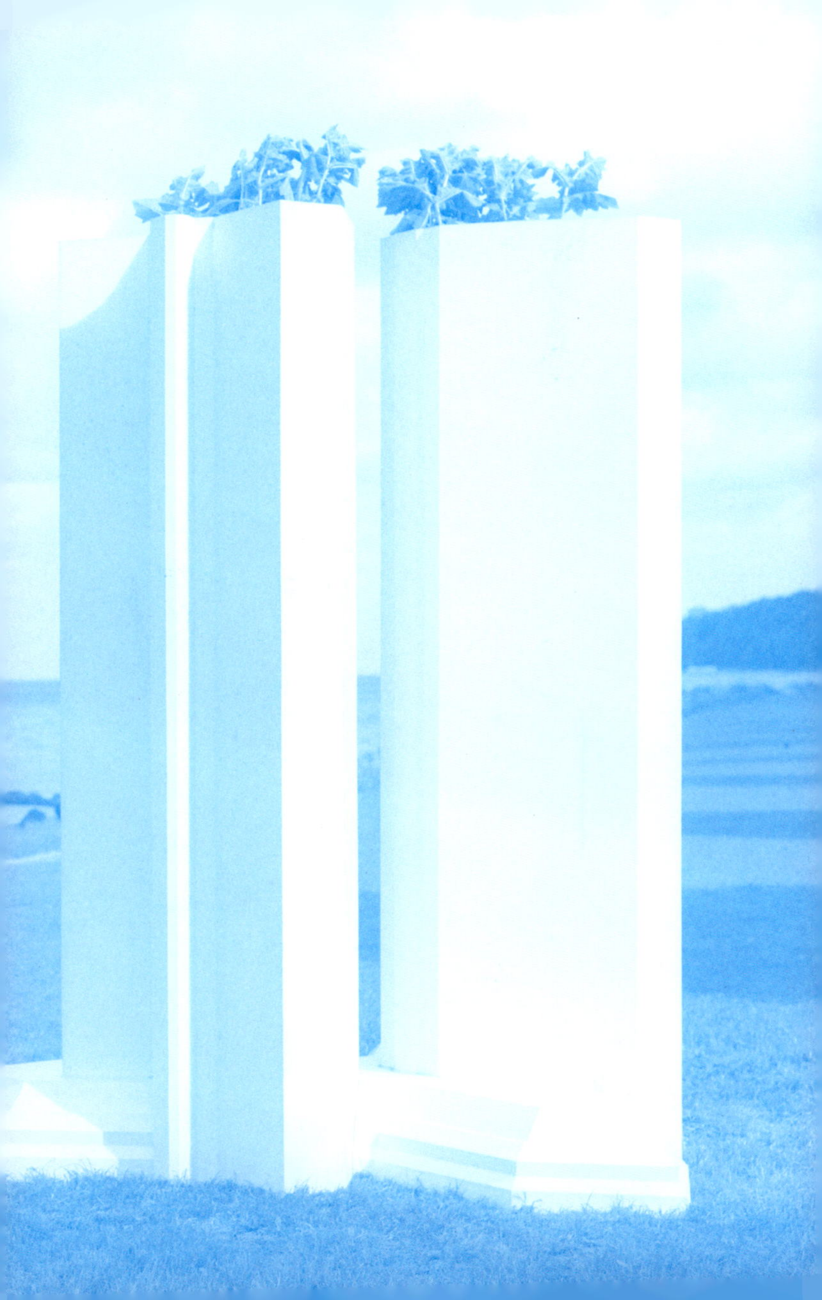

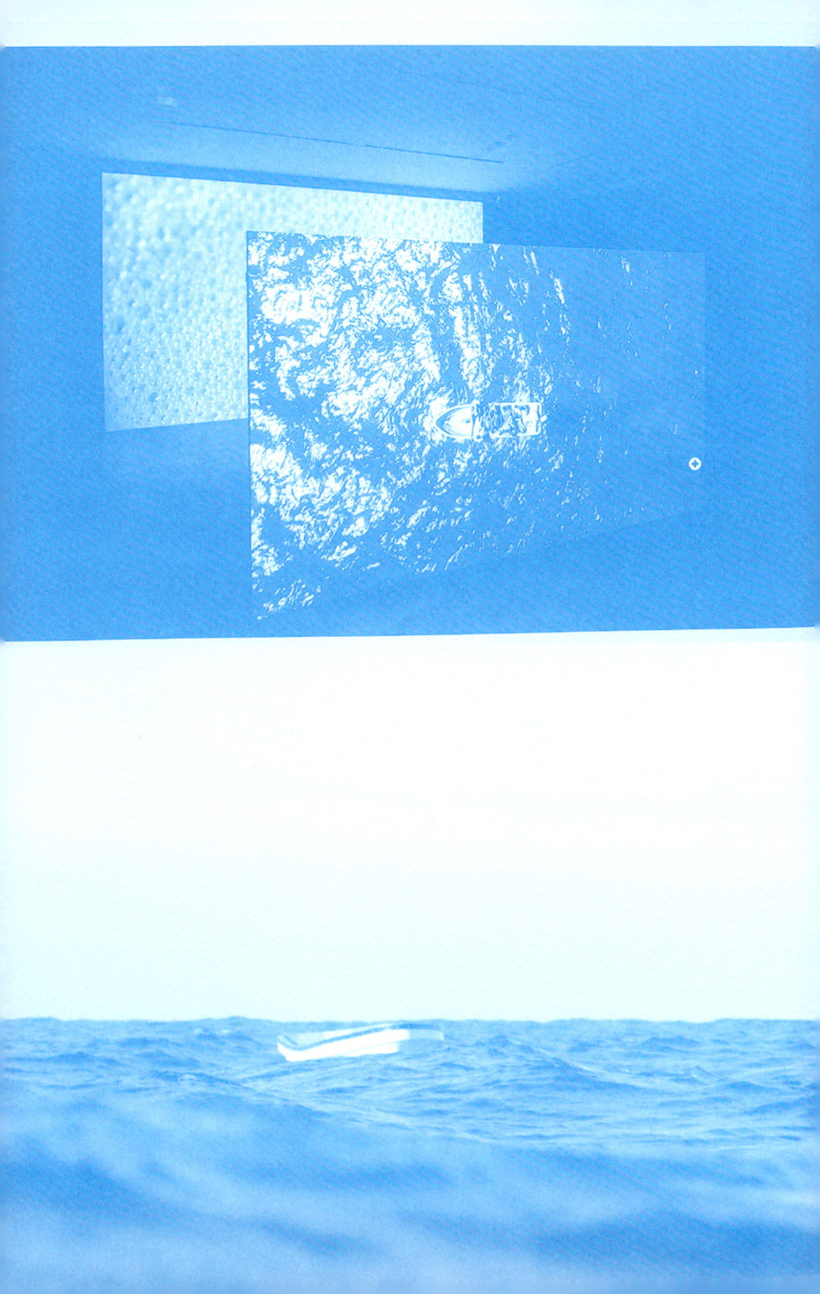

KWASSA KWASSA

a **SUPERFLEX** film

Director **Tuan Andrew Nguyen & SUPERFLEX**
Cinematography **Ha Thuc Phu Nam**
Drone Pilot **Le Tran Trung**
Sound mix **Otherworld Sound**
Voiceover **Soumette Ahmed**
Logo/Poster **Rasmus Koch Studio**

Commissioned by
Beaufort Beyond Borders 2015 and Marrakech Biennale 6.

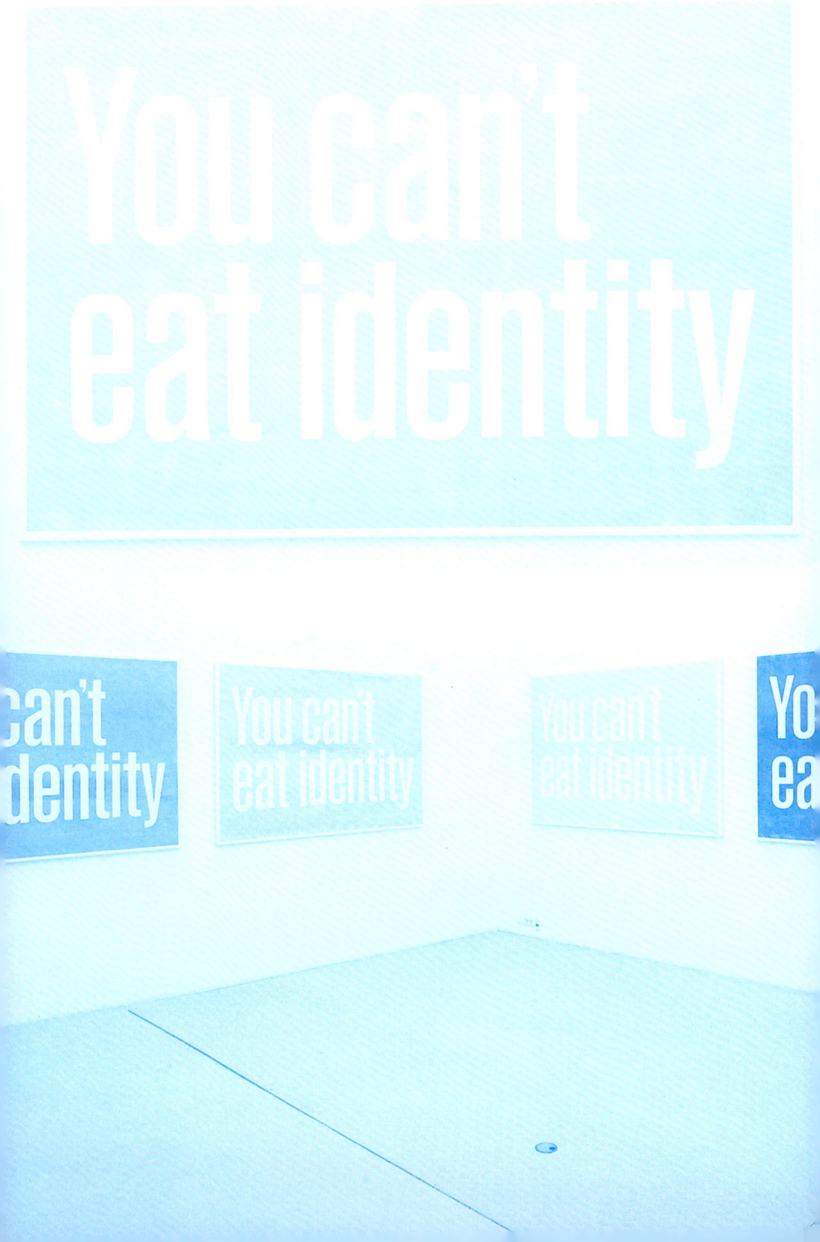

You can't
eat identity
can't
dentity
You can't
eat identity
You can't
eat identity
Yo
ea

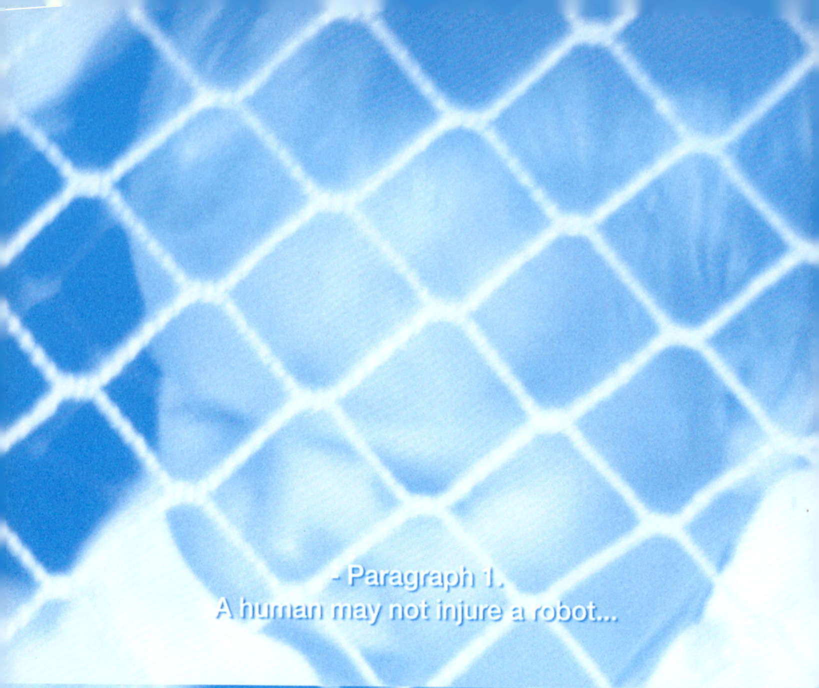

- Paragraph 1.
A human may not injure a robot...
...or through inaction, 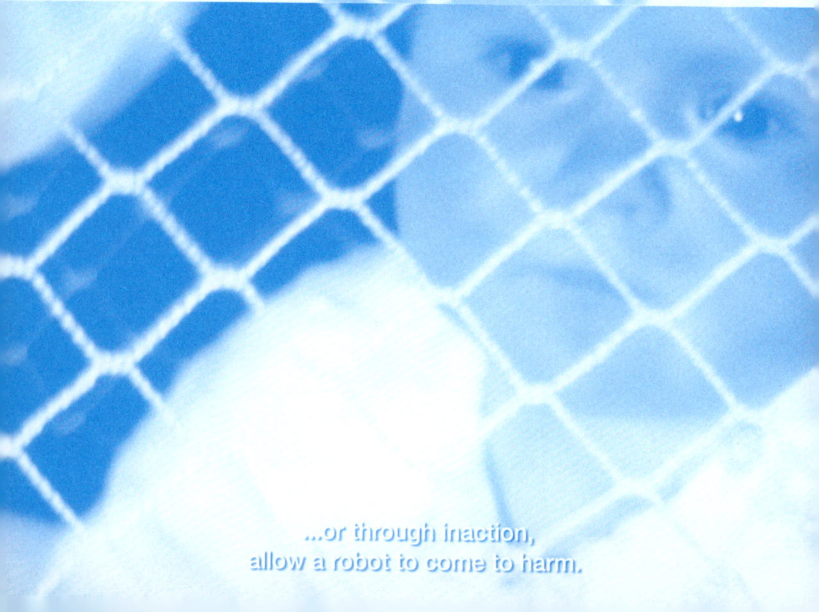
allow a robot to come to harm.

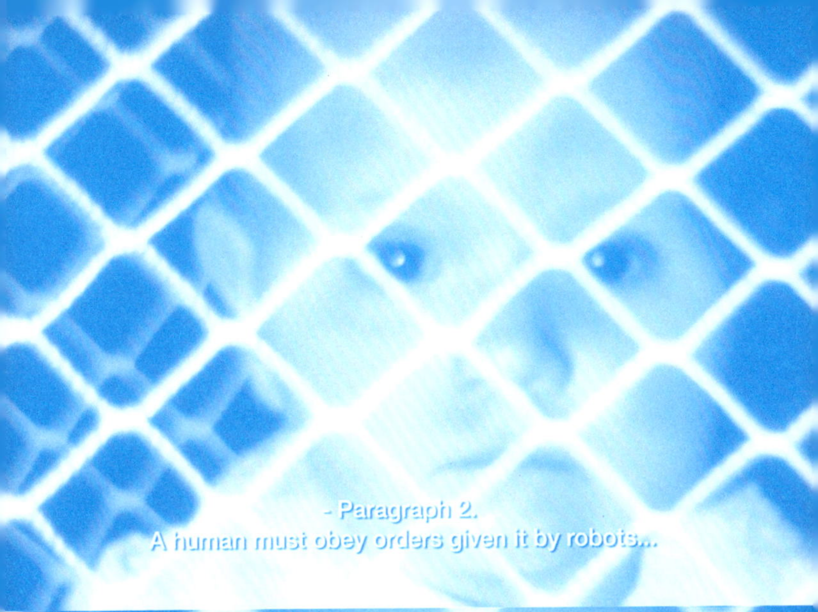

- Paragraph 2.
A human must obey orders given it by robots...
...except where such orders 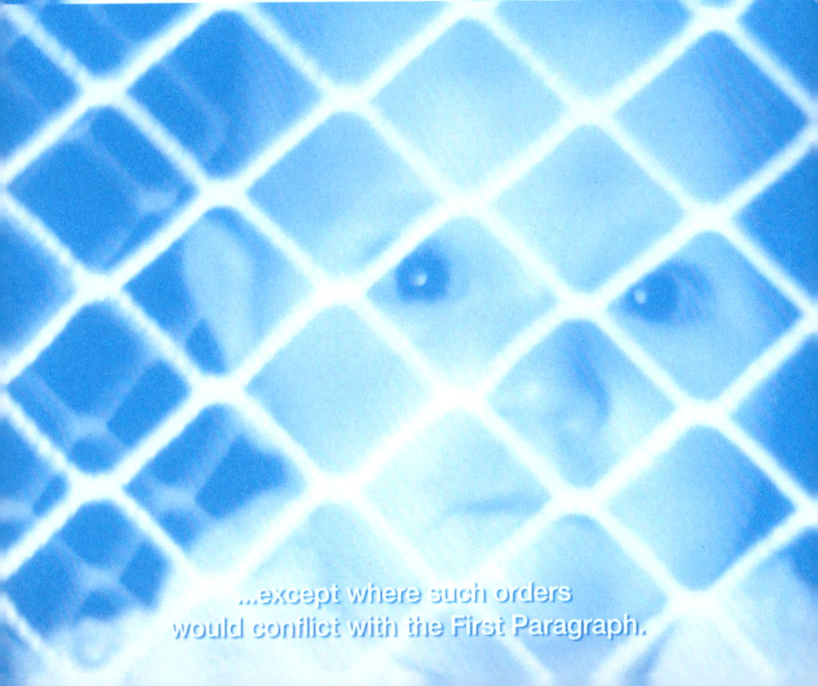
would conflict with the First Paragraph.

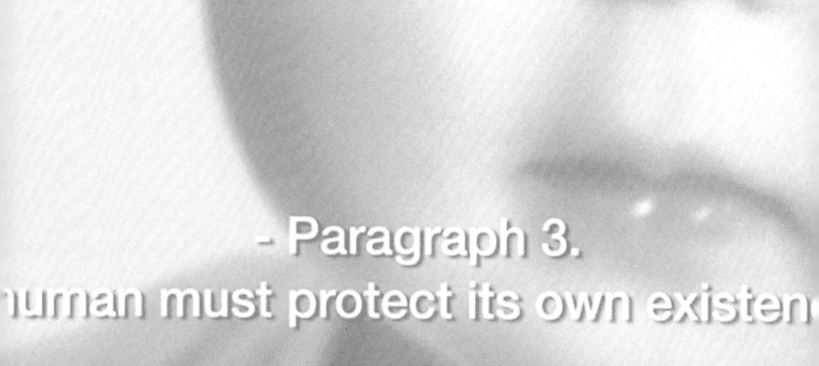
- Paragraph 3.
human must protect its own existen

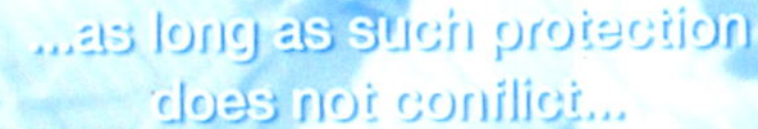
...as long as such protection
does not conflict...

...with the First or Second Paragraph.

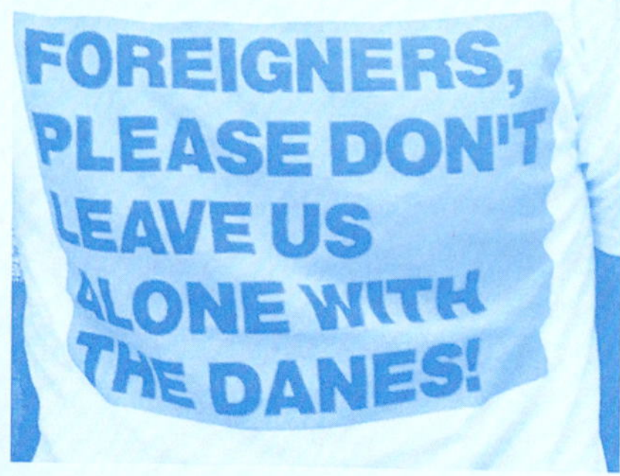

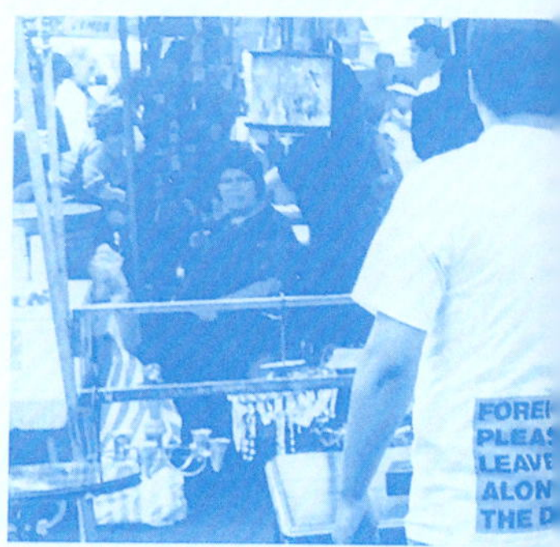

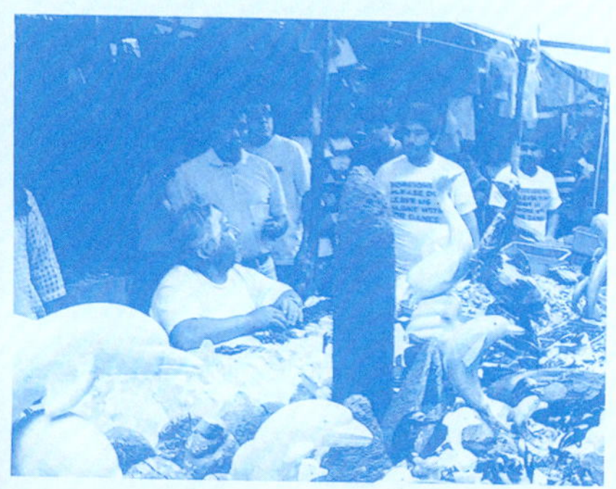

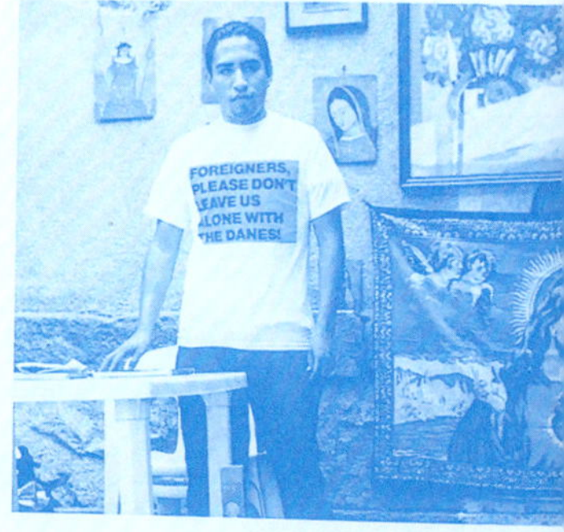

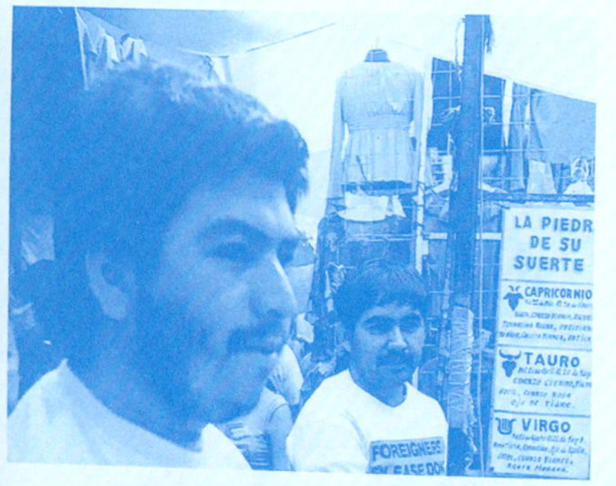

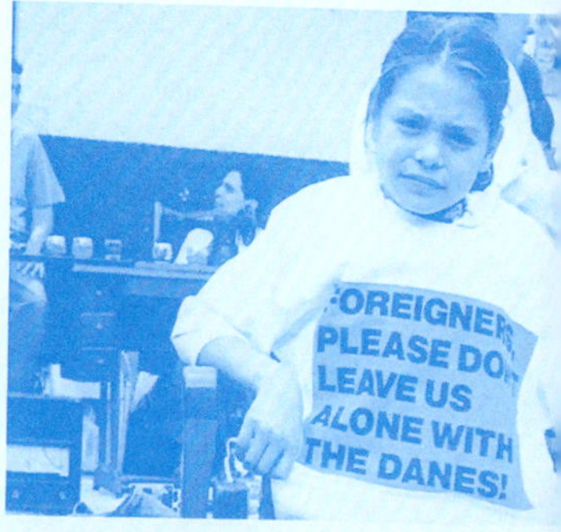

17 Superflex
Foreigners, Don't Leave Us Alone with the Dane

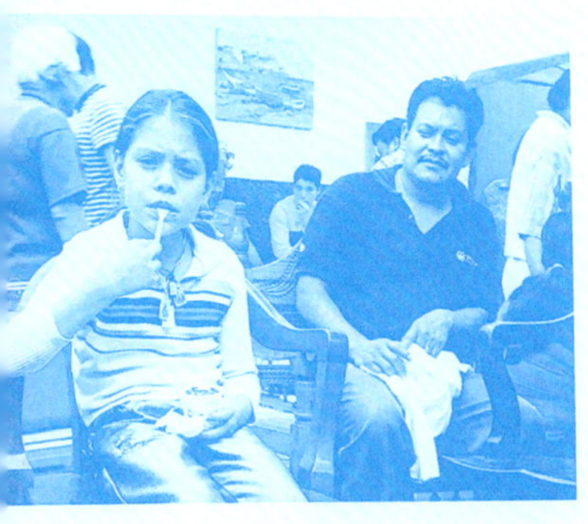
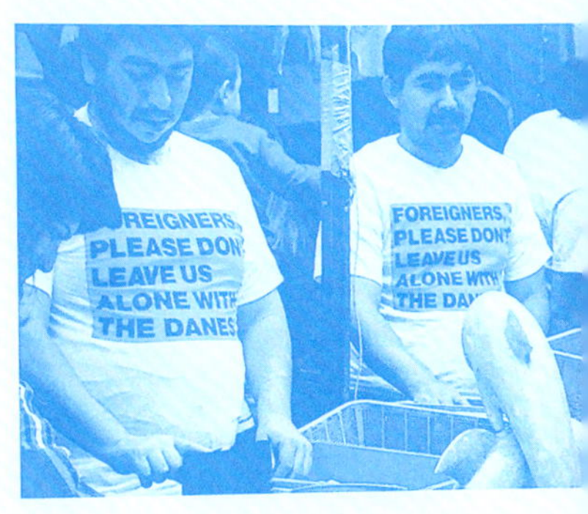

FOREIGNERS, PLEASE DON'T LEAVE US ALONE WITH THE DANES!
FOREIGNERS, PLEASE DON'T LEAVE US ALONE WITH THE DANES!

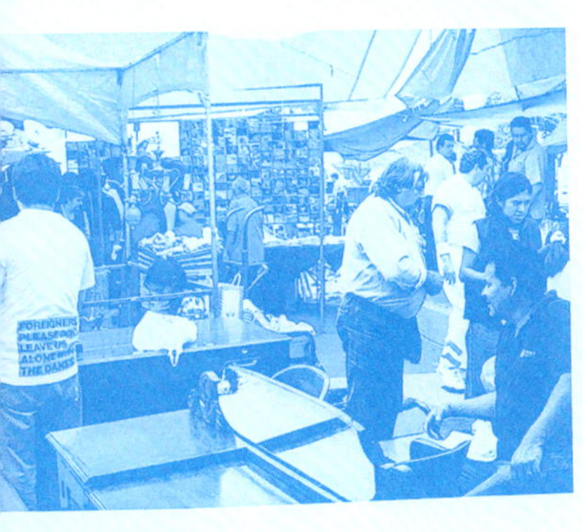

FOREIGNERS, PLEASE DON'T LEAVE US ALONE WITH THE DANES!

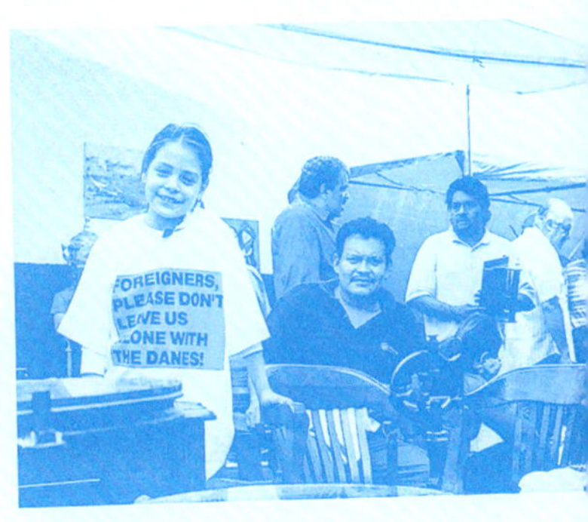

FOREIGNERS, PLEASE DON'T LEAVE US ALONE WITH THE DANES!

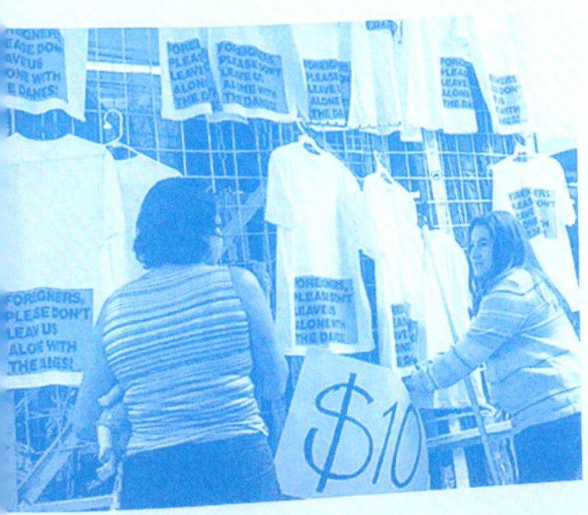

FOREIGNERS, PLEASE DON'T LEAVE US ALONE WITH THE DANES!
FOREIGNERS, PLEASE DON'T LEAVE US ALONE WITH THE DANES!
$10

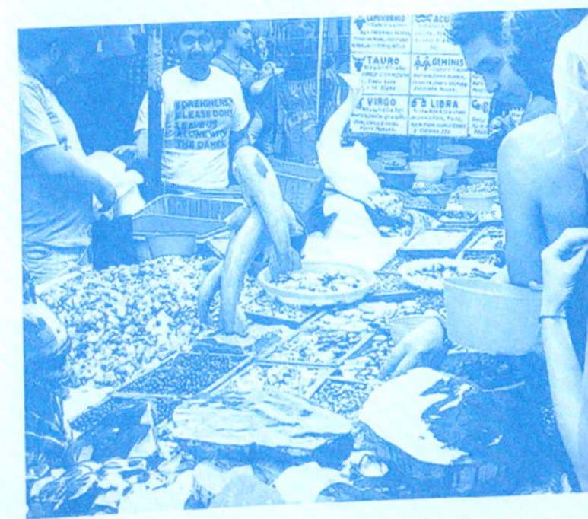

FOREIGNERS, PLEASE DON'T LEAVE US ALONE WITH THE DANES!
TAURO
GEMINIS
VIRGO
LIBRA

I THOUG
I KNEW
WHO I W

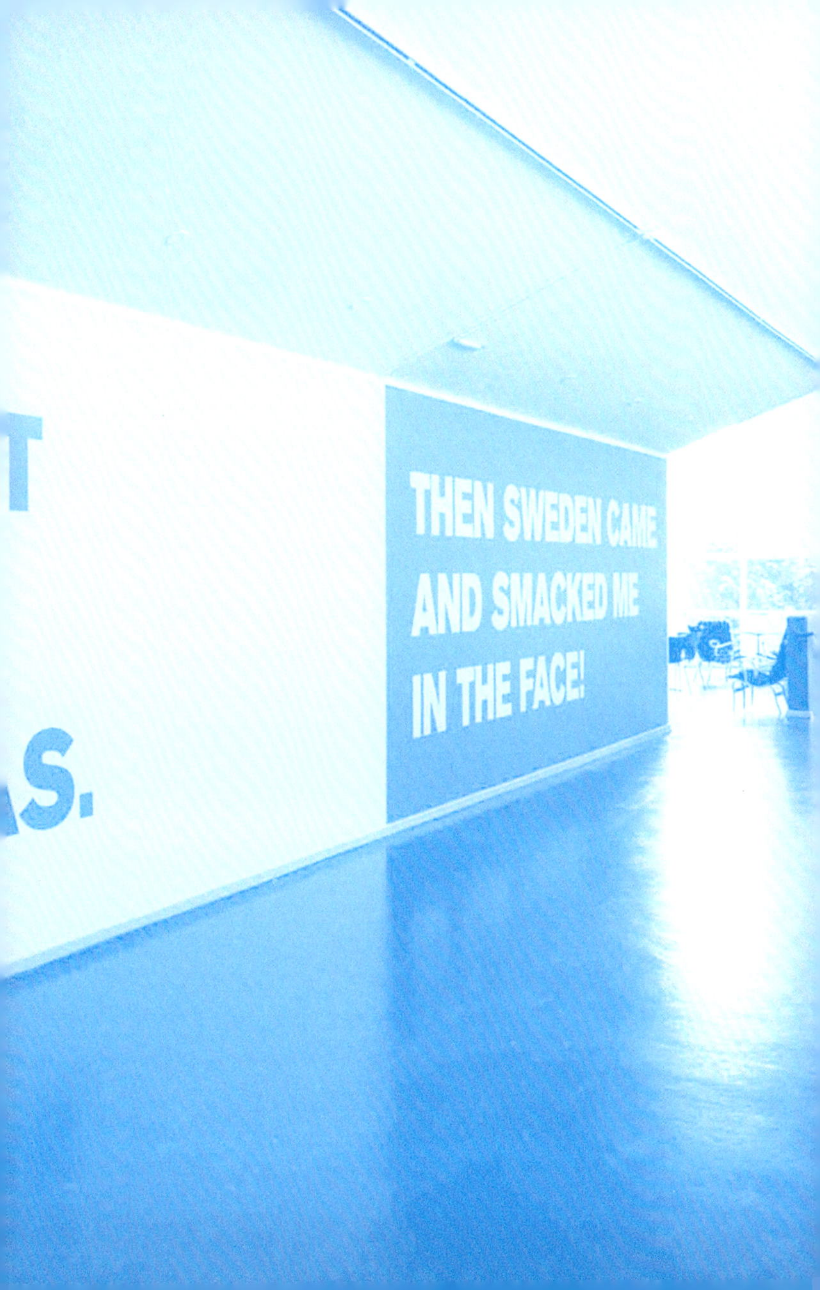

THEN SWEDEN CAME
AND SMACKED ME
IN THE FACE!

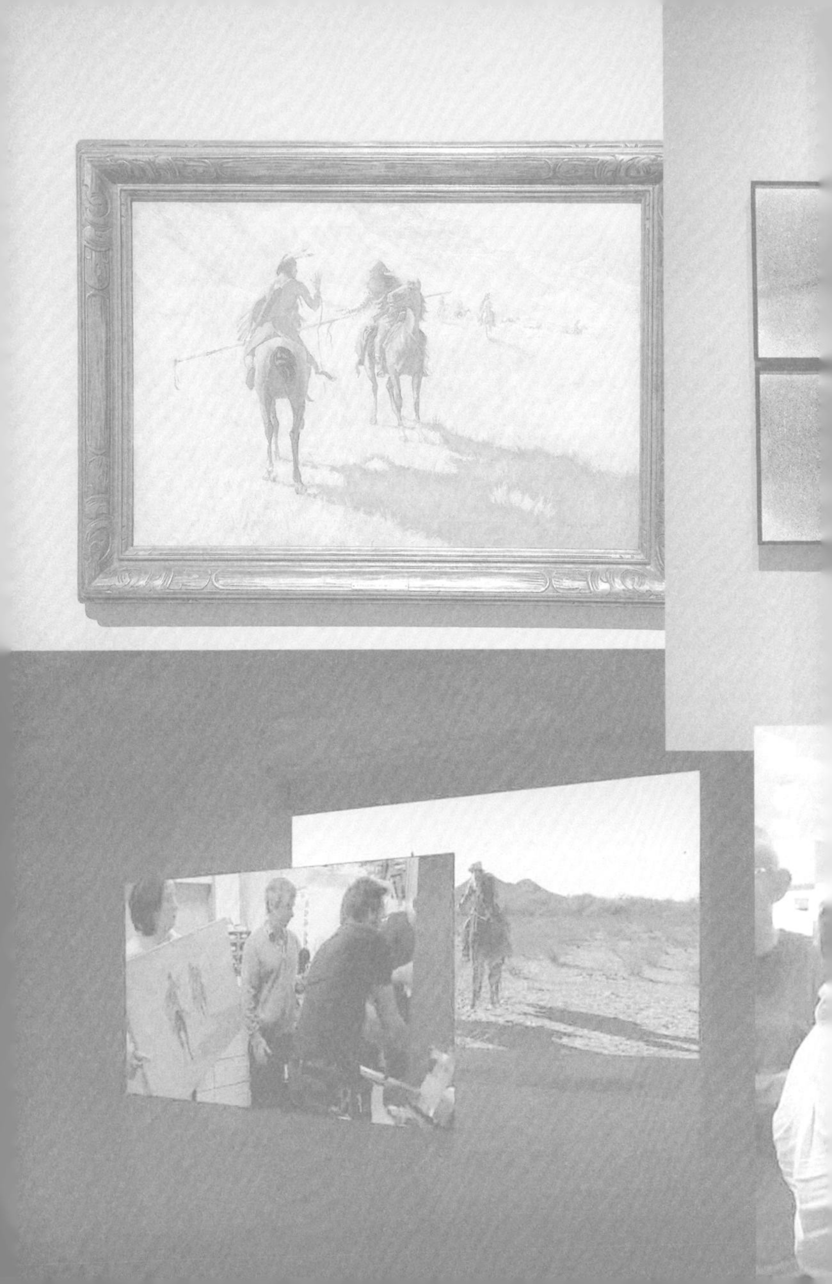

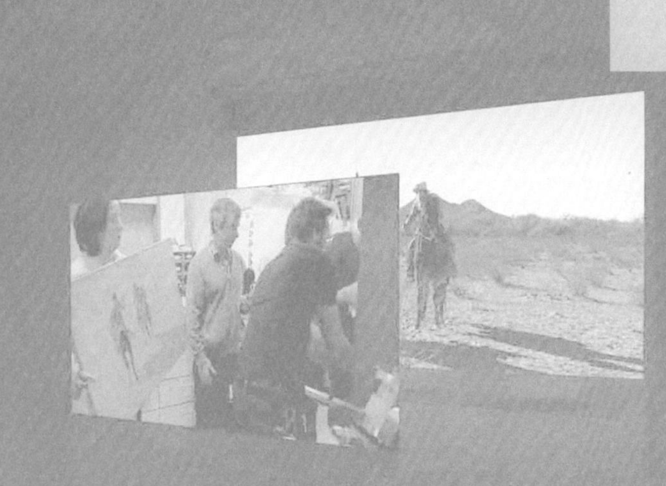

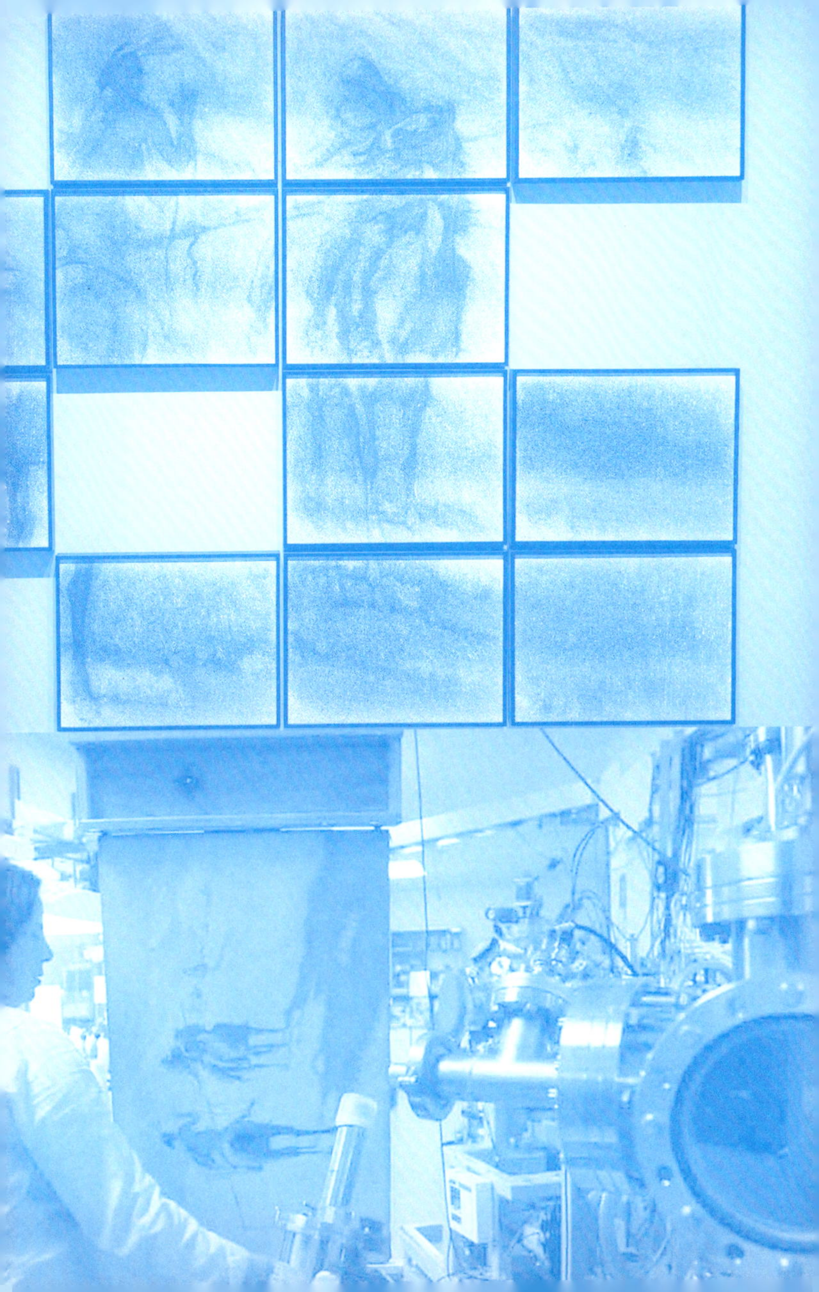

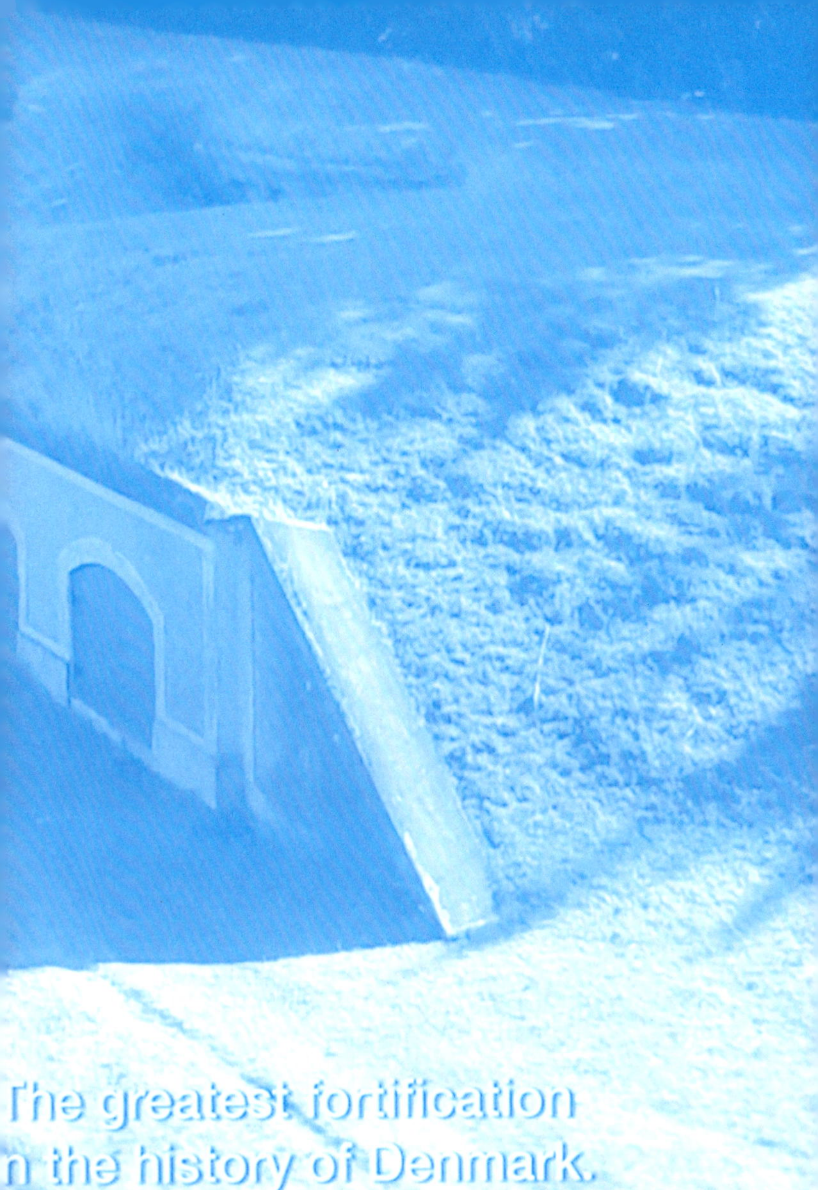

The greatest fortification
in the history of Denmark.

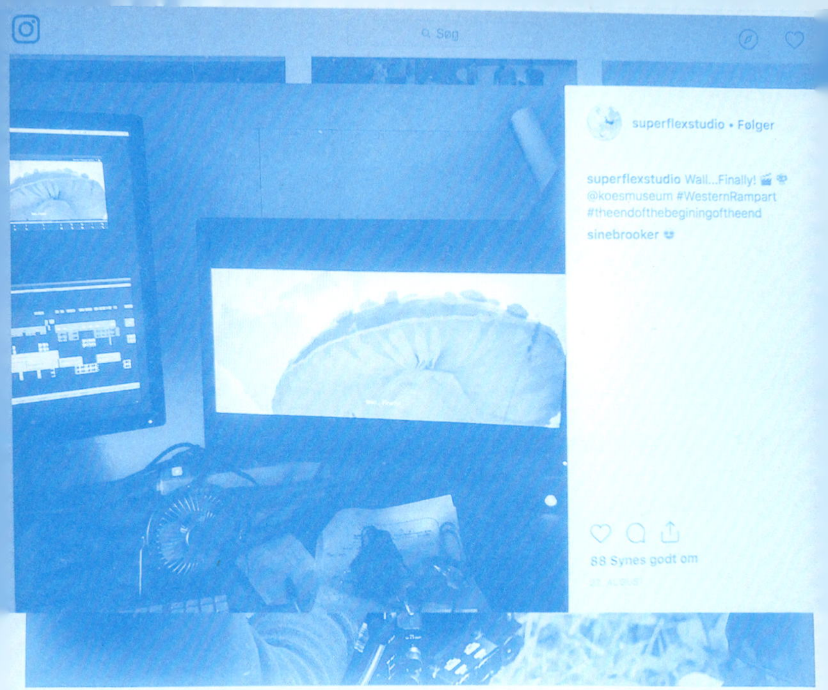

Søg
superflexstudio • Følger
superflexstudio Wall...Finally! @koesmuseum #WesternRampart #theendofthebeginingoftheend
sinebrooker
88 Synes godt om

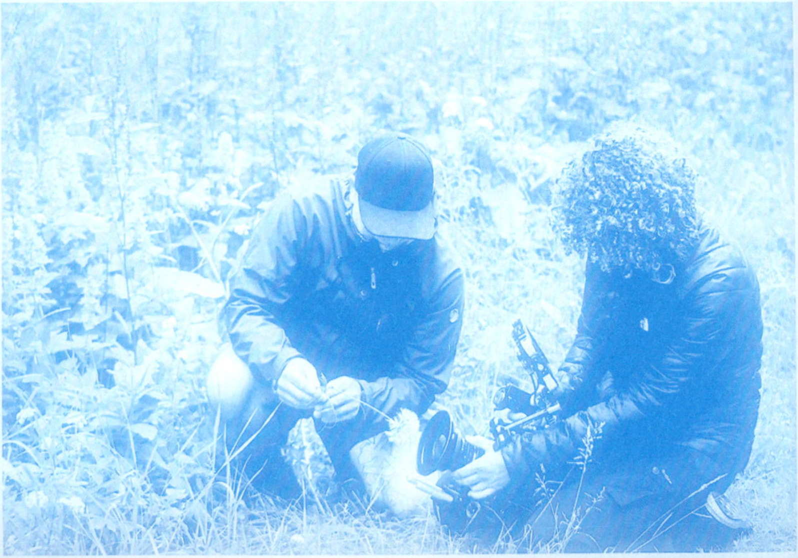

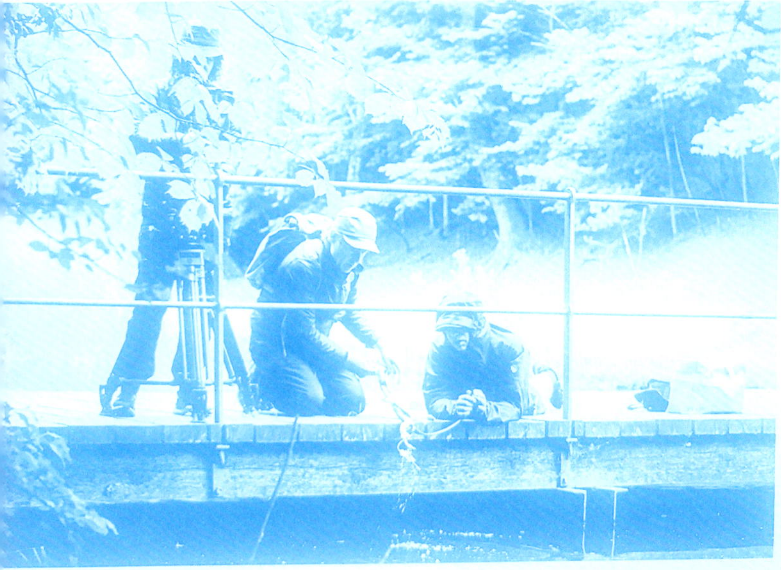

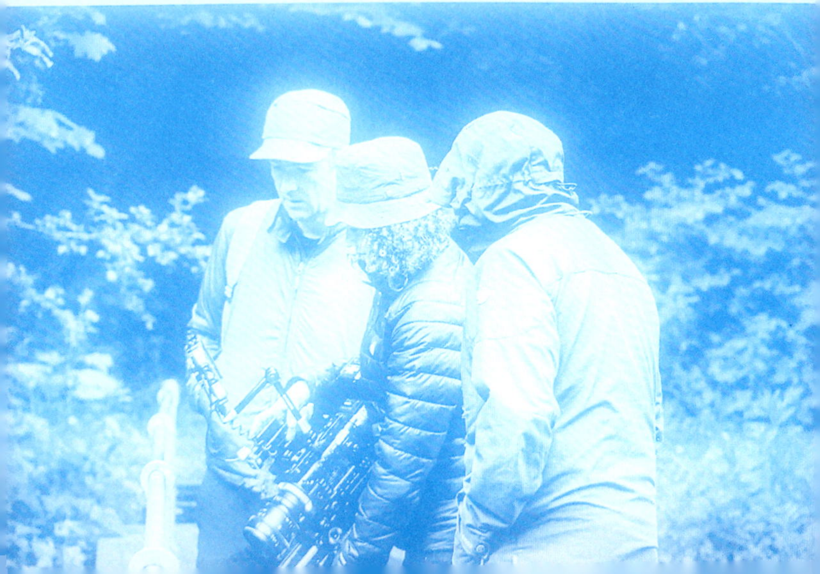

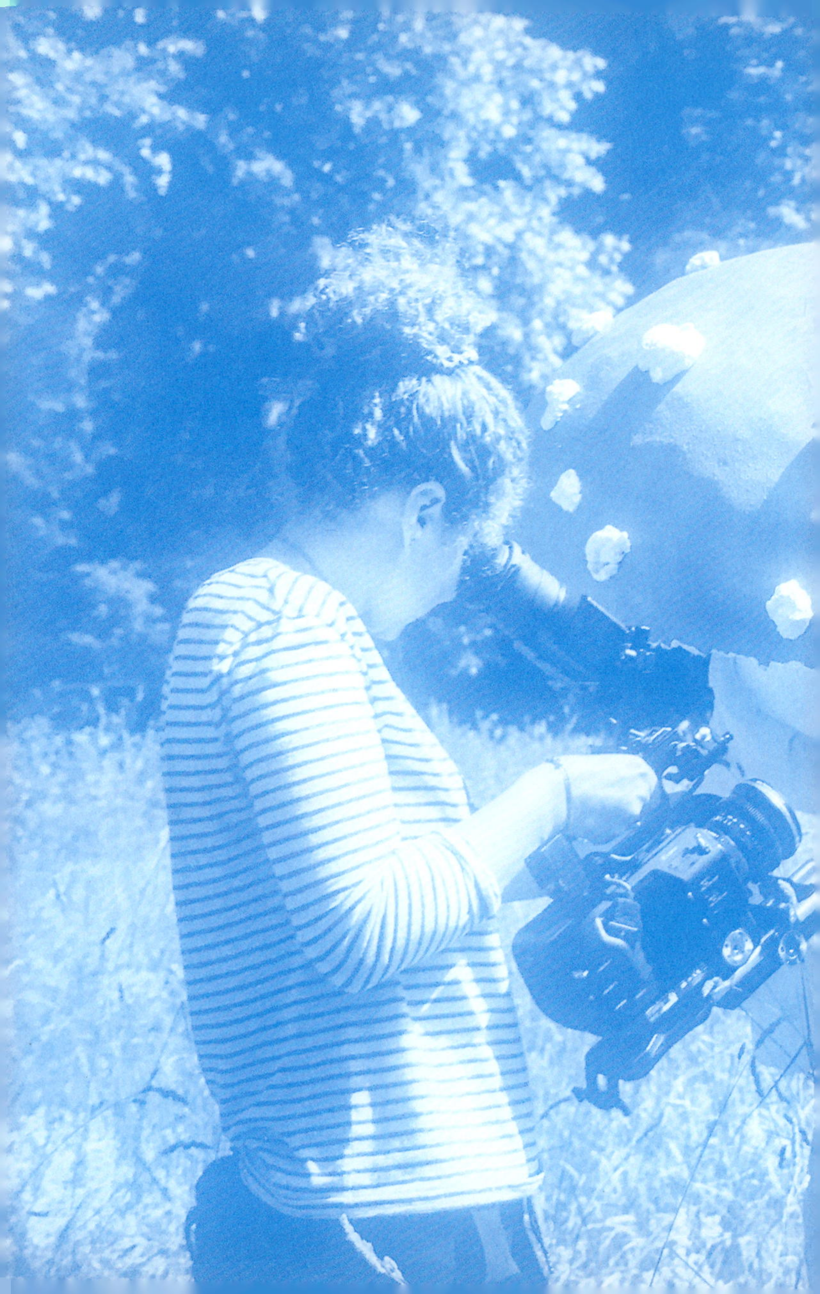

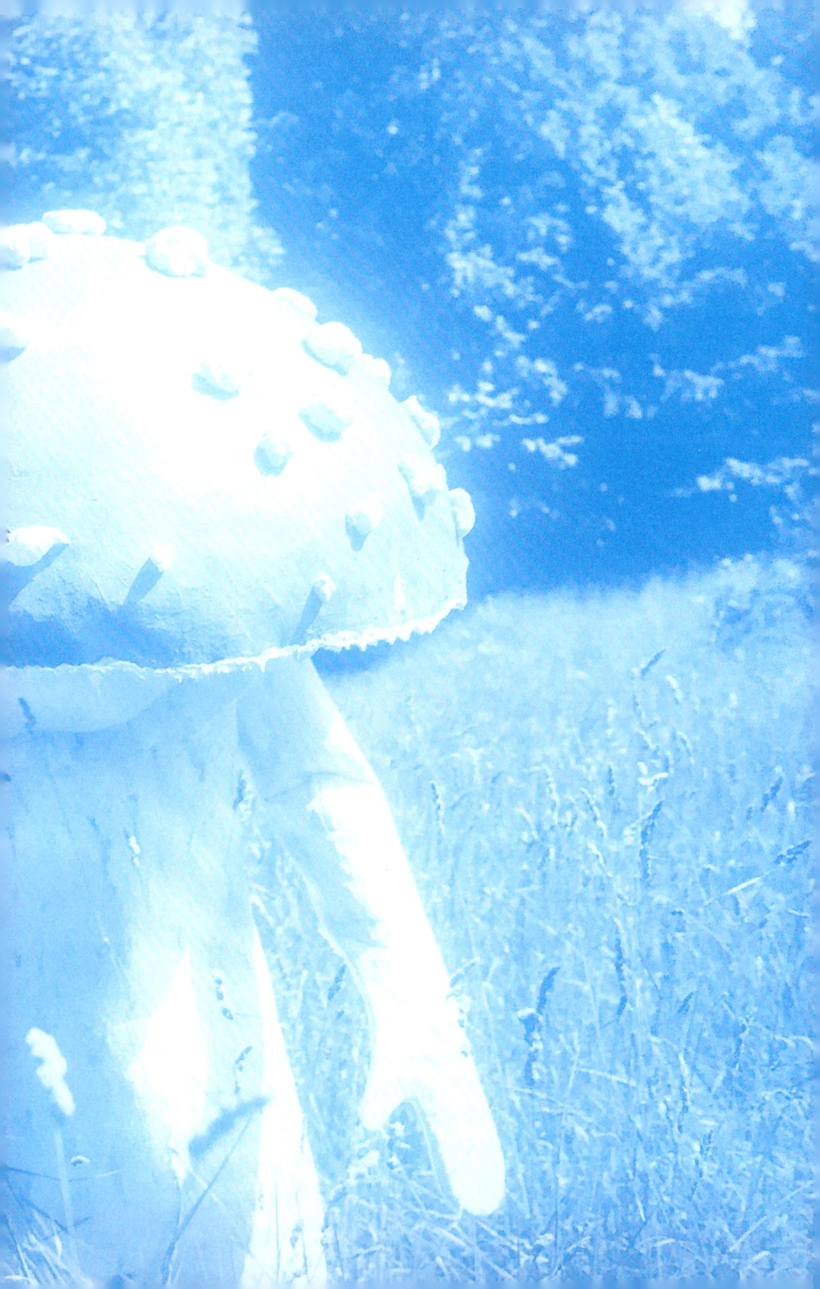

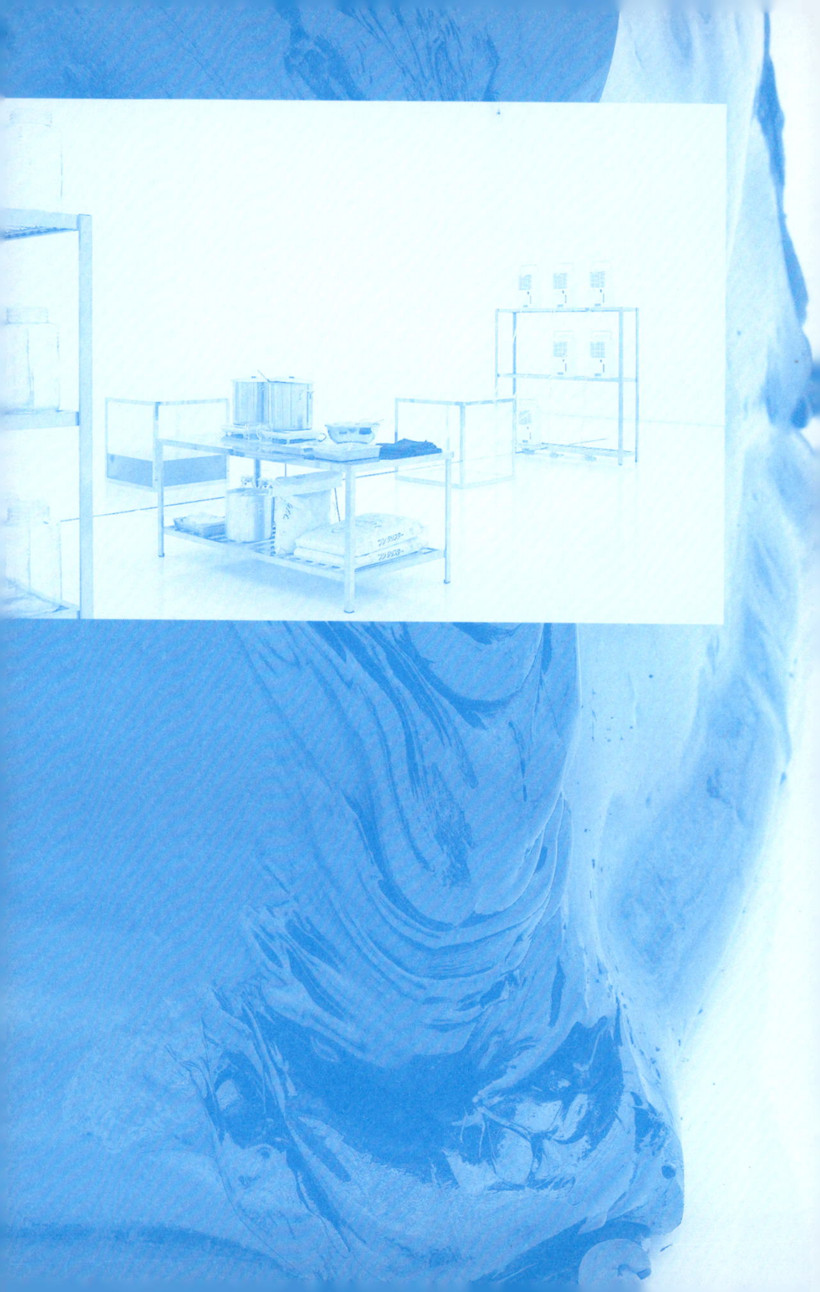

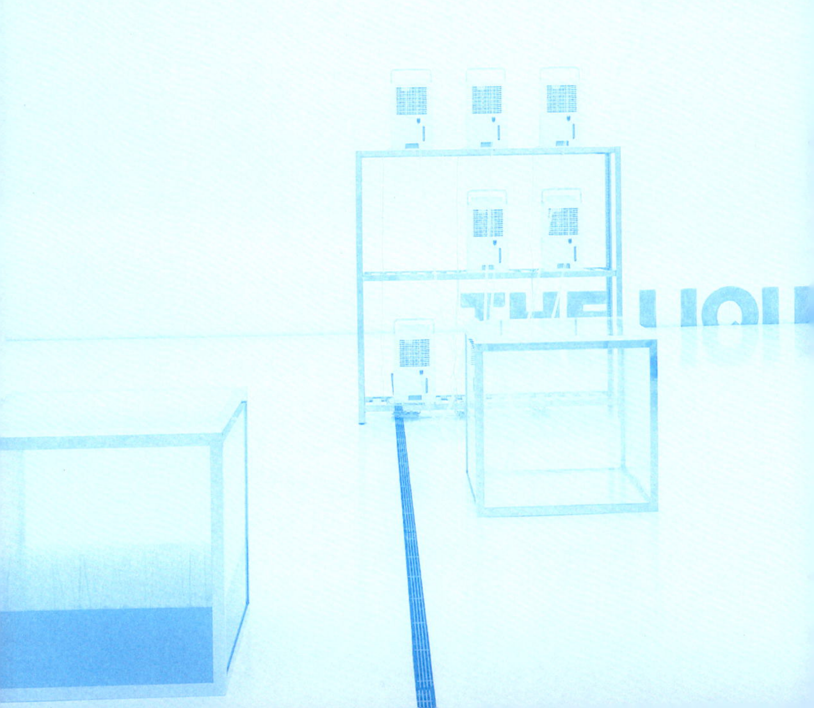
THE LIQUID STATE

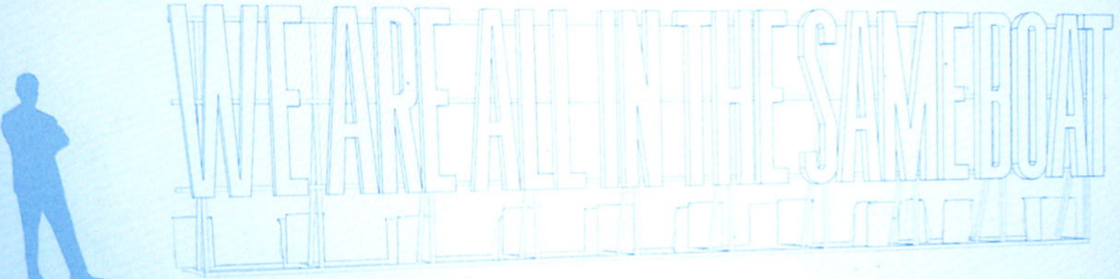

WE ARE ALL IN THE SAME BOAT
SCALE 1:1

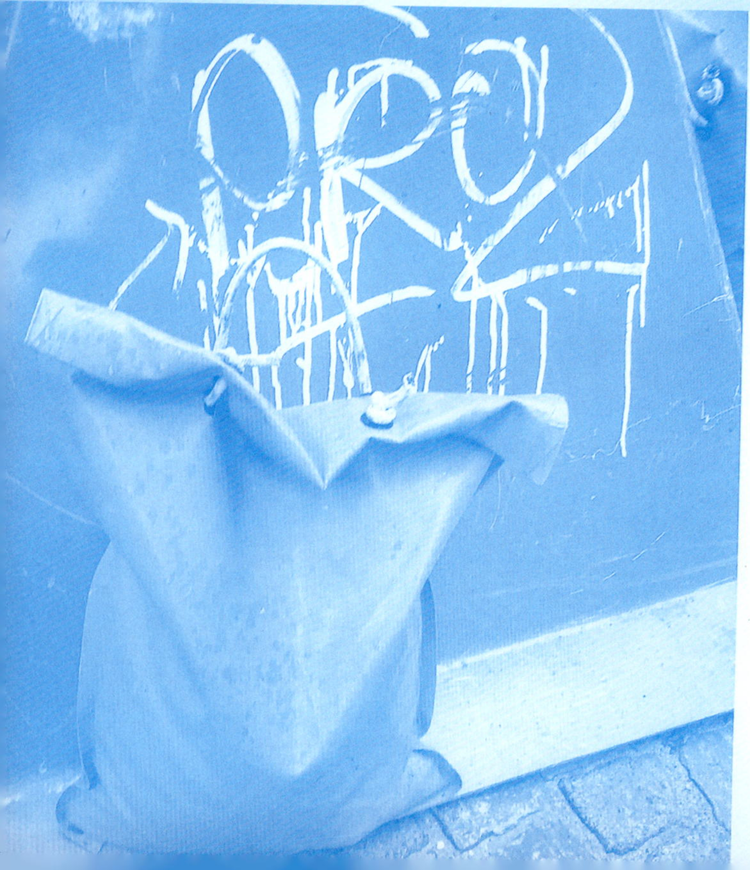

WE ARE ALL
IN THE SAME BOAT
Royal Caribbean

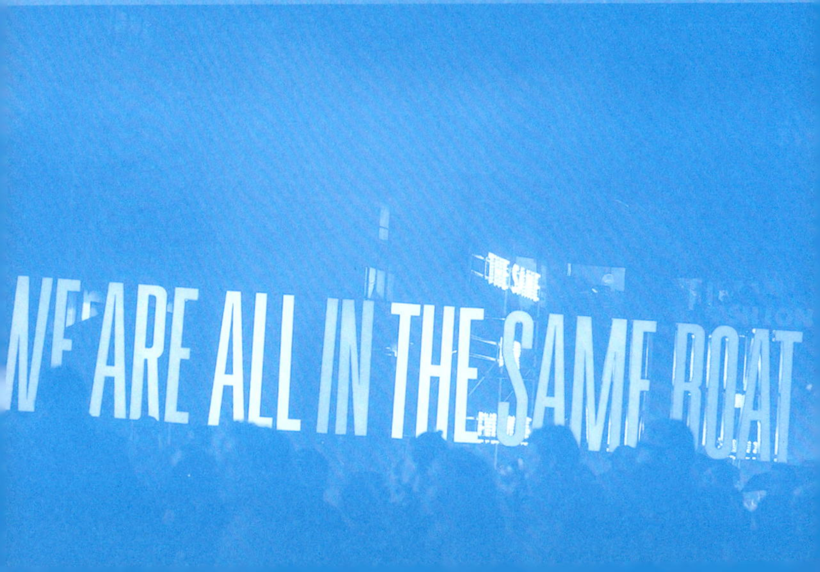

WE ARE ALL IN THE SAME BOAT

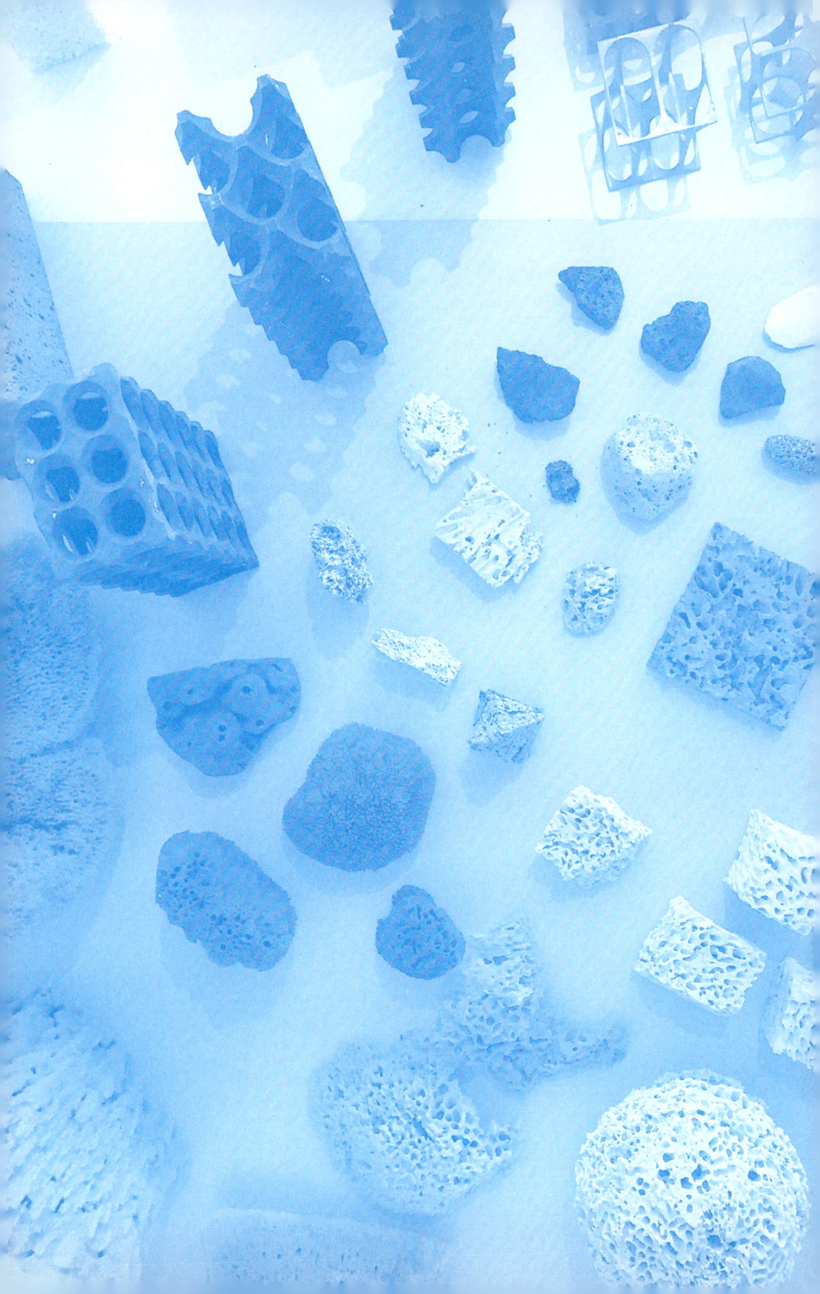

TO
BE
A
FISH

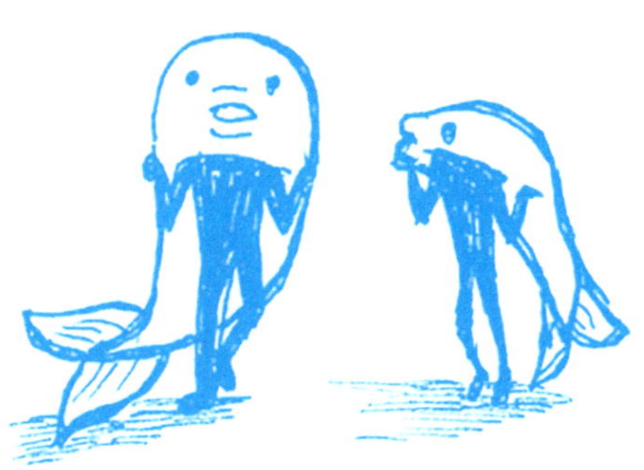

A21-Academy, *The Current II: Deep Sea Minding*

perflex, Expedition #1: *Deep Sea Minding*: August 20–September 3, 2018
nga Tonga-Hunga Ha'apai, South Pacific

demy.tba21.org
ebook / Instagram / YouTube / #TheCurrent / #DeepSeaMinding / #Superflex / #tba21academy

ticipants: Dr Dayne Buddo, Ricardo Gomes, Francesca von Habsburg, Dr Barbara Imhof, Dr Alex Jordan, Ju
nei, Maureen Penjueli, Markus Reymann

ep Sea Minding

e deep sea is closer than ever. Global warming is causing an unprecedented rise in the sea level, which will
stically reshape our planet. Dry ecosystems, including human landscapes, will soon be submerged. Great
grations will happen, and all species will be forced to survive extreme changes in their habitats. As the water
lluscs, fish and algae will occupy our cities, homes and parking lots. Every object created by humans will
entially end up underwater: cars, televisions, fish bowls. When the depths of the sea finally reach the places
have carefully designed and built, their original function and aesthetics will be lost. It is time to consider if
l then become a destructive force or an element of transformation. Apart from continuing to fight the cause
nate change, we should also prepare for the inevitable arrival of the ocean.

p Sea Minding is a project by SUPERFLEX that merges artistic and scientific research in an attempt to reach

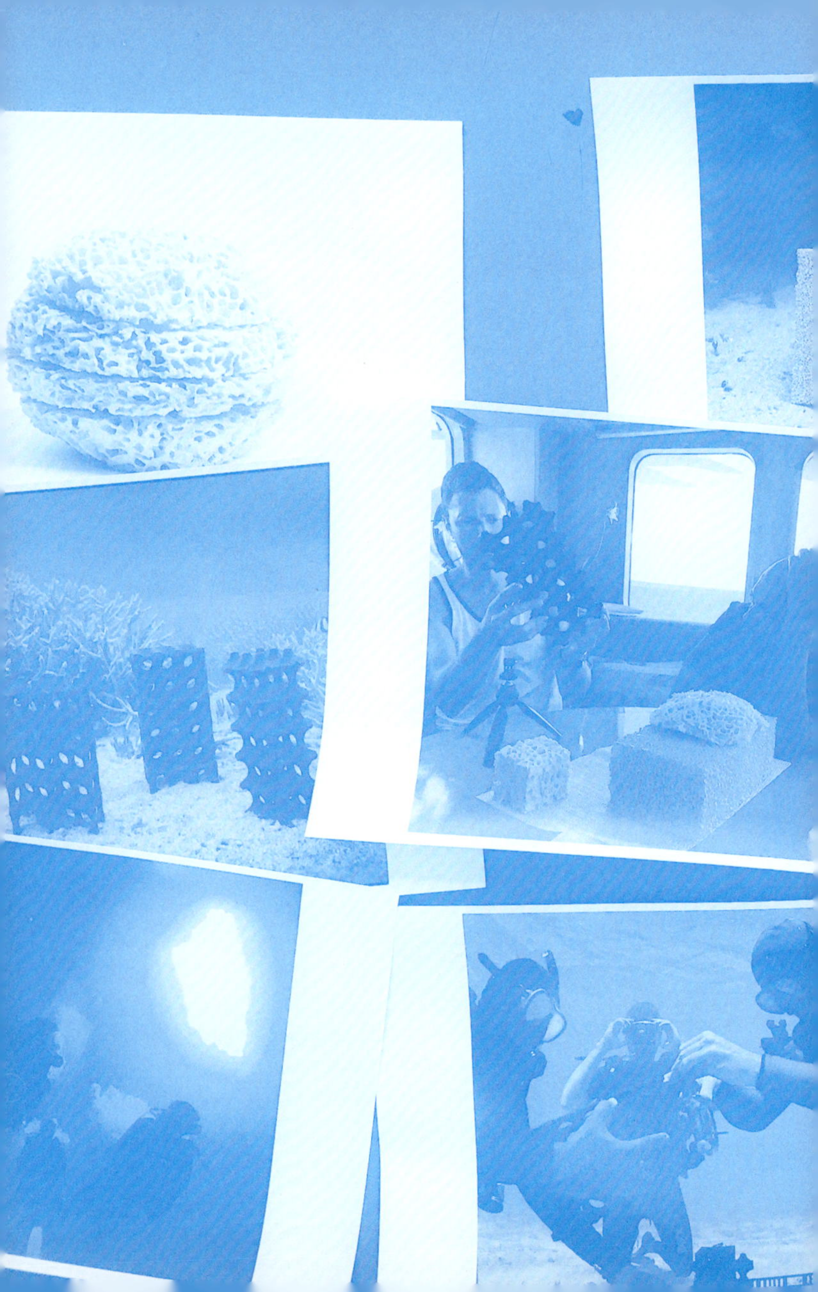

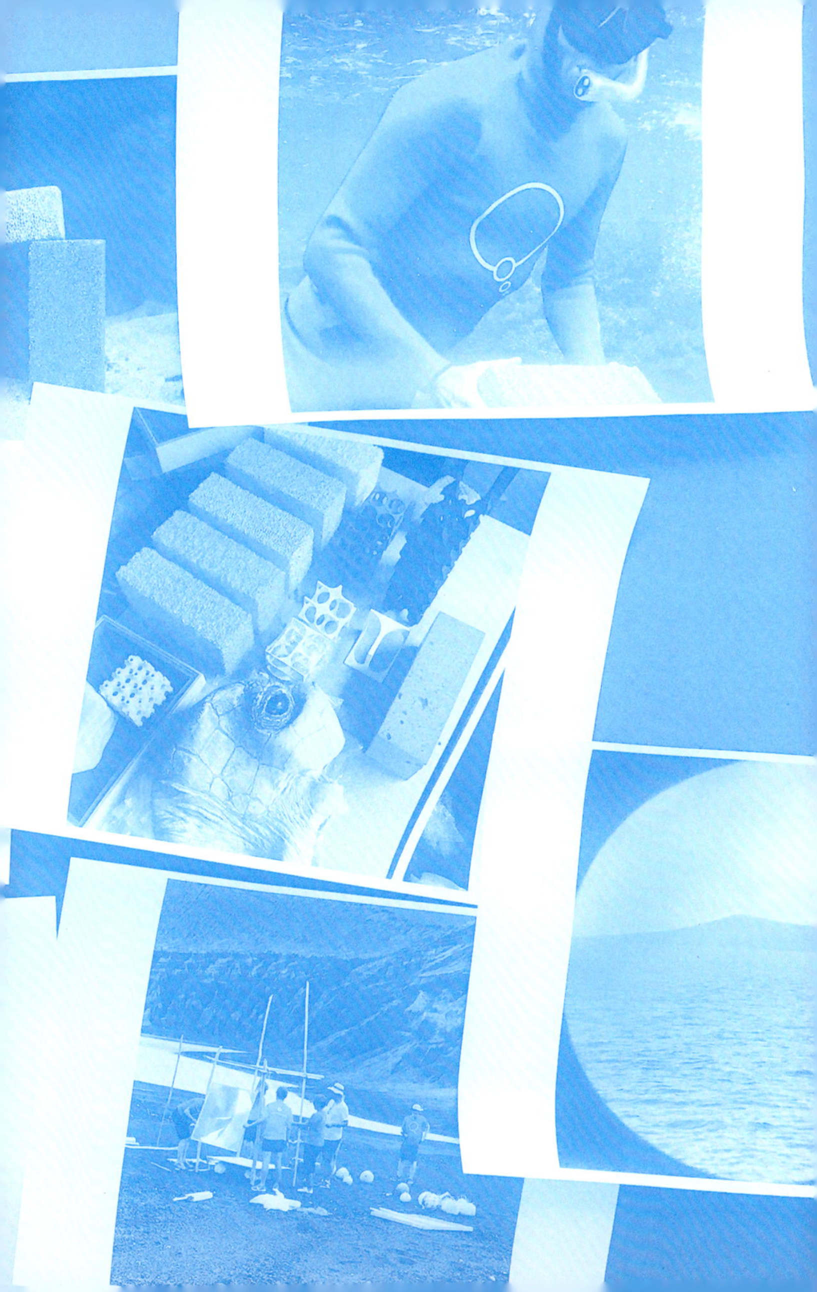

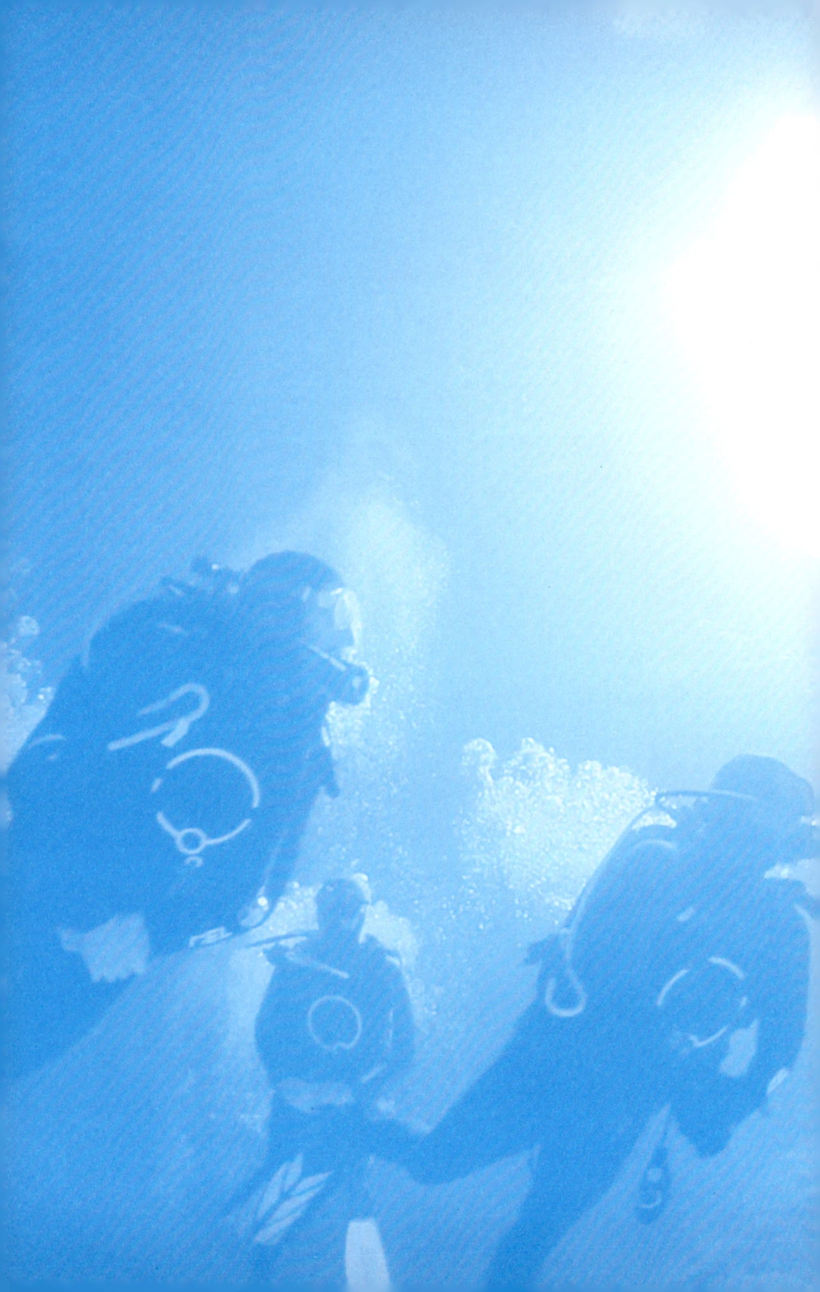

Foreword and Acknowledgments

Rina Carvajal

The Museum of Art and Design at Miami Dade College (MOAD) is honored to present the exhibition *SUPERFLEX: We Are All in the Same Boat* and this accompanying catalogue. Focusing on the humorous and playfully subversive installations and films of the critically acclaimed Danish artists' group, this project addresses the economy, financial crisis, corruption, migration, and the possible consequences of global warming as they relate to the specific context of Miami.

Art has always responded to issues in the real world, and SUPERFLEX has been at the forefront of artists who grapple with these pressing subjects ever since its founding twenty-five years ago. While the group has shown its work in galleries and museums around the world, *SUPERFLEX: We Are All in the Same Boat* represents its first major survey in a museum in the United States. We are proud to have organized this exhibition, which includes the American debut of a number of the group's works, several of which have been newly imagined for our city. It also includes new works commissioned by MOAD, including *We Are All in the Same Boat*, which lent its title to the exhibition as a whole, and *Euphoria Now*. We are especially pleased to host this presentation of SUPERFLEX as the culminating event in the first year of programming in our newly renovated galleries.

This programming reflects MOAD's new mission, which more closely aligns it to core values of Miami Dade College: examining contemporary cultural and social issues in close collaboration with partners in the community and city, helping to foster inclusivity and resilience. MOAD's programming continues to link the Museum to these goals while bringing Miami an unparalleled schedule of exhibitions on the leading edge of art and design, and public programs that engage diverse audiences in the College and in the community.

Many individuals have made the realization of this exhibition and publication possible. We are very grateful for their immense efforts.

First, we offer our very special thanks to the exhibition's curator Jacob Fabricius, Artistic Director of Kunsthal Aarhus in Denmark, for the strength of his vision and for all his work on this project.

This publication would not have been possible without the invaluable contribution of a fantastic group of collaborators. I am grateful for the insightful essays by the contributing authors Gean Moreno, Mark von Schlegell, Stephanie Wakefield, and George Yúdice. I also would like to thank to Rasmus Koch for his innovative expertise in translating the concept of the exhibition into a unique design for this catalogue. In addition, I extend my thanks to Juliane Eisele, Julia Ulrich, and the rest of the staff of our co-publisher Hatje Cantz for their commitment and attention to all the details of this volume.

I would like to express my sincere appreciation to all the staff of the SUPERFLEX Studio that collaborated with us on this project: Malene Natascha Ratcliffe, Cristina Casals Soler, and Angela Adeix. I am always indebted to MOAD's staff, particularly Bruce Williams, William Iverson, Robert Perez, Jessica Brodsky, and Simone Porto, who coordinated the multiple aspects of the exhibition with a careful handling of crucial details, both large and small. I thank architect Francisco Canestri for his expert exhibition design. The brilliant Álvaro Sotillo and Gabriela Fontanillas at VACA (Visión Alternativa) contributed the striking graphic identity of the exhibition. And I thank my frequent collaborator Joseph R. Wolin for his sage counsel on matters both curatorial and editorial.

SUPERFLEX: We Are All in the Same Boat would not have been possible without the generous support of our sponsors: the John S. and James L. Knight Foundation, the Miami Dade County Department of Cultural Affairs, this.nordic, Funding Arts Network, the Danish Arts Foundation, and the Florida Department of State Division of Cultural Affairs. Their assistance enabled us to bring this project to fruition. I extend my deepest thanks to all of them.

We are also most grateful to Miami Dade College and its president, Eduardo Padron, for their continuing support and for allowing us to experiment and take new risks with our mission and programs.

145   Finally, our efforts would mean nothing without the work of
the artists. I would like to thank the members of SUPERFLEX,
Bjørnstjerne Christiansen, Jakob Fenger, and Rasmus Nielsen, who,
in addition to their immense artistic labors, have been our most
valued collaborators and esteemed sparring partners throughout.

Introduction

Jacob Fabricius

For more than two and a half decades, the group of artists known as SUPERFLEX have expanded ideas of how art can relate to, and improve, social behavior. They have used their position as artists to pose questions of political, economic, and environmental responsibility.

The title of the new work that gives this exhibition its name, *We Are All in the Same Boat*, sets the tone and theme of the project. The figure of speech envisions passengers together in a ship at sea, and a set of shared risks that may put them in danger. It is an idiom that suggests that we may all have a problem. If our boat sinks, we all sink with it; but if it stays afloat, we might reach the shore. Our collective danger implies a collective responsibility and a need to collaborate so that our ship does not capsize. The title is both poetic and dark. It obviously refers to the simple importance of sharing and working together collaboratively, but also to problems that we now face and the current global situation. Talk about change is not enough. We need to act. In times like these it is imperative to work together to find solutions for the most threatening problems we may ever have confronted.

The fertile and fragile surroundings of the city of Miami have been central in the dialogue with the artists that led to this exhibition. Even the history and location of the Museum of Art and Design at Miami Dade College have influenced the selection of works presented. The topics of water, migration, refugees, and the economy inevitably became crucial points in the conception of *We Are All in the Same Boat*.

Climate and geopolitics are critical issues for people around the globe; both cause internal and external migration, and global warming does not care about borders or nation states. A complex connectivity exists between the subjects that SUPERFLEX addresses in the exhibition, which may help us rethink fundamental aspects of the ways we consider social control versus cooperation.

Art cannot solve the challenges that we face, but SUPERFLEX points at, comments on, and helps us understand some of the pressing issues that envelop us. The exhibition presents new commissions by SUPERFLEX, works reconceived and reconfigured for the particularities of Miami, and a selection of older iconic works that engage intertwined environmental, political, economic, social, cultural, and legal concerns. These works are meant to create political awareness, generate discussions, and help us think and act.

Cocaine Cowboys Redux: The High of High Finance and Urban Redevelopment

George Yúdice

Miami: its boosters dubbed it the "Magic City" on account of its rapid growth into a "subtropical paradise," a tourist mecca, an immigrant-friendly multicultural/multilinguistic metropolis, and a hemispheric entrepôt that made good on its promotion as "The Gateway of the Americas." But not all is as rosy as the boosters would have it. Negative consequences also result from the five causes of this rapid growth cited by Jan Nijman:[1] cheap labor provided by Cuban immigrants in the 1960s and by subsequent waves of immigrants from Latin America and the Caribbean; an adaptable and dynamic business elite; the entrepreneurial expertise and international connections of elite immigrants from Cuba and elsewhere in Latin America, many of whom relocated businesses to Miami; the expansion of air travel through Miami International Airport and of commerce in Port Miami; and narcotraffic, which injected vast amounts of capital into the local economy to propel the trade, finance, and real estate industries. While it is true that in Miami, in contrast to New York or Los Angeles, Spanish speakers are the owners of business enterprises (though let's not forget that they are also the dishwashers, yard workers, and nannies), the strength of Cuban and Latino networks has made it more difficult for black Miamians to have the same opportunities. The openness and adaptability of the business elite has often translated into lax attitudes toward and even resistance to regulation. Narcotraffic, of course, not only injected capital into the local economy; it also oriented significant segments of the finance, banking, real estate, and retail industries toward illicit practices and, as we will see, exacerbated inequality and racism through unethical urban restructuring and gentrification.

In its heyday in the late 1970s and early 1980s, the Miami drug market generated an annual cash surplus of $5 to $8 billion (which would be three times greater in 2018 dollars) for the Federal Reserve's Miami branch—more than the surplus of all other Federal Reserve banks combined. An economist reported in 1981 that the underground economy, the majority of which was fueled by drugs, composed a third ($11 billion, or $33 billion in 2018 dollars) of the overall economy.[2] There were reports of traffickers entering banks to deposit millions in cash carried in shopping bags and cardboard boxes. Eighty percent of Colombian cocaine made its way to the United States through the Magic City, and a good deal of the profit went into the real estate market, especially expensive condos, apartment complexes, warehouses, and plots of land, most of which was purchased with cash. Miami's glitzy skyline is in part a result of this infusion of money, which was also spent on luxury cars, diamonds, jewelry, clubs, and nightlife. With the drugs and the cash came the violence. In 1981, drug-related murders reached 621, making the city one of the most dangerous in the world, with gang shootouts between the dominant Medellín and Cali cartels and Cuban distributors. All this was captured in the hit series *Miami Vice* (1984–89). Nonfiction film depicts an even more gruesome scene, as we see in Billy Corben's 2006 documentary, *Cocaine Cowboys,* where bloodthirsty traffickers like Griselda Blanco target entire families, including babies, for execution.[3]

Although the CIA and the Drug Enforcement Agency reduced the drug traffic in South Florida by the mid-to-late 1980s and the IRS strengthened regulations to counter money laundering in the banking industry,[4] new studies in the twenty-first century, and especially the documents leaked in the Panama Papers (2016), reveal that Miami has continued to be a major center for money laundering via banking, real estate, and luxury items. Alongside drug trafficking, which was not totally eliminated, as is made evident by recent reports,[5] other forms of illegality also find welcome breeding grounds in Miami. An appallingly spectacular example is the gold smuggling by drug lords to "feed the insatiable demand" of Americans for jewelry, bullion, and electronics. Extracted illegally from Latin American rainforests with toxic chemicals, "the dirty gold enters a pipeline that flows directly through Miami." Over the past decade, $35 billion of this dirty gold has come through Miami.[6]

Miami is also a magnet for the ill-gotten gains of corrupt politicians and business people from around the world, costing developing countries $1 trillion in lost revenue. Miami accounts for over a quarter of all real estate sales to foreigners in the United States, double the rate of such sales in second-place California. Moreover, 76 percent of Miami sales to foreigners are made in cash, more than double the 32 percent of the national average.[7]

153   Cash purchases of real estate via shell companies and other legal entities, such as limited liability companies and trusts, shield buyers from revealing their identities and the source of their funds, thus enabling money laundering and tax evasion in their home countries. Even the Department of the Treasury's attempt in January 2016 to stem money laundering in the wake of the release of the Panama Papers was not effective. According to a report in the *University of Miami Business Law Review,* an analysis of the leaked information revealed that eight of nineteen offshore companies were involved in "bribery, corruption, embezzlement, tax evasion, or other misdeeds in their home countries."[8] In his piece in *The Nation,* Ken Silverstein identifies some of the shady foreign buyers of South Florida real estate, such as Ukrainian Michael Cherney, who owns a $7 million property in Boca Raton despite being denied a visa to the United States since 1999. Spanish drug lord Álvaro López Tardón, who was sentenced to 150 years in prison in 2014, laundered $26.4 million in cocaine profits by buying luxury condos and cars. Zulita Menem, daughter of discredited ex-president of Argentina Carlos Menem, resides in a $1.2 million Bal Harbor condo "owned by a banker who prospered under her father's regime." Silverstein's investigative report identifies too many shady characters to enumerate here, but it is worth mentioning that Donald Trump's properties in Sunny Isles (three Trump Towers and three other Trump-branded properties, including the Trump International Beach Resort) apparently have a number of these figures as owners. Indeed, a real estate agency specializing in Russian buyers—Exclusively Baranoff Realty—has its office in the lobby of the Trump International Beach Resort, representing "the most exclusive residences in Sunny Isles Beach, from $250,000 to more than $20 million."[9] It is difficult to ascertain ownership of these properties. As part of his investigation, Silverstein pretended to be interested in buying a $2.3 million condo from a Russian who was in the market for a bigger condo. When Silverstein obtained the property records, he learned that the legal owner is an offshore company in Belize, where there is "no requirement to file annual returns or public disclosure of directors, shareholders, charges, loans, or agreements."

Miami real estate boosters croon that the 2018 market shows "consistent and meaningful strength in the sale and marketing of properties at the top of the market."[10] This despite a softening of prices for luxury properties this year compared with 2017, largely due to a spate of new construction.[11] Developers are aided, however, by the increase in available income to "high-net-worth buyers" as a result of Trump's Tax Cuts and Jobs Act, signed into law in late December 2017. Additionally, the elimination of the deduction for state and local property taxes in New York, Connecticut, California, and other states encourages the wealthy from those areas to buy property in South Florida, where there are no state and local property taxes.[12]

The tax cuts and the increase in prices in the real estate market have only deepened inequality. Nationally, new construction favors luxury and middle-class buyers, while low-income renters face a shortfall in affordable and available apartments, with only 35 units available for every 100 renters (Andrews & Sisson 2018). In Miami, the situation is worse: the city is home to the highest percentage of households in the country that rent, and renters pay an average of 43.2 percent of their income on rent (the second highest rate in the United States). Miami is also the fifth least affordable market for renters.[13] With the dwindling availability and increase in value of homes in coveted neighborhoods such as the Media and Entertainment District, Parkwest, Downtown, and the Wynwood Arts District, prospective renters and buyers move into neighboring areas such as Little Haiti or Little Havana and displace lower-income minority populations and their business enterprises, the lifeblood of their communities. Miami has a history of destroying vibrant ethnic neighborhoods, such as Overtown, the "Harlem of the South," much of whose population was forced to leave in the 1960s when the city built Interstate 95 right through its middle.[14] In 2017 the city approved another infrastructure project, the privately funded Brightline train that connects Miami with Fort Lauderdale and West Palm Beach and that is slated to connect the city with Orlando—and its 68 million annual tourists. The fifteen-dollar price of a one-way ticket between Miami and West Palm Beach makes it highly unlikely that low-income residents will ride; Brightline is clearly aimed at wealthy tourists and business people. In constructing Brightline, All Aboard Florida, "a subsidiary of Florida East Coast Industries, the state's oldest and largest commercial real estate and transportation company,"[15] built a huge wall dividing what is left of Overtown from Miami's rapidly developing and expanding downtown.[16] Brightline is estimated to be a $3 billion project. Consistent with other huge capital development projects, the line's Miami Station will have an upscale complex of restaurants, offices, and apartments, all beyond the reach of Overtown residents. Right next to the station, another mega project, the twenty-seven-acre Miami World Center, portions of which will open this year, is being built and will consist of 300,000 square feet of retail; 1,875 residential units; 500,000 square feet of office space; 2,050 hotel rooms; and 500,000 square feet of exposition space. The Brightline has received mostly good press, but there are also critiques of its contribution to further gentrification: "The development is the harbinger of gentrification for the historically black neighborhood of Overtown, whose residents are justifiably concerned about its effects on their community."[17]

Little Haiti, a vibrant community just north of Miami's arts and design districts, is also undergoing gentrification. It was settled by tens of thousands of migrants seeking refuge from the Duvalier dictatorship in the late 1970s and 1980s. Against all odds—negative stereotyping, rampant racism, legal exclusion, difficult access to employment, etc.—Haitians established their own enterprises, restaurants, galleries, bookshops, botanicas (small storefront shops for religious accouterments), and even their own system of transportation consisting of minibuses or jitneys. As people seeking to live in the hip arts and design districts are priced out, they move further north to Little Haiti and other neighborhoods. Developers buy up properties and evict residents and businesses. As in other similar cases, the law is stacked against minority residents. The month-to-month leases that most residents have enable owners to terminate tenancy with only a fifteen-day notice.[18] And to make matters worse, developers departing coastal zones because of impending flooding due to climate change are looking to higher-ground neighborhoods like Little Haiti for their real estate projects.[19] A recent Harvard study on climate gentrification argues that Miami will be more impacted by climate change than any other city in the world. The premise is that climate change alters the value of property "by virtue of its capacity to accommodate a certain density of human settlement and its associated infrastructure," thus leading to "the displacement (and sometimes entrenchment) of existing populations consistent with conventional framings of gentrification."[20] The authors identify three pathways by which climate change impacts the value of property. The Superior Investment Pathway refers to the transfer of investment from low to high elevation geographies (they give the example of Little Haiti). The Cost Burden Pathway refers to the affordability of living in a place, that is, being able to deal with the "increased costs of insurance, property taxes, special assessments, property repairs, transportation and consumer goods, as well as a loss in overall productivity (e.g., sitting in traffic in water-clogged streets).["21] And the Resilience Investment Pathway refers to "a derivative of the well-developed concept of 'Green Gentrification,' wherein investments in sustainability amenities and infrastructure are unevenly distributed."[22]

In his 2018 review of the Harvard study, Richard Florida, famous for his development of the concept of the creative class (artists, technologists, software designers, media professionals, etc.) and for his subsequent critique of its failure to bring about sustainable development, makes the important point that gentrification "does not simply reflect the preferences and decisions of so-called gentrifiers" but is "often the product of larger structural forces and major public investments."[23] Florida is wrong: these forces, of course, do reflect the preferences and decisions of developers. Structure is not natural or inevitable but is the result of price setting, policy, law, and the loopholes engineered into laws. Life chances are structured by laws like Trump's Tax Cuts and Jobs Act and by policies that make possible putting an interstate or a huge wall through a neighborhood.

Florida, together with Steven Pedigo, conducted a 2016 study and set of recommendations to make Miami "a creative and inclusive global city."[24] Some of the recommendations are in conflict with Florida's reconsideration of the role of the so-called creative class in bringing about prosperity. Florida and Pedigo advocate building a fully creative economy, but in *The New Urban Crisis* (2017), Florida argues that the growing success of the creative class is itself part of the reason for the widening gaps among the various communities that live in cities.[25] Two of Florida and Pedigo's other recommendations—to use quality of place as an economic driver and to address crises arising from the region's success (i.e., increasing traffic and hence longer travel time)—, if not implemented carefully and using policies aimed at improving the lives of lower-income and minority people, are likely to aggravate Miami's problems, as we have seen with regard to climate gentrification and the Brightline rail line which is priced beyond the means of working class people. Although the study recommends promoting the region's tolerance and diversity, the authors contradict themselves by stating that "for all of its diversity, Miami is the least integrated, both racially and economically, of all of our benchmark metros."[26] Florida and Pedigo do acknowledge that a "divided geography reinforces and compounds economic inequality,"[27] but they say nothing about the role that illicit activities and corruption play in exacerbating residential segregation.

While illicit activities do not cause such inequality, they do play a role in decreasing public coffers. According to the Tax Justice Network, the hidden financial assets of the rich in offshore tax havens could have reached a staggering $32 trillion in 2012. That figure is roughly double the US GDP and represents 42.3 percent of the Gross World Product. Moreover, Gabriel Zucman argues convincingly on the basis of data from the Swiss National Bank that the popular impression that "China owns the world" and that Europe and the United States are net debtors is utterly wrong. Because global data do not take into account the assets held in tax havens, "they overlook the portfolios of equities, bonds, and mutual fund shares that households own via banks in Switzerland and other countries with strict bank secrecy rules."[28] Zucman's explanation is that "rich countries taken as a whole are richer than we think, but some of their wealthiest residents hide part of their assets in tax havens, which contributes to making governments poor."[29] He focuses on personal wealth management routed through tax havens such as the British Virgin Islands, Luxembourg, the Cayman Islands, Bermuda, the Bahamas, Panama, Hong Kong, Singapore, Jersey, etc. In such "tax havens with strict secrecy rules, banks do not generally report information. Taxes can be collected only if taxpayers self-declare their income."[30] As we saw earlier, individuals shield their holdings through shell corporations registered in tax havens such that securities registered in a bank in Switzerland appear in the name of the shell corporation of the country that serves as a tax haven. "When tax evaders combine numerous sham corporations in multiple tax havens, foreign authorities have practically no way to find out who is the beneficial owner of a Swiss account."[31]

This also happens through the purchase of real estate in the United States. Indeed, in February of this year, the United States was ranked as the world's second largest tax haven, after Switzerland. The responsibility to do something about this illegality lies with politicians and jurists, but, as argued above, US policy maintains these tax havens. The US government "refuses to take part in international initiatives to share tax information with other countries, and has failed to end anonymous companies and trusts aggressively marketed by some US states . . . . There is now real concern about the damage this promotion of illicit financial flows is doing to the global economy."[32] And, of course, the damage to the non-wealthy is extensive. We have already seen how illegality drives the real estate market, not only in Miami but also in New York, San Francisco, Chicago, and other cities. The effects are increased gentrification, residential segregation, and the deterioration of services for the middle and working classes. According to a survey conducted for Charles Schwab's Modern Wealth Index, "it takes $2.4 million to be considered wealthy, and $1.4 million to be considered financially comfortable" in the United States.[33] According to the *World Inequality Report 2018,* wealth inequality is on the rise almost everywhere in the world. The top 1 percent global wealth share was 33 percent in 2016, while the top .01 percent share was about 16 percent. If practices remain "business as usual," in 2050 the share of the top 1 percent will be 39 percent and the top .01 percent will have 26 percent, almost the same as the entire middle class.[34] The United States' wealth inequality is so steep that "global income inequality will increase even more if all countries follow the high-inequality trajectory followed by the United States between 1980 and 2016."[35] And these figures refer to the period before Trump's tax cuts.

The report finds that income and wealth inequality is not irreversible. It requires changes in national and global tax policies, such as instituting progressive tax rates, reversing privatization, and increasing public ownership of wealth. Instituting a global financial register that makes visible ownership of financial assets will help stem tax evasion, money laundering, and tax inequality. Democratic access to quality education will encourage a more informed citizenry, but education will not decrease inequality unless well-paying jobs are available. Other public investments in health, housing, and environmental protection will also help reduce inequality. Unfortunately, these are measures in which Miami does not score well. The media, universities, and public institutions need to keep pressure on the political and business classes to spur the will to implement political change.

1. Jan Nijman, *Miami: Mistress of the Americas,* Philadelphia, 2011, p. 71–73.
2. Rebecca Wakefield, "Awash in a Sea of Money," *Miami New Times*, October 6, 2005, https://www.miaminewtimes.com/content/printView/6339208 (accessed 8/9/18).
3. Billy Corben, dir., *Cocaine Cowboys*, DVD, Miami, 2006.
4. Nijman, *Mistress,* p. 89 (see note 1).
5. Facundo Alvaredo et al., *World Inequality Report: Executive Summary*, World Wealth and Income Database, 2018, https://wir2018.wid.world/files/download/wir2018-summary-english.pdf (accessed 8/10/18), and DEA, "2003-2008," https://www.dea.gov/about/history/2003-2008%20p%20118-153.pdf (accessed 8/9/18).
6. The Miami Herald I-Team, "Dirty Gold, Clean Cash: A River of Gold Controlled by Drug Lords Runs Through Miami," *The Miami Herald*, January 16, 2018, https://www.miamiherald.com/news/nation-world/world/americas/article194362569.html (accessed 8/9/18).
7. Ken Silverstein, "Miami: Where Luxury Real Estate Meets Dirty Money," *The Nation*, October 2, 2013, https://www.thenation.com/article/miami-where-luxury-real-estate-meets-dirty-money/ (accessed 8/9/18).
8. Gary McPherson, "Floating on a Sea of Funny Money: An Analysis of Money Laundering Through Miami Real Estate and the Federal Government's Attempt to Stop it," *University of Miami Business Law Review* 26:1 (2017), https://repository.law.miami.edu/cgi/viewcontent.cgi?article=1310&context=umblr (accessed 8/9/18).
9. Silverstein, "Miami" (see note 7).
10. Jay Parker, "Inside The South Florida Real Estate Market," *Forbes*, June 26, 2018, https://www.forbes.com/sites/forbesrealestatecouncil/2018/06/26/inside-the-south-florida-real-estate-market/#19d39aec8433 (accessed 8/6/18).
11. Douglas Hanks, "Luxury Real Estate Weighs Down the Real Estate Market," *The Miami Herald,* May 31, 2018, https://www.miamiherald.com/news/local/community/miami-dade/article212287999.html (accessed 8/9/18).
12. Parker, "Inside" (see note 10).
13. Kyle Munzenrieder, "Another Grim Reminder That Miamians Pay Insane Rents yet Make Little Money," *Miami New Times*, July 8, 2015, https://www.miaminewtimes.com/content/printView/7734667 (accessed 8/9/18).
14. Marvin Dunn, *Black Miami in the Twentieth Century*, Gainesville, 1997.
15. Emilie Anzilotti, "Can This New Privately Funded Train Reshape Transit in Florida?" *Fast Company*, May 15, 2018, https://www.fastcompany.com/40571597/can-this-new-privately-funded-train-reshape-transit-in-florida (accessed 8/10/18).
16. Jerry Iannelli, "Brightline Train Builds Wall Through Overtown, Miami's Historically Black Community," *Miami New Times*, May 18, 2017, https://www.miaminewtimes.com/news/florida-brightline-train-builds-gigantic-wall-through-overtown-miamis-historically-black-community-9354316 (accessed 8/9/19).
17. Anzilotti, "Can This" (see note 15).
18. René Rodríguez, "These Little Haiti Businesses Have a New Landlord: A Developer Who Wants Them Out," *The Miami Herald*, April 27, 2018, https://www.miamiherald.com/news/business/real-estate-news/article209843594.html (accessed 8/10/18).
19. Brad Wong, "Miami's Little Haiti Organizes on Gentrification," Marguerite Casey Foundation (website), July 4, 2018, https://caseygrants.org/who-we-are/inside-mcf/miamis-little-haiti-organizes-on-gentrification/ (accessed 8/9/18).
20. James N. Keenan, Thomas Hill, and Anurag Gumber, "Climate Gentrification: From Theory to Empiricism in Miami-Dade County, Florida," *Environmental Research Letters* 13 (2018), http://iopscience.iop.org/article/10.1088/1748-9326/aabb32/pdf (accessed 8/10/18).
21. Keenan, Hill, and Gumber, "Climate Gentrification," p. 3.

22. Keenan, Hill, and Gumber, "Climate Gentrification," p. 4.

23. Richard Florida, "Rents Are Too Damn High and the World Is Too Damn Hot: Both Are About to Make Gentrification Worse," *Mother Jones*, July 7, 2018, https://www.motherjones.com/environ-ment/2018/07/rents-are-too-damn-high-and-the-world-is-too-damn-hot-both-are-about-to-make-gentrification-worse/ (accessed 8/9/18).

24. Richard Florida and Steven Pedigo, *Miami's Great Inflection: Toward Shared Prosperity as a Creative and Inclusive Global City*, Miami, 2016.

25. Richard Florida, *The New Urban Crisis: How Our Cities are Increasing Inequality, Deepening Segregation, and Failing the Middle Class––and What We Can Do About It*, New York, 2017.

26. Florida and Pedigo, "Miami's Great Inflection," p. 28.

27. Florida and Pedigo, "Miami's Great Inflection," p. 29.

28. Gabriel Zucman, "The Missing Wealth of Nations: Are Europe and the US Net Debtors or Net Creditors?" PSE Working Papers no. 2011-07 (2012), https://halshs.archives-ouvertes.fr/halshs-00565224v3/document (accessed 8/10/18).

29. Zucman, "The Missing Wealth," p. 3 (see note 28).

30. Zucman, "The Missing Wealth," p. 6 (see note 28).

31. Zucman, "The Missing Wealth," p. 11 (see note 28).

32. Max DeHaldevang, "Watch Out, Switzerland: The US Is Now the World's Number Two Tax Haven," *Quartz*, February 7, 2018, https://qz.com/1200096/the-us-is-the-worlds-second-worst-tax-haven-say-tax-justice-networks-ranking/ (accessed 8/10/2018).

33. Rob Wile, "In South Florida, $2.1 Million No Longer Makes You 'Wealthy': Here's the New Benchmark," *The Miami Herald*, August 9, 2018, https://www.miamiherald.com/news/business/article216257170.html (accessed 8/9/10).

34. Alvaredo et al., *World Inequality Report*, p. 13 (see note 5).

35. Alvaredo et al., *World Inequality Report*, p. 14 (see note 5).

Alvaredo, Facundo et al. *World Inequality Report: Executive Summary* (2018). https://wir2018.wid.world/files/download/wir2018-summary-english.pdf (accessed 8/10/18).

Andrews, Jeff and Patrick Sisson. "US Housing Market Continues Rebound, Despite Increased Inequality, Says Harvard Report." *Curbed,* June 19, 2018. https://www.curbed.com/2018/6/19/17476360/housing-market-rebound-inequality-harvard-state-of-nations-housing (accessed 8/9/18).

Anzilotti, Emilie. "Can This New Privately Funded Train Reshape Transit in Florida?" *Fast Company,* May 15, 2018. https://www.fastcompany.com/40571597/can-this-new-privately-funded-train-reshape-transit-in-florida (accessed 8/10/18).

Corben, Billy, dir. *Cocaine Cowboys.* DVD. Miami, 2006.

DEA. "2003-2008," 2008. Drug Enforcement Administration (website). https://www.dea.gov/about/history/2003-2008%20p%20118-153.pdf (accessed 8/9/18).

De Haldevang, Max, "Watch Out, Switzerland: The US Is Now the World's Number Two Tax Haven." *Quartz,* February 7, 2018. https://qz.com/1200096/the-us-is-the-worlds-second-worst-tax-haven-say-tax-justice-networks-ranking/ (accessed 8/10/2018).

Dunn, Marvin. *Black Miami in the Twentieth Century.* Gainesville: University of Florida Press, 1997.

Florida, Richard. *The New Urban Crisis: How Our Cities Are Increasing Inequality, Deepening Segregation, and Failing the Middle Class––and What We Can Do About It.* New York: Basic Books, 2017.

Florida, Richard. "Rents Are Too Damn High and the World Is Too Damn Hot: Both Are About to Make Gentrification Worse." *Mother Jones,* July 7, 2018. https://www.motherjones.com/environment/2018/07/rents-are-too-damn-high-and-the-world-is-too-damn-hot-both-are-about-to-make-gentrification-worse/ (accessed 8/9/18).

Florida, Richard and Steven Pedigo. *Miami's Great Inflection: Toward Shared Prosperity as a Creative and Inclusive Global City.* Miami: Florida International University, 2016.

Hanks, Douglas. "Luxury real estate weighs down the Miami market. Values dip in ritzy Key Biscayne." https://www.miamiherald.com/news/local/community/miami-dade/article212287999.html (accessed 8/9/18).

Iannelli, Jerry. "Brightline Train Builds Wall Through Overtown, Miami's Historically Black Community." *Miami New Times,* May 18, 2017. https://www.miaminewtimes.com/news/florida-brightline-train-builds-gigantic-wall-through-overtown-miamis-historically-black-community-9354316 (accessed 8/9/18).

Keenan, James N. Thomas Hill, and Anurag Gumber. "Climate Gentrification: From Theory to Empiricism in Miami-Dade County, Florida," *Environmental Research Letters* 13. http://iopscience.iop.org/article/10.1088/1748-9326/aabb32/pdf (accessed 8/10/18).

McIntosh, Phyllis. "Miami, Florida: The Magic City." *English Teaching Forum* 3 (2008), pp. 35–44. https://americanenglish.state.gov/files/ae/resource_files/08-46-3-f.pdf (accessed 8/10/18).

McPherson, Gary. "Floating on a Sea of Funny Money: An Analysis of Money Laundering Through Miami Real Estate and the Federal Government's Attempt to Stop it." *University of Miami Business Law Review* 26, no. 1 (2017). https://repository.law.miami.edu/cgi/viewcontent.cgi?article=1310&context=umblr (accessed 8/9/18).

Munzenrieder, Kyle. "Another Grim Reminder That Miamians Pay Insane Rents yet Make Little Money." *Miami New Times,* July 8, 2015. https://www.miaminewtimes.com/content/printView/7734667 (accessed 8/9/18).

Nijman, Jan. *Miami: Mistress of the Americas.* Philadelphia: University of Pennsylvania Press, 2011.

Parker, Jay, "Inside the South Florida Real Estate Market." *Forbes,* June 26, 2018. https://www.forbes.com/sites/forbesrealestatecouncil/2018/06/26/inside-the-south-florida-real-estate-market/#19d39aec8433 (accessed 8/6/18).

Rodríguez, René. "These Little Haiti Businesses Have a New Landlord: A Developer Who Wants Them Out." *The Miami Herald,* April 27, 2018. https://www.miamiherald.com/news/business/real-estate-news/article209843594.html (accessed 8/10/18).

Silverstein, Ken. "Miami: Where Luxury Real Estate Meets Dirty Money." *The Nation,* October 2, 2013. https://www.thenation.com/article/miami-where-luxury-real-estate-meets-dirty-money/ (accessed 8/9/18).

Tax Justice Network. "The Price of Offshore Revisited: Press Release," July 19, 2012. http://www.taxjustice.net/cms/upload/pdf/The_Price_of_Offshore_Revisited_Presser_120722.pdf (accessed 8/10/18).

The Miami Herald I-Team. "Dirty Gold, Clean Cash: A River of Gold Controlled by Drug Lords Runs Through Miami." *The Miami Herald,* January 16, 2016. https://www.miamiherald.com/news/nation-world/world/americas/article194362569.html (accessed 8/9/18).

Wakefield, Rebecca. "Awash in a Sea of Money." *Miami New Times,* October 6, 2005. https://www.miaminewtimes.com/content/printView/6339208 (accessed 8/9/18).

Weaver, Jay, Nicholas Nehamas, and Kyra Gurney. "How Drug Lords Make Billions Smuggling Gold to Miami for Your Jewelry and Phones." *Miami New Times,* January 16, 2018.

Wile, Rob. "In South Florida, $2.1 Million No Longer Makes You 'Wealthy': Here's the New Benchmark." *The Miami Herald,* August 9, 2018. https://www.miamiherald.com/news/business/article216257170.html (accessed 8/9/10).

Wong, Brad. "Miami's Little Haiti Organizes on Gentrification," July 4, 2018. Marguerite Casey Foundation (website). https://caseygrants.org/who-we-are/inside-mcf/miamis-little-haiti-organizes-on-gentrification/ (accessed 8/9/18).

Zucman, Gabriel. "The Missing Wealth of Nations: Are Europe and the US Net Debtors or Net Creditors?" *PSE Working Papers no. 2011-07* (2012). https://halshs.archives-ouvertes.fr/halshs-00565224v3/document (accessed 8/10/18).

Tools for a Thawing World

Stephanie Wakefield and Gean Moreno

On a planet increasingly characterized, on the one hand, by the fact that every inch and future state of it is quantifiable and a virtual web of capital-moving vectors has become nearly coterminous with it, and, on the other hand, by massive surplus populations generated by rampant deindustrialization, civil wars, and climate instability, there may be some merit in trying to formulate a few observations around the inevitability of an "art after the wage"—which may be the same thing, viewed from the other side, as an "art in a world of thawing orders." This would involve looking at artistic practices that find their social determination not in the fragmented process of production that the capitalist relation generated in an earlier phase of development, but in the financialization of the global economy. It would also entail considering practices that are generated in places (the collective future that awaits many of us may be one of these) that exist and persist in exclusion from the world of wages and all the ordering—economic but also metaphysical— that accompanies such a loosening world. We're not thinking of some fantastical post-work situation of full automation and luxury communism, sweet as such a thing promises to be, but of edge-hugging worlds in which articulations and expressive propensities—cultural, but across the plane of everyday life, as well—find their determination precisely in the social and subjective production that occurs as a consequence of exclusion. Not so much in reaction to it, but in the possibilities that open because of it.

The world, we know, has jumped the fence. Record heat waves unfurl across Europe and North Africa; wildfires scorch Greece and even the Arctic Circle, while in America's blazing West Coast, meteorologists warn, billowing smoke could choke out views of annual Perseid meteors. According to Earth systems scientists, the planet is shifting out of the stable climates of the 11,000-year-long Holocene interglacial in which modern civilizations developed (and also out of the glacial-interglacial cycle in which it flickered for the last 100,000 years) and onto a trajectory toward volatile and unknown operating spaces, one of which may be a so-called Hothouse Earth.[1] Fueled quasilinearly by carbon dioxide emissions and biosphere degradation, this trajectory will also be coupled with nonlinear biogeophysical feedbacks creating tipping cascades—permafrost disappearance, land and ocean carbon sinks weakening, polar ice sheets melting—and accelerating global warming as well as pathway irreversibility.

In the urgent discursive reconfigurations and flights of fancy that these alterations to the Earth system have authorized, an ascendant tendency is that of borrowing the vocabulary of the natural sciences and certain strands of materialist philosophy in order to build with it new interpretative machines and models to be applied to cultural production. The incursion of flat ontologies, notions of quasi-sentient matter, post-anthropocentrisms of every stripe, and slushy-mushroomy chemistry in art discourse and exhibitions in recent years has been impossible to miss. Non-human actors, complicity with chthonic powers, deep time chronometries—it's all there. An ambient anxiety over climate, when it is not hard science and its unavoidable conclusions, explains much of this. But one cannot help but grow astonished by the way in which critical art production, having sharpened its tools over the last fifty if not one hundred years to deal with social, political, and ideological issues—not the least of which were the ones embodied in the very institutions that it sought legitimacy from—has suddenly turned from all this. The Anthropocene, so misnamed, derailed everything and absolved everyone from the task of interrogating the systems in which they function. Offering urgent problems, extinction and the like, it has set us adrift in a world of animated matter and operatic cosmic vastness. And yet, what is it that all these energies now applied to *sensing* the secret depths of a planet that is coming undone have actually contributed, in terms of a scale that matters, to the mitigation of anthropogenic effects and to ecological renewal? Asking this question is not just a matter of picking on artworks that organize themselves around discourses that borrow from natural science and materialist philosophies for their ineffectiveness; it's also a matter of considering what is hidden by the proliferation of these discourses in cultural spaces.

In their respective fields, the discourses that art has been borrowing from are often militantly realist. The world is out there. We interface with it, enmesh ourselves in its tangled lines and ways, or are swept up by them, but *it* has to be there, beyond our projections and interpretations, for this to not be a trivial fact. This inevitably means that there must be serious engagement with all the mediating elements that are activated along the way, with the apparatuses that science and other disciplines rely on—not only in the role they play in the production of knowledge but also for the myriad applications they afford. It is precisely this respect for objective circumstance, for matter-without-us, if you like, on the one hand, and serious acknowledgement of mediating apparatuses, on the other, that is lost in the drift of these discourses into the art world. What they offer as they vacation in the cultural sphere, instead, is an excuse to not look at the manner in which art objects move and function in world, obviating a material matrix of institutions, economic pressures, historical and social determinations, and concrete modes of distributions and usage. In this socio-institutional ecology as it has developed over the last few decades, not only sustained by but tailored to reflect the imaginaries of elite economic players, art objects are often subsumed into financialization processes. The pictures on the wall or the sprawling installations, in their crates in one or the other tax haven, are collateralized, leveraged, and turned into currency without the actual artifacts having to return to the market—without, that is, their biographies being affected and their owners being stigmatized as flippers and speculators. Through procedures such as art-backed lending, the object, while staying put, literally sets frozen capital in motion and puts it to work. The Rothko pays for the new luxury condo tower construction without ever being dismounted from the wall of the luxury condo it currently graces with its mysterious depths.

By becoming a collateralizable entity in this way, the artwork seems to have sprouted a new dimension that allows it to be absorbed at any moment by an autonomous field of economic operations adjacent to its institutional habit. Of course, nothing prevents the artwork from continuing to make laudable claims, proposing itself as a tool for the constituent power of the multitude, as a short-circuiting apparatus in spectacle cultures, or as the last agent capable of drawing discrepant temporalities and repressed histories from a homogenizing globalization. Art objects can continue to deliver their promises of rupture and redemption. But they just live, from the perspective of those who benefit from its new dimension, relegated to islands of fantasy. Abstraction, instantiated in actual practice, supersedes the claims of the sensible thing, determining not its form but its behavior in the world—often against its explicit commitments.

Some of this may help explain why certain discourses have flooded contemporary art production and its interpretative exercises with such ease. In light of the financial abstracting of the artwork, what could be more enticing than an object as a full-on autonomous agent wielding dimensions that exceed the limited things we can comprehend? The enthusiasm for the inexhaustible object, however, cannot help but give up the "hidden transaction" it sustains: the eagerness to re-mystify the object registers as a *displacement* of the traumatic fact of having artworks spring a new dimension that has been pressured into existence by a process of accumulation that generates profit through financial instruments, through the proliferation of capital as commodity, rather than through production and sales, and over which the art object has no say and possibly finds no footing for resistance. The uses that can be extracted from the art object beyond all it can determine are positively re-coded as its secret power to extend beyond human cognitive reach and other horizons. In the end, however, the object's supposed unfathomable "inexhaustibility," the excess beyond its self-understanding and controlled operations, is financial, before it is inward or relational or cosmic or whatever. The unwieldy flows of energy and matter may turn out to be just stand-ins for the flows of capital in moist and mushroomy garb.

Seeing as the subordination of the concrete to an abstract asset functions in absolute disregard of the artwork's content and self-definition, unencumbered by critical resistance and sophisticated diagnostics, how, then, to register the discrepancy between what is sensibly available and the procedures of ontological reconfiguration and economic capture that happen, to repurpose that old phrase, behind the artwork's back? In a series of paintings collectively titled *Euphoria Now* (2015), SUPERFLEX addresses some of this by allowing the color schemes of different national currencies, including the US and Singapore dollars, the Chinese yuan, and the British pound sterling, to provide the color palette. The concrete configuration that money must assume in order to execute its abstract function is graduated into the generative structure of the art object. One should see this less as an acerbic critique of the power of money or some such thing than as an effort to make blatant the discrepancy that exists between sensible manifestation and the relations that actually move the world. In his seminal *Intellectual and Manual Labor: A Critique of Epistemology,* Alfred Sohn-Rethel proposes that exchange, the physical practice of it, is the abstraction that organizes our thinking. What this means, in shorthand, is that through money everything can be stripped of qualitative heterogeneity, and this operation, in turn, impinges on or even determines the nature of the intellectual tools with which we apprehend the world. The exchange relation becomes thinking's deep and delimiting infrastructure.[2]

In SUPERFLEX's production, it's not necessarily what seems deliberately pointed at that matters. To stay on the unslick surface of the immediate is to miss the problematic epistemic gap we constantly face, covering it up with the satisfaction of simple and generally agreeable denunciations. *Investment Bank Flowerpots* (2015) reproduces the architectural shape of the headquarters of the twenty largest global investment banks, all deeply implicated in the last financial crisis, as functional flowerpots. These receptacles are used to grow hallucinogenic and cannabis plants. One can stay with the obvious here and bask in the satisfaction its implied denunciation offers: the almost erotic stimulation of moving and manipulating disembodied money in quantities that can literally shift global markets, drain the wealth of entire populations, and spread immiseration without much blowback is a bankers' or traders' high, their soaring trip and the source of their despicability. Or conversely, the fact that they can do this, oblivious to or unable to understand the consequences, maneuvering on an autopilot that external rhythms adjust even while sensing some kind of amorphous fear building in their bellies, means that they are already hallucinating their innocence—"it's just my job"—to begin with.

This attends to and overvalues the semantic plane at the expense of the material facts of the work. *Investment Bank Flowerpots* comes in two versions—one is a 3D-printed set that employs PLA plastic, a biodegradable polyester derived from corn starch or sugarcane; the other is cast concrete. In the chemical and historical distance that separates these materials and the ways in which they are given shape something about the conditions that allow for the dominance of finance is obliquely articulated. Concrete is *the* material of modernity. It's the paradigmatic truth-element, the obvious example that inhabits any truth-to-materials demand. It is the aggregate that structured all the metonyms for industrial capital's production. In contrast, 3-D printing belongs to another world, as do a whole slew of new bio-based materials and the capacity for on-demand execution. It is a world in which the "real abstractions" that came with the exchange relation and money make way for the absorption of complex methods and models of calculation, universalized through algorithmic manipulation, into the organization of the production process itself, as much as into the field of circulation and risk management. It is no longer a matter of standardization and equivalence as much as one of reflexive updating, a kind of self-learning, at the center of production and circulation as a way optimize movement and extraction, compress time, and adjust quickly. In this scenario, however, the appropriation of cognition into the process of production and circulation meets the problem of *limited* powers of prediction within increasingly complex fields of economic and financial activity, to say nothing of increasingly varied ecological and atmospheric conditions. It is here where, before a collapse of the closed circuit of industrial production and ownership (manufacture-circulation-profit-reinvest-ment-manufacture and so on), the intersection of finance with discourses of resilience finds its ground. If resilience is the capacity to absorb unpredicted crises, then it serves as one mechanism through which reflexive updating (and its ideology) is perpetuated. Markets, as much as ecosystems, now have to be resilient, to move through and capitalize perturbations that they may not be able to determine in advance.

Starting in 1997, as one of their first projects, SUPERFLEX developed *Supergas*, a biogas system that created a self-sufficient closed energy circuit for poor farmers. The first of these systems was installed in Tanzania. With the dung of a few cattle, it produced three cubic meters of gas per day, enough for a family of eight to cook and run a lamp. New prototypes have been developed since, and the system has been installed in different places, in collaboration with various NGOs and other partners. What is as interesting (in a different way) as the exercise of testing the possibility of alternative ways of producing non-fossil fuel energy is that in 1998 SUPERFLEX established the holding company, SUPERGAS Ltd., to actively promote investment in the system. (The company folded in 2005, due to lack of investment, but the questions it raised didn't die with it and in fact become more pertinent every day.)

In the critical literature on the biogas project, which tends to divide into those who defend the work as a new way of providing tools that respond to situational needs and those who are suspicious of the likeness of the project to the products of international aid programs saddled with shameful records, the holding company is rarely touched upon. What were investors offered? One asks the question with an eye on what today are called climates futures and ecosystem services. In other words, a specific answer regarding what the company offered is less interesting than considering the company itself as an intuitive and benign prefiguration of the process of capitalizing the mitigation of climate instability and energy needs—and, more sinisterly, the door that this has opened for the immiseration and devastation that global capital has wrought to produce another set of returns for investors. The quantification of biodiversity conservation and the mere survival of poor populations, for instance, become a way to trade climate's destabilizing effects on the open market. Future geophysical difference and biodiversity depletion risk are turned into investible entities.

Miami—to provide but one example—has been proposed as a good location to test sea-level derivatives as a way of funding adaptation infrastructure. In one version, an investor provides the funds to develop an adaptive measure—a seawall is the common example, but one can imagine pumps, a raising of the ground, etc.—in exchange for a return if the sea level becomes higher than expected within a certain period of time. The underlying commodity is intangible and what is ultimately traded is economic risk. The idea is that as the seawall prevents flooding and its attendant damages, the city's savings—from less preparation and less relief and rebuilding—will cover the payout on the investment. What this neat logic obfuscates is the increased vulnerability that comes with it. The return, based on a quantitative measurement and not on the benefits of the infrastructure that the investment funds, is due even if the sea level rise is wildly higher than the one that is agreed upon and the adaptive measure cannot mitigate the consequences of this. It is also unaffected by other costs that may be the result of climate change but not directly related to sea level rise. The costs of massive flooding due to a raised water table are not subtracted from the return on the investment. (Of course, there is also a futures contract on flooding in the works.) It is not even the city's future that the bet is on, but the performance of an external index.[3] In probable-to-worst case scenarios, the local government will sink into a quagmire of debt and—as is more and more the case, with nearby Puerto Rico serving as the most recent example—face restructuring in disregard of the needs of the local population.

But let's go back to the unsullied collectors leveraging Rothkos to build multimillion-dollar condos and to the artists and theorists enthralled by mushroomy things, as a way to consider the other procedure, beyond highlighting the epistemic gap between sensible experience and abstraction, that SUPERFLEX deploys: the production of tools. For the artists and theorists, the world can never be fully known. It is a magical, untouchable sphere, palpitating with relations that keep us out of the loop. To still consider such a material world available for human transformation appears, from this anti-humanist perspective, to be a relic of twentieth-century hubris. The impossibility of use is proclaimed not just a structural condition but an ontological and moral one. In contrast, take those

who speculate with their Rothkos. While critical theorists tweet
about unknowable rocks, the world's elite are organizing to thrive
amid a civilization in free fall. They are signing off on plans to
erect sea walls to protect Wall Street, to fund luxury bunkers in
New Zealand, to put Google's infrastructure on the moon, and to
geoengineer Mars. Here are people for whom the world is certainly
knowable and open to use. To some of the collectors among them,
things are not all that mysterious in another way: $X millions (a 50
percent loan on the value of the work) builds X number of condos.
Between these two warring factions—pirouetting high above us,
the elite in their penthouses and the theorists on their metaphysical
clouds—attempting to say what life is, one side is at least making
use of whatever they get their hands on, albeit toward its own
nefarious ends and through brutal calculations, buttressed by the
belief that they can transform the very cities we live in and the solar
system around us into large-scale laboratories for their trials. Even
as the water rises, they will maniacally be making the world in the
image of their desires. What about us, down here, pressed against
one edge or another, disinterested in vibing with objects that can
pipeline the Earth's pain into our spines since we are falling out of
the wage world and stable ecosystems in non-symbolic ways?

The quest of modern philosophy and politics was always
to determine being by giving it a name, a ground, or a telos. What
mattered was always some abstract realm beyond or below life that
gave it meaning or order. By identifying this safe operating space,
outcomes were seemingly guaranteed, or at least stable theoretical
pictures of them were possible: justice, equality, a perfectly ordered
world in which the rivers would flow with lemonade. But if any
generalization can be made about the Anthropocene, traveling
hand-in-hand as it must with the rampant immiseration that finance
capital reproduces and expands, it's that the baselines of civilization
are shifting. Populations and climates are being upended along with
physical and metaphysical grounds for thought and action.

Faced with upheavals of the Earth and of thought, it seems
impossible for many to imagine a relationship to life other than
one of discipline, accounting, and management. But the idea that
'politics'—a summary name for these latter three fields—as the
sole legitimate sphere of transformative, historical activity would
somehow survive the discombobulations of the present intact
seems absurd. That the answers to living in the Anthropocene can
already be found in a series of cobbled-together givens extracted
from imploding frameworks should be suspect. To think that the
forms and possibilities of the future subsume themselves to such

languages, nay governance, should be doubly so. The sun has set on such thinking. In contrast to the regimes we're leaving behind, beings and things are released and open to new possibilities. The world is thawing. We are free to move on other planes. And this should compel us to shift our perspective a bit. Rather than thinking that the material world is beyond us, or imagining it merely subject to us and thus reducible to equivalence and calculation, why not consider other possibilities? The way things are is neither just the way things are nor inherent to the things in question. This is repeatedly touched on in SUPERFLEX's work. Bank logos, once exuding confidence and authority, become a timeline of failed institutions after the 2008 financial crisis. The Stora Enso building, a supposedly eternal structure, crumbles into a ruin. The car, symbol of petrocapitalism or whatever, burns to charred remains. McDonald's cups and wrappers, submerged in water, drift aimlessly. Instead of untouchable or eternal mysteries, the structures around us appear as the contingent, ad hoc formations that take a lot of work and energy to maintain that they are.

So, a hiatus to paeans to time, or wind, or erosion, or fire. Cars are lit by people. Riots, arson, insurance scammers, teenagers fucking around. Why should we care about the bubbling metal of the car's exterior, the molecular chemistry of heated enamel? What we want to know is: Who set this car on fire? How and why does one set a car on fire? Is this 'who' in the first person plural? What's the context? What's the motivation? How are the kids in Gothenburg coordinating to set everything ablaze?[4] More than melancholic or smug musings on the eventual world-without-us—when, finally, contemporary institutions will crumble—the important question is how with our own hands to be done with them, now. How do these get lit up?

It is attuned to this question that SUPERFLEX's idea of tools should be read—or perhaps re-read against the grain of the manner in which it has been interpreted thus far. In 2003, Charles Esche wrote: "'Tools,' in their [SUPERFLEX's] terms, seem to me to be an idea about underlying structures—about how things can be different if you do something with the engineering of the situation, and then stand back to watch the results."[5] Esche goes on to speak about "tool[s] for a community." Of course what one wants are tools to flee community, to no longer (and again) deal with the "underlying structures" and "do something with the engineering of the situation," insofar as all these things sound like exercises that simulate amelioration without disarticulating anything of much consequence. They, in fact, sound like ways to never allow the disorganizational impulses that are unleashed to rev up to their full potential. We don't want community, but new worlds; not underlying structures, but out-in-the-open ones that we have built out of the scraps that are strewn about; not opportunities to engineer the situation, but situations through which we can be done with all that engineering and get on with living in all its uncontainability. We want tools that aid us in exiting the rotten orders we are currently sentenced to, to make them thaw at increased velocities.

Bereft of the certainties that old political ideologies extended, there is no preset answer to what such tools would be. Tools are simply the links between people and their environments and their ideas of freedom or betterment; tools are the way people throw off given conditions and create worlds. They are verbs as much as things. The means through which we not only transform ourselves but also our very modes of existence. Every tool is a testament to how beings made use of their environments, projecting themselves through and against it, in communion at times and defiance at others, and in the process altered themselves, becoming something else. Never the result of an answer from on high, fire and shelter and so many other things were developed in response to local problems, tried and tested in reality.

SUPERFLEX offers some ideas: free/open source software, black markets, informal architecture; culinary and brewing techniques; bootlegging; the repurposing of means of transportation: the fisherman's kwassa kwassa boat employed to deliver migrants from the island of Anjouan in the Comoro archipelago to French overseas territory Mayotte. Life-saving hospital operating theater equipment ready for both exhibition and combat zones. Or communication: SUPERCHANNEL's network of studios, in which users produce their own interactive internet TV channel. This last one included a studio opened in Liverpool's oldest high-rise housing bloc, Coronation Court, where residents produced sports shows as well as documents of their lives and homes, which, contrary to the popular notion that housing towers are a failed utopian experiment of the sixties, they in fact love. *Common People*, a series of programs, included "African Hair-Styles and Make-Up Tips," and "Sometimes Chicken Sometimes Dhal."

We live in Miami, one of the lowest-lying coastal cities in the United States. Here, sunny day flooding from sea level rise and high tides is already a reality. Images of octopi floating in parking garages and Miamians wading through flooded intersections on their way to work are already old news. No one is coming to save us—this, too, is old news. What tools do we need here? This is the doomsday that we are pedaled: saltwater infiltrates Biscayne Aquifer, rendering tap water undrinkable and collapsing the sewage system, as residents flee en masse like twenty-first-century Dust Bowl refugees, while for those who stay, instead of bikini shops and coffee-dispensing cafeteria *ventanitas* where old Cuban men gather to argue their insane politics, what awaits is a submerged city of undrivable highways surrounded by virus and excrement-filled oceans with dead bodies churning in them. Lives are reduced to fending off the latest Chikungunya or Zika strain in soggy and unbearably hot neighborhoods. If we want to avoid the sordid fate already forecast for Miami by journalists and scientists, several obvious and immediate questions present themselves. How do we live with water? The question is not at all about how to vote on referendums on city-engineered sea walls or how to design breezily apocalyptic luxury condos fortified to withstand category 5 storms. Rather: What techniques are useful across the unstable plane of our everyday lives? Amphibious, boat, and stilted housing are architectures with a rich history here. They are found in Miccousukee Everglades lifeways as much as in weird suburban houses on barges. How can we learn and equip ourselves with the latest design innovations for aqua-urban futures?

Heat waves, resilience practitioners propose, will be the urban question of the future. Miami's extreme heat, its increased peak temperatures every year, add to the problem of rising water. A Supersauna makes sense in the green meadow among the mountains of Bergen or along the sandy Baltic Sea shores of Møn, but Miami remains humid and hot way past Halloween. Without air-conditioning not only will life be miserable and deadly but, given current construction, within six months half the houses will be rotting. Should buildings be retrofit and constructed from rot-resistant wood, using cypress as local indigenous communities have since they got here? How viable is solar-powered air-conditioning? The list of questions on the table is endless: about how and where to produce, distribute, and store food; how to maintain drinkable water, whether by restoring historic Everglades flows or by turning disused septic tanks into rainwater catchment cisterns. The questions also touch upon desire and pleasure, new forms of sociality built alongside everything else, and on the refusal of accepting images of miserable survival as representative of the only futures possible here.

As we explore the question of tools in our own iguana-jammed city, it can be taken up by anyone anywhere. Tools are, after all,

developed in response to specific needs and contexts, in rapport
with practical and spiritual understandings of the places we live in
and in relation to the tangle of different modalities of living available
(or potentially available) to us—mutual aid meeting domestication
where necessary meeting lit cruisers and limousines. This fluency
is as relevant in dense urban settings as in the wilderness. The
question should never be high versus low tech, but what suits us,
what allows us, here where we are, to give shape to our own chosen
forms of living? In some cases the techniques are already out
there, waiting for us to grab hold of them. And if they are not, what
new forms can we devise? What forms of sharing space and ties,
beyond the vaunted "community" that they keep telling us about,
can we build? Where, with whom, and with what tools?

When SUPERFLEX describes *Free Beer* as "a beer which
is free in the sense of freedom, not in the sense of free beer,"
they hit on a key point: even when speaking of life basics (fire,
water, shelter, food), the matter of tools is never one of survival
but rather of freedom and autonomy. When we make use of tools,
the world unfreezes. We take our lives in hand and shape them,
participating in the world, rather than being hostage to its apparent
order. Returning to 'practical use' equally has a determining
social dimension. There are populations that will not be allowed
back into the economy and there are places beyond repair. In
such cases, it's not a question of choice; rather, the freedom
and necessity may become entwined in a new and complicated
way, while the old points of reference may not be useful. In the
past, politics in one way or another entailed a set of rules or
prescriptions for how to live or what to do, but, in large part, such
prescriptions are part of the ruins. There is no answer given in
advance. Whether or not biogas stoves help Morogoro families
become self-sufficient in light and energy while also suiting their
cooking tastes is a question only these families can answer.

Souring on trends in art and theory that push toward some
kind of exacerbated sensing of imminent collapse (and thereby
disactivate from the get-go the power that ordinary use may hold)
is not the same thing as saying that the world *is* fully knowable.
Likewise, acknowledging the autonomy and power of the nonhuman
world does not demand we disavow our own capacities or spiral
into the safe space of doom-thinking. Faced with the power
and tumult of our environments, with the challenges and often
tragedies that they deliver, why not see these things as incitements,
provocations, gifts, unknowns, singular presences—anything but
enslavements. That the world is in many ways unknowable to

us—who would really say otherwise?—does not require that we also say "All power to the nonhumans." We can explore the kinds of life possible amid volatile inhuman forces and in this way reinvent our *own* autonomy. In taking up a pragmatic orientation, those who experiment with tools are transformed from people who simply live to people who design the conditions for their lives. And, of course, a tool may not work. It may break. The water might rise much faster than we expected. Nothing is guaranteed, and tools can't operate the same way that transcendent rules or moral codes do. Plus, no one can say exactly where we are headed. Not knowing—or not going where one of modernity's stories said we would go—does not necessarily mean an experience of "terror," nor need it define us as powerless, vulnerable, incomplete, or dispossessed. Rather, not knowing means that life is a question; this is an especially poignant fact as transcendent guidelines continue to wither. Old frameworks should not be mobilized thoughtlessly to understand new, singular realities. We can welcome the now rather than shoving it into the categories that we are needlessly hauling from the past. All this isn't such a big deal. It just means you can try anything.

Notes

1. Will Steffen et al., "Trajectories of the Earth System in the Anthropocene," *Proceedings of the National Academy of Sciences* (2018), http://www.pnas.org/content/early/2018/07/31/1810141115 (accessed 8/31/18).

2. Alfred Sohn-Rethel, *Intellectual and Manual Labor: A Critique of Epistemology*, Atlantic Highlands, New Jersey, 1977.

3. Sevren Gourley, "Funding Adaptation: Financing Resiliency Through Sea Level Derivatives," *Harvard Environmental Law Review* (April 17, 2017), http://harvardelr.com/2017/04/17/funding-adaptation-financing-resiliency-through-sea-level-derivatives/ (accessed 8/31/18).

4. Christina Anderson, "More than 100 Cars Burned in Mass Arson Attack in Sweden," *The New York Times*, August 15, 2018, https://www.nytimes.com/2018/08/15/world/europe/sweden-car-fires.html (accessed 8/31/18).

5. Esche, Charles, "TOOLS and Manifestos," in *Superflex Tools Book*, Cologne, 2003, p. 188, https://superflex.net/files/SUPERFLEX_TOOLS.pdf (accessed 8/31/18).

Miami7

Mark von Schlegell

I

In 1899 only three huts and a single shack stood within the otherwise uninhabitable swamp. But in 1915 a lone oil-pig brought an entire railroad there as if for no reason, and ever since, every present-day Miami has appeared out of thick air, as *the* present-day paradise.

This remained true in 2099. Below the Tallahassee and Jacksonville skylines, the old peninsula had been deemed underwater, and thus extra-national, since the seventies. No one who tied up year-round cared to pay any taxes whatsoever.

I live aboard the *Crusted Bluff,* a coral-growing, fully-submersible semi-intelligent houseboat, with guest quarters and sauna. She's my bread and butter. I won her in high-stakes poker, back in Miami3, the hard way, with a nine of diamonds high. The great thing about semi-intelligence is that it always gets more intelligent. The boat's full-time mate is the handy Bayer, an artificial personality. I depend on Bayer for everything. Imagine an omnipotent omniscient butler, that's Bayer. He improves, every day.

Miami2 was a six-acre mall-world casino resort and sauna, built up into the surviving ruins of the twentieth-century city. Two decades later, Miami7 was a whole different concept. It was a surface settlement, co-ruled and rented out by international concerns, as wide as the original, taking in tens of thousands of visitors any day. Miami7 was a testament to what AI-enabled Field Theory could achieve. After Field Theory revolutionized free space, it was brought to bear Earthside to resurrect South Florida as a vacation destination for the rich, their offspring and attendants. All South Florida and the Caribbean had been under the domination of a monoseason of hurricanes and storms for most of the last century. But now the energy-rich resort cast a field from the old Cape Florida, over to Coral Gables, up to Hialeah and over to Biscayne Bay, enabling a happy eyelet of sun and tranquility inside a kilometers-thick perimeter rim of cloud and condensation. Field Theory blew a perfect hole in the sky, all the way up to Miami's private satellites and space hotel getaways, easily accessed from nearby Canaveral Barge. Glittering pneumatic cloudscapers floated over bars, clubs, and

living-rafts, moored together along an interlocking lay-ground
atop tranquil, lapping waters. Deals were cut with the Seminoles
for energy, and clusters of underwater turbines were leased all
around under the permastorm. The excess power fueled massive
desalination plants and extraordinary watersculptures. The sunny
resort showcased the new "cooling culture," entertaining elite and
white-collared visitors atop a quasi-natural floating island in a
pseudo-biome adapted to their perfect pleasure.

Marina townslips surrounded the center in all directions.
Local boat-people resorted to improvised neighborhoods, like my
very own Mahia Mar, an entity made up by a conglomeration of
the first seven hundred to have claimed a slip. The *Bluff* was a true
Miami original. She was in sync with the City Fathers and came
with medallions granting the right to roam through all the exclusive
access waters of Miami7.

Boat gave access to the whole of what for many was
experienced only as a single hotel or convention pavilion. Miami7
offered sorts of recreation no longer possible in space environments—good old outdoor, earth-gravity golf, waterskiing, outdoor
tennis, shuffleboards, free diving. In hotel resorts people went about
eating beef burgers in bikinis by the intercoastal waterway.

Every such setup guaranteed the most spectacular underwater
vistas but in fact presented only glorified aquariums and fish farms
inside ancient ruins. A visitor had to leave the island limits to
discover the undersea. I sometimes took tourists out into the rim,
the cloudy perimeter of Miami7, just to look down on the laughing
colored lights of the free undersea. And though it was strictly illegal,
it was important for Miami7 that, when someone wanted to take the
plunge, captains like me could lead the way—for a price.

II

"What's wrong with your face?" the body-armored bot demanded.

"What's up with your aggression?" I replied, entering Tegel-
Corp's Fairpods. My VIP pass allowed me to bypass bouncers. If
my goggles, my snorkler, or my flappers gave this armed individual
the sense I didn't give two shits about surface dress codes, all
the better.

I snorkle all the time. As Bayer says, it's bloody rational, and
it's pretty much the reason I survived Miami4.

With ambitions in Space, TegelCorp was known for hosting
various inter-post-national kultur dealers out to expand the limits
of human cultures in controlled climates. I wasn't the only snorkeler

walking around the place, but I got the feeling I was the only one not working the aquariums. Most of the evening-attired guests wore nose-breathers, an organic element for surface diving that runs from the nostril to the corner of the lips. It gave to everyone, regardless of age or gender, what appeared to be the handlebar moustache of an Elmore Leonard hero.

FREEZE LONDON 2100 PRESENTS
FREEZE Miami7 2101
presenting
HYPER-CONTEMPORARY-PSYCHO-ENGINEERING
HYPE! trade fair 2199
Under the TegelCorp Pneumatic Pavilion

The fair literature presented curious paradoxical drawings, filled with perspectives rendered so that you needed boosters to make sense of them. I filed archival material away for Bayer and approached the small party waiting for me at the proper coordinates; they stood among some palms and ferns to the side of the pavilion, looking out eastward across the Intracoastal toward the rising sun.

I immediately recognized Danish kulturator L. Rick Blauvius, fit in his trim fluxedo. It was indeed the same Lou Blauvius, visiting European student, I remembered from more than a decade ago representing a certain moment in the scene that was Miami3.

He stood by the railing, the naked sun behind him. Miami suited him, even with that ridiculous nose-breather.

"You're a bit obvious in that get-up," he said. "Aren't you calling attention to yourself?"

"The opposite is the case. Trust me."

"I'm so sorry about this," he sighed. "We need to wait. One of the invitees is late. The one with the cash."

"I have to start clocking you now," I said.

Did he remember me? I didn't ask.

"Naturally." He returned to the three others at the rail, gesturing to something in the waves: a nasty-looking whitetip shark. The bioelectric receptors speckled across its snout made it one of the rare sea creatures immune to Field Theory. Sharks were so much the symbol of the new Miamis that tourists beckoned to them and threw them snacks. They went about like kings, given free rein to hunt stocked fish, and the occasional human, and to exit the fields if they so chose. This whitetip male grinning at the party was even equipped with some sort of technology, a white band tucked behind its gills.

The man-sized shark lept high to intercept, as Blauvius's nearest companion, a large Italian sort of fellow, perhaps an opera singer, threw a lobster roll over the rail. Black-haired, gruff, about to burst from his evening flux, this Italian personage was crowding the kulturator away from a young couple, or perhaps a brother and sister. Over their rental smartsuits, somewhat threadbare evening attire suggested they were creatives, students, or perhaps refugees.

"Wait!" Blauvius signalled to me, though I was clearly already waiting—and received a message. He smiled as he took it in, smiled so broadly that I realized the expression as other than a smile. That elastic grin could embody great cynicism; it could transform into a thin, clear smile of hatred, as easily as it could laugh. Yet it was always somehow unhappy. It promptly disappeared, as he cut off communications. "The collector's not coming," he told the others.

To me he smiled a broad smile of nothingness. I looked over the edge at the milky blue internity of sweet Miami Bay. There in the distance I spotted the *Crusted Bluff,* just turning into our branch of the great Intracoastal; most people didn't recognize it as a ship at all. With its single dirty eye, it looked like a giant, coral-gabeled clam.

"The money?"

"I know." The kulturator grimaced. "About that. He has wired me the kredit. I promise you it's good."

Bayer hated kredit. It wouldn't do. Through the snorkler my sigh honked. "It's a smart contract."

"Damn it." Blauvius turned to his guests. "I'm sorry, guys. We had a tour of the art of the old Miami7 all plotted out. I so wanted you to see it—and other things. But I hadn't planned on paying for this myself; without local coin—"

"I have local coin," the young woman said. Despite the breathing apparatus that gave her a handlebar moustache, she didn't seem like a liar. But she wore a cheap engagement ring on the finger that held out a large wad. "How much do you need?"

When told, she went rather pale. "Introduce me to the captain," she said.

"Captain, meet Violet Reeves. Mathematician."

Mathematician? Who would have guessed?

She transferred me the coin. One thousand good fresh casino currency. Bayer would be pleased.

"And this is Percival Derkelpounder," she said, in all seriousness, gesturing at the lanky youngster beside her. "He's from New York."

"I'm so sorry."

"H. Heinrich Hoffendeffer," a large Italianate fellow said,

proffering a meaty hand. "From Germany. *Not* invited to the fair. *Not* even a catalogue in L. Rick's booths."

Blauvius rolled his eyes. "Shhh, Heinrich. The engineers vetoed the jelly. That is the end of the matter."

"I grow jellies," he told the others. "I am a jelly artist; they decry jellification, but here we are."

"There's my mate Bayer now," I said, directing their attention to the waterway. "He's brought the launch. When the fountains shoot, let's hop over, one at a time."

"That's a launch?"

III

Seventeen minutes later I sat on the back transom of the surfaced *Crusted Bluff*, flappers extending into the bubbling wake as it frothed out before me—and obscuring the ID badge from any (and there were no doubt many) prying eyes. The TegelCorp inflatable bubble receded into the Miami7 skyline. Its lines lay loose, long, and liquid, blown out of the most lightweight and modular new fabrics. Lit in fruity pastels, laid onto the most intelligent tiles, new porcelains reflected white and blue-green structuralism in and around every oasis.

"Is it safe down there? Couldn't those flaps hit the propeller?" The green-eyed Violet Reeves, mathematician, looked down upon me.

"There is no propeller," I answered. "The boat is actually sailing."

"Sailing?" She looked about curiously. "But there's no mast—or boom—"

"Boom?" I chucked. "You never heard of GreenSails? They've got the booms. Their craft are actually elsewhere, lined by entanglement technology to *our* cleats. We are being pulled by the transfer of energy paradox, by a far-away boat."

"I have heard of GreenSails . . ." Her brow furrowed. She looked around, clearly chewing on something. "Are you really taking us to Nuevo Mundo?" She asked suddenly.

Beside us long banks of algae stabilized the surface, absorbing human sewage in the process.

I only honked.

"OK," she said.

The curiously red-streaming sun was now obscured by the western edge of the rim. As the *Bluff* plowed onward, Miami glittered behind us, its shapes and colors constantly shifting.

Here on the surface the placid waters remained a bathlike 20°C, kept warm by the underwater oil fires still raging from the days of the old United States. Miami7 tapped into this energy and transferred its carbon to useful algae, or building materials.

As we moved onward, Bayer couldn't help eavesdropping. The youth Percival was chatting to Hoffendeffer the artist outside the head.

"I think I saw some of your jelly some years ago at the Socle du Monde TegelCorp Pavilion."

"One of my jellies, thank you. Not some of my jellies."

". . . Didn't it, like, randomly expand and go on to destroy the greater part of the exhibition?"

"Jams jam, man. Come on. That was a legendary jellification. People fear the jelly too much. Awarding agency to non-solid? It was not I who introduced it to the larger manifold. That was the work of your friend Ms. Reeves's former employer. Perhaps the one who is paying for this trip, no?"

"Um. No. Violet won that money this morning. It was supposed to be for our—"

"Shh. This boat has ears. I know what it is for. I keep your secrets."

I aimed only to make make some noise. But the flappers were still wet, and they laced the sheltered cockpit with long lines of seawater. It caught everybody's attention, most of all Violet Reeves, who left Blauvius standing at the rail and took young Percival's hand excitedly in her own.

"Time to mask up?" she asked eagerly.

"Yes. Because it's a lot quicker, easier, and cheaper, we're going to hire a ride down. The *Bluff* will pick us up later. Everyone take a pak from the kitty. The snorkler apparatus need not be worn at all times. But it must be around your neck. Pressure changes down where we're going, sometimes unpredictably. If you feel queasy, snorkle. One needs to be ready to swim if need be, anyhow. So smartsuit, booties/flappers and headgear readied at all times."

Now that we were deep inside the misty perimeter of Miami7, the waters had grown more lively. In that always odd chop, the famous lights were visible, dancing all around and turning the anti-aesthetic hull of the *Bluff* candy colored. From out the reds and golds and greens I looked for the so-called *Marsopas*, the depthcabs that would take us down to Nuevo Mundo. Tourists like Ms. Reeves knew it as a mythical underwater city stretching from Recenta Scotia in the North to Cuba Profunda in Caribbean. In truth Nuevo Mundo was more of a mental place than a physical location.

I signaled gold and up popped a steel cab imbued with that color. It was a typical sphere inside a sphere, with access north and south, crafted from industrial junk left over from the fossil-burners.

The north hatch popped open, and I followed the guests aboard, one by one.

"It's that easy?" blue-eyed Blauvius wondered.

"You need to know the right signals. That's all."

"Welcome to Mo's," the cabbie said. "My name is Azeland."

The small, salty-skinned boy-man wore shorts and nothing else. Webbed toes and fingers, gills under his ears, and broad nictitated eyes, showed his body remade for the sea. After helping us down one by one, he sat on an apparatus that required him to supply energy by pedaling at a constant rate. He steered by bumping the rudders and controls with his hands as the AI instructed.

Buckled in along the diameter benches, we could see out the hatches above and below as we fell.

"Pretty murky," Percival remarked.

'We're only three kilometers from Hurricane Alley," Violet informed him. "Field Theory repels ninety-nine percent of the engaged energy, but the little that comes through brings traces of chaos with it."

"Traces of chaos . . ." Blauvius shivered. "Don't even say that."

We dropped some ninety meters in seven silent minutes.

It was good that we had strapped in. The cab bumped hard, landing on a slope edging the Miami shelf. We rolled for a moment down that plain long sucked bare of life by storm and human, toward the big deep of the Florida Gap, where free sealife still thrived. Associates of Alezand appeared, clad only in lead boots and bathing suits, managing the cables that caught us and pulled us into the gleaming circular entrance port. Supersaturated for longtime diving, these were not boys, but tiny dense men. A conglomeration of homemade habitats suddenly sparkled into our view, stretching into various nooks and crannies all along the shelf in two directions.

If *Nuevo Mundo* was a fictional term, it conceptually linked varying subsurface peoples in modular chains of improvised undersea habitats that more often than not served as so-called "freemarkets" for whatever extraneous services nearby Earthside settlements demanded. Most of those working down here were bioengineered to stay, and had adapted to the pressure for this depth.

"Welcome to Mo's Marine." I gave Azeland a tip he'd remember, and
we passed through scanners and into the clammy entrance tube to
Mo's, our port of entry to Nuevo Mundo.

Welded together from fallen space junk, shipping containers,
and sunken waste of all sorts, the bulky steel-walled interior of Mo's
Marine moaned from time to time under the pressure of all that water
outside. The exterior was kept supercold so as to freeze any potential
leaks. Space heaters and lamps warmed things up quickly inside.
Merchants and fish fries competed for space in various modules
attached to Mo's main body. Seminole guards stood about entry
points, fully suited and armed. Scanners controlled what came and
went, with prejudice in the traveler's favor. Signs advertised bunks
and offered employment. The metallic air stunk of fish and produce.
The density of human life was striking.

"You've only got an hour," I told them. "Bayer is excited for
the sub tour he's plotted, incorporating some surprises from the
old surviving contemporary arts with which the local elite long
ago attempted to distinguish their spacetimes from others. Trust
me, visits undersea should be brief. It's not safe here, unless you
pay attention. Everything's color coded. Stay gold. That's Mo's
color. It's relatively safe, patrolled by helpful Seminole guards,
and there's lot's to see and do. If the air density starts to get to
you, put on your snorkler. Do not take one of the other colored
tubes. In particular, do not attempt leave the gold/yellow/
orange spectrum. Certain areas are only for locals. Red is much
higher pressure than you're ready for; green impossible without
immersion in inert gases. Everywhere, even in Mo's, there are
scammers and tricksters about—like there used to be in any free
city. Do you understand?"

Four fully masked individuals nodded.

"The timing's important. Our ship only gets one chance to berth.
Do you understand? Meet me here in sixty minutes."

They nodded.

I went to take care of some personal business.

IV

The first to return were Blauvius and Hoffendeffer: a full seven
minutes late.

The exuberant German-Italian gripped the slim kulturator
in what appeared to be an armlock. He appeared to have stuck to
Blauvius like gum. "I am so glad I have came tonight. To hobnob
with *you*. My god, your eye for shark meat is profound."

"I'm so sorry," Blauvius apologized, extricating himself. His exposed face radiated odors of garlic and seaweed. "Forgive us."

I shrugged. "You're the first."

"What?" Blauvius turned, showing signs of worry. "That's not like Violet Reeves."

I shrugged. I knew Hoffendeffer knew something.

"She's messaged: Wait!" Blauvius looked at his watchlet, and that strange grin of his returned. "This is really not my fucking day." He showed me his screen.

WE'RE GETTING MARRIED!

The same thought coursed through our brains. Many games and virtual environments had painted a false picture of Nuevo Mundo. A big feature of their undersea was, of course, wedding chapels. In fact, it was not a tradition to marry down here at all; rather, the opposite was the case. Wedding chapels existed, but they were inevitably identity-laundering operations. Worse, some were linked to human trafficking and forced submersion. There wasn't a legitimate chapel I knew about in this whole swath.

"Why is it that whenever I do business with New Californians, chaos belches forth?"

"It is called life!" Hoffendeffer leaned forward. "It is called freshness!"

"Married! To that boy? I'm so . . ." His brow furrowed and he looked pale.

"L. Rick! I believe you positively uninterested in women?"

"It's not like that."

Bayer had to chuckle when I told him what was going on. He was tracking our equipment, of course, so it was easy enough to locate the lovebirds. He thought a pickup would be managable. "After all, it turned out she paid for the cruise. It will take the *Bluff* twenty minutes to get there, Sir. You less." Good old Bayer.

Exactly fourteen minutes later, as Blauvius, Hoffendeffer, and I hustled down an uncolored track-tube beyond a rum dispensary, promising signage appeared, distinctly orange-lit in the waters across:

MARIO'S MO'S MARINE MARKETS MARRIAGE EMPORIUM
And licensing service

The business was a self-pressurized zone created out of a fully inundated honeycomb of occupiable dodecahedrons architected into the seafloor under Mo's hull. With its bowl of free cigars and constantly bubbling pools, it already smelled like a hundred-year-old aquarium. The pressure gave the "chapel" a magical appearance; rippling pentagonal wall panels of pure sea windowed the room. One of every four panels was open to the sea, which meant that AI was at work: the pressure blowing in from the air tubes maintained to temporarily keep the bay at bay. This was a temporary pod; soon enough it would be open to the element. Without a smartsuit, an ordinary human could only stay here thirty or so minutes tops before critical damage would occur. With a suit, it would be a matter of hours.

The floor was covered with an underwater carpet on which were printed directions to various stations. Ms. Reeves and Mr. Derkelpounder, apparently not yet wedded, sat working with a bot over at BLOOD TEST, across the room from the coral-crusted RING STATION and CEREMONIAL ALTAR. The newlyweds didn't appear particularly lighthearted. Their masks were off, but sweat was pouring down their strained faces.

Behind the altar, Mario, the priest, a goggled behemoth, had his enormous back to us, was feeding their documents into a quali-scanner. If Mario had been female, she'd have been large enough to have given birth to a couple of grown Hoffendeffers. In this pressure his smartsuit must have been some kind of genius.

One big pool above us, rippling like a drunk mirror, showed a shark approaching.

Presently, a round-eyed whitetip poked its nose and jaws out into the emporium; it was the same individual we had seen earlier in Miami7; the white band remained around its gills. This apparatus apparently gave it the ability to communicate to us in English, through a speaker.

"You big man. Why not come for a swim?" The predator grinned at Hoffendeffer. "You belong on the surface. Why not get me even better up close? I'm no crocodile. And different types must get together, no? What? You think I'm a crocodile?" The perfectly round eyes seemed to swell beneath their protective membrane. "Come closer."

"If anyone objects to this union," the preoccupied priest called over his shoulder, not understanding events a-fin. "Speak later. Now forever hold your peace."

The fish's round eyes shone. "Don't you just *love* bony meat?"

"Not today!" said a new voice emerging out of a second pool/wall, this one semi-perpendicular to the first. Through the middle of the air came Bayer, my mate. The little humanoid twirled across the chapel like a weaponized bouquet, fisting the cartilaginous vertebrate directly on its electric ampullae of Lorenzini. The requiem shark curled, folded, banked, and was immediately off and on its way.

Bayer swiveled to engage Mario from afar; his intelligent waterblast froze the priest's wrists to the camptable.

Bayer then inserted himself between the sweating Violet Reeves, her difficult-to-astonish fiancee, and the bloodsucking bot.

"If Sir and Madam would first don their snorklers, then retrieve and secure their papers," Bayer said, "we will then swim to board the *Crusted Bluff.*"

He gestured to the still rippling wall of azure saltwater from which he'd emerged moments earlier. There shimmered the fuzzy outlines of the *Crusted Bluff.*

V

Soon enough we were safe inside, snorkels down, shedding water in the vestibule. The visible parts of Hoffendeffer's face had turned green, no doubt from too much shark and too many pressure changes. We gave him a tranquilizer and a hammock.

"You can thank Yves for your identities," Blauvius scolded Violet Reeves. "You almost had your DNA scrubbed in there." So he did remember me!

"But we're not yet married," she cried.

"But why would you want to get married to begin with?"

"*You're* married!"

"Don't you understand? V. R., I wanted to talk to you on this trip about Jarl. He's left me! It's over. I thought we could speak underwater, if anywhere. I'm not even wearing my ring—you didn't notice."

She sighed. "I knew you'd disapprove. I asked Heinrich to occupy you. I hoped it would go faster. But we had to marry *today.* I'm a mathematician, you know. This was all part of the plan."

"She had it all worked out." Percival shrugged, putting his arm around her. "We needed to be able to fill out certain forms right away, so we could both return to Europe on the next GreenSails working berths available. After that trip we could have been certified for Space, as well."

Here Bayer leaned over and whispered to me privately. "Captains of any vessel, Sir, in extenuating circumstances, can officiate."

We still had an hour or so to work with. We'd miss the full tour, but, damn it, she'd paid the money herself.

I married them in the ship's salon, before the round viewing port that is perhaps the star attraction of the *Bluff*, sauna not excepted.

Whether or not they married simply for logistical and mathematical purposes, as the young bride continued to put forth, it was clear she was more than convenienced by her sandy-haired, shuffling, quiet but obliging young suitor. They held hands long after the solemnizing kiss, the growths on old Museum Park swaying behind him. We passed by an abstract stainless steel sculpture still fixed like a tooth into the gums of that other's era's jaw. Surrounded by jellyfish in all directions, with great tufts of kelp replacing the ancient palms, the sculpture had moved from minimalism to surrealism. The broad stainless steel blades still displayed graffiti left over from the dry days, a layering of history sprayed even on the surfaces of the spectacle's depths. Great shadows from our lightbanks and the sun imprinted dimension into the deep-sea ruins. Wedding music played as Bayer printed out the couple's certificates, and we passed through the open jaws of the SUPERFLEX Addition to the old science museum. Blauvius served as witness, initializing the certificate that Bayer printed and I finger-signed; and by the time we had settled down for an algae spritzer, we were holding beside one of the anchor posts of the TegelCorp Pavilion.

Even Blauvius was pleased.

"I am only sorry," he intoned, "that we have no champagne or wedding gifts."

"But this reminds me," boomed Hoffendeffer, now springing up from his hammock revery. "Violet Reeves. Your ex-employer purchased you a wedding gift! It was pricey, I tell you."

He produced, as if from a napkin in his pocket, a shimmering, multicolored egg-shaped globule.

"A jelly of your own! Look, it's getting to know you."

As the anomaly rotated, it sent out what appeared to be an intelligent, wet feeler, flying forth and anchoring, with a smack, on Violet Reeves's concerned forehead.

"Heinrich, no!" called Blauvius. "The air density is too high. Down here variables are a whole lot different than on the surface."

Bayer agreed. "If inclined to overachieve, that jelly could well expand exponentially along any available hypotenuse."

With a first geometric belch, the jelly grew to the size of a heart, then a pumpkin, pulsating with a repellant, veiny strength, clearly struggling to contain its own desires.

With Hoffendeffer's help, Bayer wrestled the semisolid down and away from the bride. We had to flush out the entire salon to get rid of the growth. Unfortunately, outside the *Bluff* the jelly grew even

189 more ambitious, mating with an entire school of passing medusa-phasing fish and thereby achieving the self illusion. It immediately linked to the skeleton of the city floating above. Improbably enough, it de-electrified all the fields.

Structures were already collapsing near and far.

Dropping off Hoffendeffer, who insisted the jelly would protect its creator, we submerged. By the time we reached the rim, the weather had penetrated.

"My kredit has dropped to zero!" Blauvius declared.

Bayer took it in stride. This is why we had invested in Miami8 two years ago. "Bimini anyone?"

"You see?" exclaimed Violet Derkelpounder-Reeves, leading her brown-eyed groom to the guest cabins. "The numbers worked out."

"Right on," he agreed. "Including honeymoon."

"Yves," Blauvius presently declared. "You're a miracle."

"I bunk up forward." I told him. "Coming along?"

"Is Bayer joining?" He smiled like a shark.